1984

A WOMAN'S PLACE IN THE NOVELS OF HENRY JAMES

A Woman's Place in the Novels of Henry James

Elizabeth Allen

St. Martin's Press   New York

All rights reserved. For information, write:
St. Martin's Press, Inc., 175 Fifth Avenue, New York, NY 10010
Printed in Hong Kong
Published in the United Kingdom by The Macmillan Press Ltd
First published in the United States of America in 1984

ISBN 0–312–88653–5

Library of Congress Cataloging in Publication Data

Allen, Elizabeth, 1955–
  A woman's place in the novels of Henry James.

  Bibliography: p.
  Includes index.   1843 - 1916
    1. James, Henry, ~~1811–1882~~—Characters—Women.
2. Women in literature.   I. Title.
PS2127.W6A44   1984   813′.4   83-40159
ISBN 0–312–88653–5

For my mother and father

Contents

A Note on the Texts of Henry James's Fiction

In quoting from James's fictional works, I have incorporated volume and page references in the text. The editions I have used are as follows:

The American	(London, 1879)
The Bostonians	(London, 1886)
The Europeans, 2 vols	(London, 1878)

The Portrait of a Lady	vols 3–4	
The Princess Casamassima	vols 5–6	
The Tragic Muse	vols 7–8	from *The Novels and Tales of Henry James*, 24 vols (New York, 1907–9).
The Awkward Age	vol. 9	
What Maisie Knew	vol. 11	
The Reverberator	vol. 13	
The Wings of the Dove	vols 19–20	
The Golden Bowl	vols 23–4	

Daisy Miller	vol. 4	from *The Complete Tales of Henry James*, ed. L. Edel, 12 vols (London, 1962–4).
The Turn of the Screw	vol. 10	

Introduction

This work is an exploration, through the novels of Henry James, of the representation of women in the literary text. I shall suggest that the attempt to reconcile the contradiction of woman's existence, both as sign and as conscious subject, is central to many of James's major novels.

To express my ideas about women's *representational* function in culture, and the ways in which this prevents women from being 'people', I have chosen to use certain specific terms (sign, signifier, subject, etc.). This introduction is therefore an outline of these terms, and the meaning they have for me in relation to women and the presentation of women in fiction. Examples, and I hope substantiation, are to be found in the following chapters.

SIGNS

A sign is quite simply a thing – whether object, word or picture – which has a particular meaning to a person or group of people. It is neither the thing nor the meaning alone but the two together.

The *sign* consists of the *signifier*, the material object, and the *signified*, which is its meaning. These are only divided for analytical purposes: in practice a sign is always thing-plus-meaning. (my emphasis).[1]

We communicate through sign systems, our existence as social beings depends on them. The most obvious one is language itself – other fundamental ones are religion, economic systems, art and rules of matrimony and kinship.[2]

In that we all use and understand the various sign systems of our culture, our own sense of self – what I also refer to as consciousness and 'subject'-hood – is actually placed and determined by these systems. Though each subject may have the illusion of existing, separate, outside of all human made systems, s/he is in fact formed by them, as well as being productive of them.

WOMEN AS SIGNS

Any sign depends on someone using and understanding it. If we learn our sense of self through being the subject or 'I', who understands and uses signs, and for whom they are being used by others to communicate, then what do we make of the position of women, who learn through existing sign systems that they themselves are signs?

Of course all people – individuals or groups – can function temporarily as signs for other people. In the advertisements which Judith Williamson discusses in *Decoding Advertisements*, various people signify gracious living, sophistication, success, etc. What I want to suggest is that women actually learn their sense of self in a way different from men: that society demands of them always to be potential signs, carriers of meaning (whatever that meaning is) simply because they are women.

That this can be only partial, since women are inescapably also conscious subjects, results in conflict which, strangely enough, is often not seen as problematic – whereas it seems in fact to be one of the fundamental conditions of oppression. For instance Lévi-Strauss, in *The Elementary Structures Of Kinship*, formulates the problem without appearing to see it as such:

> The emergence of symbolic thought must have required that women, like words, should be things that were exchanged . . . But woman could never become a sign and nothing more, since even in a man's world she is still a person, and since in so far as she is defined as a sign, she must be recognised as a generator of signs.[3]

But 'still' being a person is not as simple as Lévi-Strauss implies. It tends to involve the schizophrenic recognition of yourself as object *for* yourself, that any female reading and identifying with such a passage as this would involve:

> It will not need, when the mind is prepared for study, to search for objects. The invariable mark of wisdom is to see the miraculous in the common. What is a day? What is a year? What is summer? What is woman?[4]

There is a total assumption that the reader, the subject to whom this communication is addressed, is a man, and as such can ponder 'woman' as a category as discrete as a year or the summer. People, in other words, are men.

What women signify, or represent, varies enormously: it may be virtue or depravity, fickleness or endurance. But in as much as any person functions as a sign, the facets of that person irrelevant to the particular meaning of that sign are ignored or denied. The person becomes limited or defined. A woman signifying motherhood is seen only as motherhood – and what is more the apparent naturalness of the equation makes it all the harder to see beyond. The whole range of potential meanings for women, which are seen as natural but are in fact socially constructed, are what I mean by the *feminine*. Representative of the contained oppositions of the feminine, women form a separate class from humankind, *in relation to which* they are placed and defined. The popular nineteenth-century notion of 'true womanhood' (which I shall discuss in Chapter 1) never appeared to beg its counterpart in 'true manhood'.

In *The Second Sex*, Simone de Beauvoir describes the function of woman for the male subject. Threatened by the assertive male other who attempts to be subject and thus reduce *him* to the inessential, he can turn to woman, who is:

> the wished for intermediary between nature, the stranger to man, and the fellow being who is too closely identical. She opposes him with neither the hostile silence of nature, nor the hard require-ment of a reciprocal relation . . . [women] accepted man's so-vereignty and he did not feel menaced by a revolt that could make of him in turn the object. Woman thus seems to be the inessential who never goes back to being the essential, to be the absolute Other without reciprocity.[5]

Women learn to constitute themselves as other, in a world which decrees that women 'be' while men 'acquire' or 'possess'. However, woman is not just an object of possession, but a carrier of potential meaning. She signifies, but she does not signify herself. Her femininity points beyond her, and in order to be socially acceptable and valuable it must function for a male subject. Woman as subject is thus divided against herself, in a rejection of her own devalued feminine self. However, the paradox of a sign who is 'still a person' reappears – the individual woman can never solely constitute herself as other:

Man wants woman to be object; she makes herself object; at the very moment when she does that, she is exercising a free activity. Therein is her original treason.[6]

Although her subordination in a male world allows woman to exist visibly as sign, her reality as conscious individual constitutes a continuing contradiction for her as well as for 'man' – a contradiction which intrudes more as her ideological existence comes more obviously into contrast with her particular conditions of social and economic existence.[7] Being other means being ambiguous – containing oppositions which yet share the quality of being concepts, of being the signified in some form – the way to maintain this is to freeze woman at a certain point, to maintain her representative function by refusing to enter into too close or reciprocal a relation:

> woman is necessary in so far as she remains an Idea into which man projects his own transcendence; but . . . she is inauspicious as an objective reality *existing in and for herself*. Kierkegaard holds that by refusing to marry his fiancée he established the only valid relation to woman. (my emphasis).[8]

In *Psychoanalysis and Feminism*, Juliet Mitchell describes how, in identifying herself with her mother and establishing her existence through being desirable, or acceptable, to her father, the girl becomes defined in terms of her gender:

> She must confirm her pre-Oedipal identification (as opposed to attachment) with the mother, and instead of taking on the qualities of aggression and control she acquires the art of love and conciliation. Not being heir to the law of culture, her task is to see that mankind reproduces itself within the circularity of the supposedly natural family . . . woman becomes, in her nineteenth-century designation, 'the sex'. Hers is the sphere of reproduction.[9]

Not controlling human social existence, women are designed to ensure and represent its continuity. But this process can be indefinitely extended. Once functioning as representative, within whatever sphere, one can subsequently be representative of anything. Not heir to the 'law of culture' woman can nonetheless represent it – can make it visible and thus stabilise it, much as she does for the notion of reproduction within the family. So we can recognise the arbitrary nature of the sign – woman as signifier is not linked to any one signified – be it sex, reproduction, artifice or culture.

Feminist criticism which has applied itself to an examination of fiction in the hope of uncovering the representation of women as a specific, distinct activity (as opposed to that which has been directed to examination of texts by women and ideas of a female language) has often concentrated on identifying and categorising the variations of the sign – the range of signifieds to which women as signifiers are attached. Thus Judith Fryer, in *The Faces of Eve*, describes the use of women to reflect cultural myths, among them those of the 'temptress', the 'American Princess', the 'Great Mother', the 'real witch-bitches' and the 'New Woman'.[10] Many Ellman, in *Thinking About Women*, also concentrates on the range of abstract signifieds – and their mutual contradiction – pertaining to femininity, such as formlessness, passivity, materiality, spirituality, compliancy and shrewishness.[11] In concentrating on the process of signification itself the precise signifieds become less important. The conflict centres in the internal falsity of woman as fundamentally sign (rather than the potential for all 'man' to be temporarily sign).

This is the kind of reading taking place in John Goode's essay *Sue Bridehead and the New Woman*, on Hardy's *Jude the Obscure*, in which he identifies the presence of Sue as image (either of womanhood or of a 'peculiar individual'), and of Sue as containing her own uttered logic, as conflicting (and thus exposing) ideology:

> Sue is not the centre of the novel, she exists as a function of Jude's experience, hence as an object for him. It is surely possible that the questions come from her inability to take shape as that object.[12]

Sue's behaviour has to be 'explained' in order to comply with her existence as image. Jude is not subect to the same demands, despite his continually inconsistent decisions. Similarly, Sue is called upon to relate herself to other women, in a way that Jude is not called upon to relate his self to other men (men being 'male' rether than 'human' here).

This kind of reading is concerned with questioning precisely the elements of a text which might most usually go unquestioned – possibly, and more easily done, in relation to a text which itself puts them forward for questioning, though usually to no avail. Most critics of *Jude the Obscure* take Sue's 'feminine' inconsistency at face value. Those of James's novels which centre round a female hero seem to me to raise the same kind of questions – though equally usually to no avail. The refusal of most readers to examine the conflicts in a text which would involve questioning their own 'codes' is described by Judith Fetterley in her account of the 'phallic criticism' of *The Bostonians*.[13] Working with a confessed interest has at least the advantage of making overt the predications of the inquiry, and thus making it more open to challenge and exploration.

JAMES'S NOVELS

Because of the very particular meaning which writers (and critics) of literature have given to the terms 'symbol' and 'symbolism', I have chosen to use as my central term that of 'sign'. I think it raises fewer preconceptions, and also seems to lend itself more easily to being split up into 'signifier' and 'signified'. However, all sign systems *are* symbolic, and in dealing with literature one is dealing with signs which are often personal to one writer and one text – whose meanings we learn as we read – and which are generally called symbols. In *The Origin of Intelligence in the Child*, Piaget speaks of 'the symbol and the sign' as the two poles – individual and social – of the same system of meanings.[14]

Signs personal to a particular culture, a body of literature, or even to one writer, need increasingly specific knowledge to recognise and interpret – their framework of reference becomes smaller. Speaking of symbolism in a literary text thus refers to a conscious process of signification, drawing on a common code yet articulated primarily within the text itself: 'The Golden Bowl' signifies little or nothing until one has read the novel (or Blake, or the Bible). As a symbol, its process is that of the sign, it is simply one extent, a pole of signification, in the degree to which it is consciously and individually selected. James goes beyond simply and consciously employing his own range of significations, and probes the nature and effect of the signifying activity *itself* – thus performing and questioning it simultaneously. There is a continuous concern in his novels with manner, style and all kinds of social codes and structures into which each individual is placed, with or without the illusion of living free from them. What appearance and behaviour 'suggest' and generate, according to the structure of significations producing and surrounding them, is seen to determine the process and progress of every subject, as early as novels like *Daisy Miller* and *Roderick Hudson*. Increasingly, the recognition of these structures creating each individual in social existence is complemented by the individual use of language to recreate the signified. The projection of society (and all the forms and formulae which that contains) creates the individual consciousness in relation to society (the constitution of the subject), and that consciousness through the further signification creates further reality. The tension between the 'free' Emersonian individual and the structures which in fact create and limit that individual are resolved potentially through the individual recognition of the structures, and attempts to establish subjecthood through individual use of them, to control meaning, or the signified, through comprehension and language.

This is central to James's later novels like *What Maisie Knew, The Wings of the Dove* and *The Golden Bowl*, where the inability to pin down the signifiers to any one clear signified creates a process of flux within which the female subject is both excessively mystified and therefore viewed as sign, and also (through her own recognition of this) attempts to manipulate this mystification.

James explores the reciprocity of the individual consciousness and the material outside through occasions of specific conflict. These are engendered variously, often by having the individual designated in some way as a social outsider, and therefore in the process of placing himself in relation to social structures (or indeed failing to do so in any fulfilling way). The nature of the 'outsider' quality takes various forms – that of being American, poor, an artist. But the most fruitful incidence is that of the greatest conflict, in which the self is not only exploring the possibility of accepting or re-working its location within social structures, but is being blocked in this by the definition and limitation imposed on it as sign by those structures. Conflict thus arises out of the intrinsic limitation of existing as other which, as we have seen, is fundamental to the experience of the female self.

I am suggesting that the importance of central female consciousnesses in James's novels lies in the development of the conflict of the woman as sign and as self. There is a sense of female potential repressed by the signification of it as part of the feminine, in a manner more intrinsic than definitions of class or occupation. The rendering of woman as object makes her visible and therefore vivid as object of study in the text. The female hero becomes a paradigm for the kinds of problems and situations I have been indicating in

James's work. The very notion of being inescapably visible suggests conflict both for the female subject and in the ensuing failure of an individual subject meaningfully to signify any fixed ordered concept:

> [The American woman's] manner of embodying and representing her sex has fairly made of her a new human convenience, not unlike fifty of the others, of a slightly different order, the ingenious mechanical appliances, stoves, refrigerators, sewing machines, type-writers, cash registers that have done so much . . . for the American name.[15]

The convenience of such visibility exists for the subject who can define himself in relation to the other in this way, and later in *The American Scene* the American Girl protests:

> All I want . . . is . . . that my parents and my brothers and my male cousins should consent to exist otherwise than occultly, undiscoverably, or as I suppose you'd call it, irresponsibly. That's a trouble, yes – but *we* take it, so why shouldn't they?[16]

The conflict between sense of self and realisation of one's existence as sign, articulated in the gradual evolution of social consciousness in characters like Isabel Archer, Kate Croy, Milly Theale, etc. is often formulated as a conflict between appearance and essence. The fact that the two cannot ever be in total contradiction – that they constitute each other – is fundamental to notions of the woman's identity residing in her appearance, an idea which can be employed at a multitude of levels, from dress and beauty to those of portraiture and subsequent objectification. Men look at women, women watch themselves being looked at: 'Her own sense of being in herself is supplanted by a sense of being appreciated *as* herself by another.'[17] How a woman appears can determine how she will be treated. To gain some control over this process, women must contain it, and interiorise it.

In using the fiction of Henry James to explore the existence of women as signs in the literary text, I am focussing on a specific pattern in his work and trying to trace a development in his use of woman as sign and woman as consciousness, and the implications each has for the other, I have thus concentrated on specific texts which seem to me to exemplify various stages of treatment in this pattern, my aim being to show the development of James's presentation of a central female consciousness and the questions this throws up within the text about woman's restriction as sign, the function of signification, and the demonstrated dependence on it of the social world and all its inhabitants. This pattern appears to me to be paradigmatic of some of James's novelistic preoccupations, though it obviously does not cover the whole range of his subject matter. Indeed the very subject matter which he uses at times to explore the limitation of women by their representative function, he may use again in a conventional way to signify values for a male protagonist.

The texts I have chosen form a chronological progression, so that in the early stories the figure of the American girl functions simply as sign for an observant consciousness. *Daisy Miller* is the paradigm of the woman as sign in James's early work, whose destruction raises questions as to the real nature of her individuality and freedom. These questions are explored in the use of the same figure attempting to be the free subject of her own experience, yet being appropriated as sign by the surrounding world, in *The Portrait of a Lady*. The disillusionment inherent in Isabel Archer's failure comes to the surface in *The Bostonians*, in which the heroine is relentlessly possessed as sign yet fails to provide stable values or to trigger creative meditation as this sign, and has either to struggle to resist complete absorption or passively to succumb. *The Tragic Muse* presents the same patterns of appropriation and restriction through naming, and suggests the development towards control of signification by women in the presentation of a woman who chooses a profession, literally, as sign. The more positive development in *The Portrait of a Lady*, Isabel's growing consciousness of her existence as object for the world, and her construction as subject out of this knowledge, is employed in texts like *What Maisie Knew* and *The Awkward Age*, where the vulnerable and youthful heroines possess or develop consciousness of their existence as sign for others in a corrupt world, and explore the demands this existence imposes.

The increasing stress on the relativity of knowledge and the creative power of individual perception in these later novels gives strength to the resistance to constriction through personal interpretation and possession of knowledge. But Maisie's and Nanda's attempt to assert a contradictory subject existence, incorporating both sign and self, can still be made only in communication with the world, in the figure of a loved man. These attempts to present themselves, directly and plainly, *as* themselves, appear threatening to the conventional social order and frightening to the man who is sustained by the concealment and mystification of the feminine world of relationships and significances. The ensuing mixture of intimate communication and regretful rejection of the unorthodox girl heralds the attempts of the two highly conscious and complex heroines – Milly Theale and Maggie Verver – to reclaim social existence by consciously signifying that which the beloved requires, mystifying and controlling the signifying process. The tragedy of failure in one case and the grim nature of success in the other endorses the oppressive reality of the need of the socially functional woman to repress her complex individuality and hold out the consoling promise of meaning inherent in signification. These heroines of James's later fiction, particularly *The Wings of the Dove* and *The Golden Bowl*, are not offered the means of escape from the function of sign – this would result in invisibility in a society which recognises women through this function. Rather, they attempt to become the subject of an existence as feminine by a conscious employment of signification, so that the woman controls how she is seen and what she represents, though at the cost of unadorned, unmystified communication, which the man is shown as being unable to take.

James's sense of women as important material for fiction emerges not only from the novelistic tradition which has long dealt with heroines, but from the American culture which was recognised from within and without to accord women a particularly prominent position. One of the emerging signs was that of the American girl – youthful femininity signifying the individualistic spontaneity, freedom and innocence of the New World. James, too, recognised the figure as particularly characteristic in commenting on the work of an American contemporary:

> The author, intensely American in the character of his talent, is probably never so spontaneous, so much himself, as when he represents the delicate, nervous, emancipated young woman begotten of our institutions and our climate, and equipped with a lovely face and an irritable moral consciousness.[18]

It was James himself who was eventually hailed as the real progenitor of the fictional American girl, developing the subject that he had seized upon so early as somehow particularly expressive and paradigmatic of the contradictions he wished to explore.

1 Woman in the Nineteenth Century

The popular idea of the American girl was one which emerged in the context of a Victorian ideology of the feminine which was similar on both sides of the Atlantic. Central was the idea of 'true woman-hood'.[1] This was not totally new, nor did it deny the range of feminine attributes, or signifieds, from earlier periods, but the emphasis was different. Idealisation of women became heavily domestic in the nineteenth century. In the aftermath of the industrial revolution, there was a growing contrast between the position of working class women, increasingly employed outside the family, and middle class women (not just a tiny aristocratic élite) sitting in the newly conceptualised home with nothing to do. One can see as at least partly resulting from this leisure both the growing demands for women's greater economic freedom and legal equality, and an increasing emphasis on any ideas and reflections at all levels which justified the *status quo* and persuaded women to remain in the private world of the home.[2] To rationalise this domesticity, the notion of the separate spheres of the sexes was popular, spheres which were 'naturally' different but equal in importance (though not in reward):

> The nineteenth century was confident that it knew the difference between the sexes and that these differences were total and innate. Women were inherently more religious, modest, passive, submiss-ive and domestic than men, and were happier doing tasks, learning lessons and playing games that harmonised with their nature.[3]

And if you weren't any of these things, then you weren't a true woman. Barbara Welter describes how the phrase 'true woman-hood' is used continuously in contemporary material (here 1820–60) but never defined, rather like Lisa Appignanesi's description of the word 'femininity':

The evocative power of the term 'femininity' makes it a word which is generally, if somewhat vaguely, understood – even though little effort is made to decipher what exactly it means. As such it constitutes what Roland Barthes calls a 'myth': a statement which bears no *direct* relationship to the object it describes (woman) and evokes a range of suggestions which is culturally determined.[4]

In other words 'feminine', like 'woman', is a signifier attached to a range of signifieds to create signs which bear a very arbitrary relation to the woman herself – arbitrary from her point of view, that is, not from her society's.

Despite lack of definition Barbara Welter extracts four 'cardinal virtues' in the true woman; piety, purity, submissiveness and domesticity. The very emphasis on the domestic sphere, which meant marriage, and on the fact that women's claim to importance was their moral influence – on men – helps explain why the revolt, the alternative, was often conceived of in terms of celibacy.[5] The idealisation of woman's moral influence in the domestic sphere obscured the glaring contradiction of ascribing woman a superior moral virtue and yet rendering that superiority inferior to masculine legal, social and economic restraint.

Both the reflection on, and rebellion against, the notion of the domestic idyll and woman's place in it, was essentially middle class. Middle class women neither went out to work, nor had any real function within the home. It was they who had the time and sometimes the education to look beyond their 'separate sphere'. Yet the contemporary demand to live as a domestic paragon was only one of the manifestations of their repression as sign. In a comparison of the two poles of response to the position of women – J. S. Mill's *Subjection of Women* and Ruskin's *Of Queen's Gardens* – Kate Millet describes how the old significations of women underpinned the contemporary bourgeois idyll:

In Mill one encounters the realism of sexual politics, in Ruskin its romance and the benign aspect of its myth. Much of the other portion of Victorian sexual myth is included in Ruskin by implication, for his virtuous matron relies for her very existence on that spectral figure of the temptress, her complement in the period's dichotomous literary fantasy – just as in life, the two classes of women, wife and whore, account for the socio-sexual division under the double standard . . . The dark woman, the period avatar of feminine evil, lurks there [in literature] in subterranean menace, stationed at intervals all the way from Tennyson's verse to the more scabrous pornography of the age. But the daytime lady in *Of Queen's Gardens* is an expression of the more normative beliefs of the Victorian middle-class at the moment of their most optimistic and public profession.[6]

And these 'normative beliefs' found their expression in the ideology of marriage, just as the point of attack was the bourgeois marriage and the absurdities it contained. Marriage and the home functioned as a kind of social glue as did the Christian religion.[7] Home cheered, calmed, soothed and stabilised the active fathers, brothers and sons. As a new lynchpin, it began to deserve the attentions of cultural response, to be worthy of fiction and now also of poetry. Discussing Coventry Patmore's *The Angel in the House* – perhaps even more than Ruskin's *Of Queen's Gardens* an apotheosis of the lengths to which the signification of woman as domestic influence could go – Mario Praz describes how the old Dantesque and Petrarchan notion of earthly love as the first stage to divine love had been domesticised and privatised. The conjugal idyll was now the paradigm of earthly aspiration, finding approval also in models nearer home than the religious: 'The reign of Queen Victoria had at its centre a conjugal idyll, the idyll of Victoria and Albert.'[8] Patmore uses the idea of Christian virtue (always a consoling religion for slaves) to justify the subservience of the better to the worse:

> Say that she wants the will of man
> To conquer fame, not check'd by cross,
> Nor moved when others bless or ban;
> She wants but what to have were loss.
> Or say she holds no seals of power,
> But humbly lives her life at school;
> Alas, we have yet to hail the hour
> When God shall clothe the best with rule.[9]

Patmore is quite clear about woman's value, it is the *extent* to which she ennobles man:

> Ah, wasteful woman, she who may
> On her sweet self set her own price,

> Knowing he cannot choose but pay,
> How has she cheapen'd paradise;
> How given for nought her priceless gift,
> How spoil'd the bread and spill'd the wine,
> Which, spent with due respective thrift,
> Had made brutes men, and men divine![10]

Yet ultimately it is not for woman even to establish her own influential virtue; she must embrace her own subservience – indeed a true woman does so 'naturally': 'She loves him for his mastering air'[11] – and signify whatever is required – her virtue, in other words, is *not* intrinsic. Her real merit is her sign status, that she will be whatever it is necessary and desirable for her to be: 'A woman, like the Koh-i-noor, Mounts to the price that's put on her.'[12]

The real nature of the true woman is that she is other, sign – she does not exist for and in herself. Mill recognised this, and he also sensed that it was somehow a contrived state of affairs:

> All women are brought up from the very earliest years in the belief that their ideal of character is the very opposite to that of men; not self will, and government by self-control, but submission, and yielding to the control of others. All the moralities tell them that it is the duty of women, and all current sentimentalities that it is their nature, to live for others; to make complete abnegation of themselves, and to have no life but in their affections.[13]

> What is now called the nature of women is an eminently artificial thing.[14]

In his attack on the legal helplessness of women in marriage, and his advocacy of their right to suffrage and to any employment they wish, he pinpoints two major paradoxes in the ideology of the true woman maintained by the notion of natural separate spheres. One is that if woman's subjection is 'natural', then there should be no need to enforce it by legal, social or economic means. The other is that if women are really better and more virtuous, they should be guiding and governing the world, rather than guided and governed by it. This again is the paradox of the human being as sign – woman's nature, woman's virtue, are attributes of the 'other' of a certain class, and have little to do with the individual person and her abilities.

The marital and maternal true woman was a central sign in America as well as in Victorian England. Barbara Welter's book *Dimity Convictions* is an exploration of this ideology in America, and Nina Baym's *Woman's Fiction* is an analysis of some of the same ideals in women's fiction in the America of the period.[15] Women function in relation to others, and on an essentially private and personal scale, even if their individual fame and aspiration has gone beyond this:

> It is believed that nothing which exhibits a true woman, especially in her relations to others as friend, sister, daughter, wife or mother, can fail to interest and be of value to her sex.[16]

The suggestion that women are viewed essentially in 'relation' to others, strengthens the sense of a woman as a member of a class, as a woman before she is an individual. If woman's national function was that of upholding morality and virtue, then her personal way of fulfilling it was in relation to those around her, and most naturally in the role of wife and mother:

> The love of woman is the highest love. Therefore girls, keep your hearts. You will want them whole and clean for such a love to enter, and for the rest, if you would receive the best a man can give, be worthy of it. To love some woman is a great lifting up of a man's heart into a region of light and purity.

> A frugal, thrifty woman is a crown of glory to her husband; by her example she may implant in him noble principles.[17]

The extent to which womanhood signified life through others; morality; example; love; in short, the lack of an independent life, is suggested in America as well as in England by the fact that women who did not marry were seriously considered largely redundant. A certain number could be absorbed in surrogate marriage – in caring for parents, in nursing and domestic service – but the thought of a superfluity beyond this was apparently alarming enough for a W. R. Greg to write a book of essays, reviewed thus in the February edition of the *Atlantic Monthly* for 1874:

> His plan for remedying the evil of the redundancy is to arrange for the emigration of one third, another third to be employed in domestic service, the other third, with so many rivals removed,

will find the struggle for life less difficult, marriage will be more common and the evil will thus gradually disappear.

Of course this was considered extreme, single women were not redundant, simply unfortunate and bound to make themselves helpful to the families around them.

The fact that many women, mostly working class, were in paid employment outside the home, was not only ignored, but elaborately and 'scientifically' denied as a possibility for more women, especially in any educated capacity. The pseudo-science of 'Sex in Education' by E. H. Clarke, reviewed in the *Atlantic Monthly*, containing such statements as

Periodicity is the type (Law) of female force and work; persistence of male force and work.

A boy may safely study six hours daily, a girl not more than four, or at least five hours.[18]

is supported by the 'feminine' language of sweet reasonableness found in *Godey's Lady's Book*:

Man is the worker par excellence, the subduer of natural forces, the ruler of the material world; woman is the help meet and her work consists in supplying incentives . . . not to plan the work, to commence it, or to carry it forward, but to complete it, to add the crowning touch, to make it 'fill perfection's round'.[19]

To convince middle class girls and women that not only were they merely the icing on the cake, but that this was their supreme destiny, greater than any incidental talent they as individuals might possess, needed a powerful mythology, and this is present not only in the 'pedestal' language of the articles on womanhood, but in the stories and serialised novels in these magazines, which are concerned with the palatable side of being a woman: love, romance and marriage (or rather, engagements and weddings). To mirror forth, to complete, to enhance, to support, to provide an example: the functions of womanhood were subsidiary, cultural in a representative rather than a creative sense, and based on the assumption of a people for whose benefit all this went on – the husbands, sons and brothers of America and England. And the subject matter forming these examples comprised morality and civilisation, forms and manners – in short, the face that the nation wished to show the world.

America was of course a very different place to England, and it might be expected that the position of women, their signifying function, would be different as well as similar. Certainly, as in Victorian England, the reality of many women's lives was vastly different to this idealised reflection. Harriet Martineau, in *Society in America*, felt that although women were 'much indulged' in America, their position was ultimately no better – marriage was still the highest expectation, and it was difficult to work honourably or in decent conditions. Yet there were important differences, and one of these resides in a particular prominence that American women had, the causes of their being 'much indulged'.

The function of 'social glue' was, if anything, more important than in England, for America was a more unstable society. Women were signs of civilisation – either in terms of lace curtains and bone china (as consumers) or in terms of morality (as upholders of law and order). Yet women had a second function – that of representing America to Europe and, by reflection, to itself. The relationship to England was a topic of vital importance to nineteenth century Americans (though the reverse was not true) – European travellers met with, conversed with, noticed and even married American girls. As representative, the American female was both a recognised and civilised woman ('we are as good as the English') and a provocatively youthful and egalitarian girl ('and we are superior in our differences'). It was the American girl who really produced the effect, though it was a surprisingly long time before she became a stock character of fiction. When she did, however, the American girl contained her own paradox in a new and vivid fashion.

In a lecture delivered in 1844, entitled *The Young American*, Emerson discussed the features of his country in terms of railroad expansion, building projects, trade, democracy and, bolstering all these, a fervent need for nationalism. There was an insistence on being American that he saw as fundamental to the maintenance of, and pride in, the institutions of his native land. That this was not a dreamed up rhetoric, but a felt want, is the import of his opening words:

Gentlemen, it is remarkable that our people have their intellectual culture from one country, and their duties from another.[20]

The 'intellectual culture' comes in a general sense from Europe, but often specifically from England, and the Americans felt a high degree of sensitivity toward the English assumption of cultural superiority. The need for the cultural framework for the politics and economics of America to come from America is the need for new conceptions of freedom (socially and politically) and expansionism (geographically and economically) to be mental as well as physical:

> The continent we inhabit is to be physic and food for our mind, as well as our body. The land, with its tranquillising, sanative influences, is to repair the errors of a scholastic and traditional education, and bring us into just relation with men and things.[21]

Of all the characteristics of America in this period, the most persistent was that of change. It is interesting that Emerson identifies the effect of the railroads on England as being to contract space, whereas that on America would be to contract time – colonising, developing and covering the new land was a more imminent prospect, work could start sooner and people spread faster. This rapid development, together with the fast progressing split of the nation into areas divided by different rates of settlement and different economic bases – the West, the South and the Eastern Seaboard – also called for a sense of unifying nationalism, for a sense of things peculiarly American. Change was not only political – the beginnings of democracy co-existed with other changes in 'social relations' and new conditions called for new codes of behaviour.

Amidst the fluidity of American life at this time (and the sense that in the need to survive as a nation, expediency was more important than tradition) one might expect to find change, even progress, in the role and status of women. What one does find is a confusing mix of old and new ideology, of women as somehow more than anything the example of the new nation with new freedoms, and yet at the same time more than anything the constant amidst flux, the paragon of perennial domesticity and, again, social relations.

As a starting point, what does become clear when approaching writing about America in this period (approximately 1830–1900) is that the position of women was somehow a definite 'fact' of American life. In Alexis de Tocqeville's *Democracy in America* (1835) 'women' form a topic, like federalism or trade, a facet of the representative reflection of America. He notes the freedom that young girls have in America, the independence that is given them – and its limits:

> Thus then, while they [Americans, i.e. male Americans] have allowed the social inferiority of woman to continue, they have done all they could to raise her morally and intellectually to the level of man; and in this respect they appear to me to have excellently understood the true principle of democratic improvement.[22]

Half a century later, James Bryce, in his *The American Commonwealth* (1889), also conscientiously entered chapters on The Position of Women, stating that:

> It has been well said that the position which women hold in a country is, if not a complete test, yet one of the best tests of the progress it has made in civilisation . . . Americans are fond of pointing . . . to the position their women hold as an evidence of the high level their civilisation has reached. Certainly nothing in the country is more characteristic of the peculiar type their civilisation has taken.[23]

So if women are a cultural index, Bryce is suggesting that American women are 'different', though this difference is viewed traditionally as being representative, in the way women are representative in other nations. Even that die hard misogynist Kipling suggested a difference: but the girls of America are above and beyond them all. They are clever, they can talk – yea it is said that they think.[24]

The contradiction centres here: women represent the culture of America, its social relations, its customs, its manners, its forms. They carry on the appearances of life which can flourish only when some civilisation has been attained. As American women, they must both signify the degree to which America is different and changing (free and easy, democratic, spontaneous, young, rich, etc.) and the very constants of life, the customs and forms.

It is significant that women as cultural and social constants were considered far more important than women as active and changing people. De Tocqueville does note that:

> They [men pioneers] take their wives along with them and make them share the countless perils and privations that always attend the commencement of these expeditions.[25]

and *Harper's Weekly*, in 1884 and 1885, reports among others a Mrs Miller captaining a steamboat on the Mississippi, a Mrs Belva Lockwood practising as a lawyer in Washington and running for presidential candidate, and various anonymous women engaging in activities as diverse as canvassing books in Pennsylvania and going down mines. We know also the prominent and important roles played by women such as Lucy Stone, Lucretia Mott, Elizabeth Cady Stanton and Susan Anthony in campaigning for reform of all kinds, including female suffrage. Yet these are not the women our attention is focussed on in surveys of the time, as Nina Baym says: 'Women who did not fit the mould were oddly invisible, their lives little noticed in their own day, and largely unrecorded for ours',[26] an observation which forms the basis of Earnest's *The American Eve in Fact and Fiction*, which examines the split between what women did and what they were seen as doing.[27]

In an awareness of a changing, emerging nation, what was considered noteworthy was not women's activities being different, but women's representational status as a symbol of her country's culture. So that when woman forms a new sign – as American and therefore more free – the important point is that it *is* still a sign, like the old ones which continued to co-exist. Women's function in an appraisal of American society was singled out as that of the sign – that it might be a sign of change must not be confused with the idea of women's *lives and functions* changing, that was a completely separate activity.

In America . . . everybody who comes into our houses savours of these habits; the men, of the market; the women, of the custom.[28]

In no country has such constant care been taken as in America to trace two clearly distinct lines of action for the two sexes and to make them keep pace one with the other, but in two pathways that are always different.[29]

Three causes combine to create among American women an average of literary taste and influence higher than that of women in any European country. These are, the educational facilities they enjoy, the recognition of the equality of the sexes in the whole social and intellectual sphere, and the leisure which they possess as compared with men. In a country where men are incessantly occupied at their business or profession, the function of keeping up the level of culture devolves upon women.[30]

No country seems to owe more to its women than America does, nor to owe them so much of what is best in social institutions and in the beliefs that govern conduct.[31]

If the status of women as the test of the progress of civilisation was not unique to the United States, then woman's very prominence in that role was seen as such. Her status was not so much altered as brought into relief in a country where the middle and upper class men worked, and society, even culture, was left to the ladies – and yet in an age of nationalism that culture had a vital role to play in expressing America, both for itself and for the European countries waiting, so it seemed to the Americans, to amuse themselves at the spectacle of the new nation. James himself was one of those acutely aware of the extent to which the necessity for nearly all men in America to work had left the women the sole representatives of the cultural scene, and the false relation which this created between men and women. Women as signs were clearly separable from the reality signified, and also totally dependent on it. Yet it left the world of signification curiously under their control, even while it existed for the economic, social and ideological benefit of men:

> From the moment it is adequately borne in mind that the business-man, in the United States, may, with no matter what dim struggles, gropings, yearnings, never hope to be anything *but* a business-man, the size of the field he so abdicates is measured . . . the lonely waste, the boundless gaping void of 'society'; which is but a rough name for all the *other* so numerous relations with the world he lives in that are imputable to the civilised being . . . his default having made, all around him, the unexampled opportunity of the woman.[32]

But this also meant the women could be held accountable for the value of what they signified:

> The scarcity of women [in the newly settled West] lowered sexual morality and certainly made life rougher, but it was not entirely without advantages for when women came later, along with their morality they brought inequality . . . The making of social distinction was woman's work.[33]

One might expect that as American women signified freedom and change, this process might result in some freedom and change 'for' themselves. But freedom for women remained strictly confined, and even if American feminine culture were to shadow forth notions of equality and democracy, American women were not going to be allowed to assume equality, or to vote. Thus the extent to which freedom was symbolised by American womanhood appears forcefully limited by the age old 'European' and culturally inherited signification of woman as domestic, moral and inferior. The weight of this ideology in the nineteenth century was massive. Its synthesis with, and division from, the democratic ideology was reflected in the existing division that De Tocqueville noted in the 1830s: 'Long before an American girl arrives at the marriageable age, her emancipation from maternal control begins.'[34] But

> In America the independence of woman is irrecoverably lost in the bonds of matrimony. If an unmarried woman is less constrained there then elsewhere, a wife is subjected to stricter obligations.[35]

As usual the notion of woman's duty could be interchanged with that of her nature:

> It should also be remembered that when an American girl marries, she no longer *entertains the desire* to interest any but her husband. (my emphasis).[36]

The young, unmarried girls had a freedom greater in America than in Europe; they went out by themselves, had 'gentlemen friends' and enjoyed themselves generally at their own leisure. Often given greater education than their European counterparts, and certainly greater freedom of knowledge they could, as Kipling said, both talk and think. Encouraged in brightness and vivacity, what better representatives of young, free and democratic society? And a role carefully controlled by its destiny as wife 'subject to stricter obligations', and by the dual obligation to be not only the freedom of America but also its conscience. Eventually these aspects combined with the other emerging fact of America, its great wealth, which was also to be displayed by its most conspicuous consumers, the women who showed forth the fruits of industry minus its more unattractive operations. The mix was a complex one:

The high hopes of the Revolutionary period, that the United States would set forth an example of democracy and enlightened rule to the rest of the world, were overshadowed by the fact that America's influence, when it became great, was largely based on her wealth and power. The American girl, who had been bred to show the superiority of freedom linked to moral purity, gained renown not as the true woman or Puritan maiden, but as the heiress . . . The dilemma of democracy had always been to retain both freedom and power; the dilemma of the American girl, to be both bold and innocent, was equally perplexing and equally unsolved.[37]

Yet, as I suggested, the specifically American role of girls and women (given their cultural prominence in the United States) needed even more to be balanced by their allegiance to their class, to their being flawed products of the prototype of the True Woman. De Tocqueville could see that the apparent freedom of American girls did not imply a radical change of role in society, merely a shift in responsibility and tactic:

> Far from hiding the corruptions of the world from her, they prefer that she should see them at once and *train herself* to shun them. (my emphasis).

> Like the young women of Europe she seeks to please, but she knows precisely the cost of pleasing. If she does not abandon herself to evil, at least she knows that it exists; and she is remarkable rather for purity of manners than for chastity of mind.[38]

As with the 'super-woman' of the 1970s, who was expected to excel simultaneously in the male career world and in the traditional feminine role of homemaker, an apparent radicalisation of the female image is in fact a further distortion, forcing the onus of her oppression on to the woman herself – appearing to give her greater freedom in order to demand exactly the same results, plus.

The freedom of the American girl was, then, a further image (subordinate nonetheless to the culturally inherited ones), the combination forming the basis of the social and cultural world that American women figured forth while their menfolk were out 'doing' everything under the sun, but primarily making the wealth of the

new nation, multiplying in that market place that Emerson in the
1830s saw as being so sorely in need of an American intellectual and
cultural cradle.

There were other notions of freedom in America at the time which
can be linked to the same origins as the democratic ideals, but which
manifested themselves in different forms to social spontaneity and
vivacity. The other side of the coin of economic individualism was
spiritual individualism, which found full expression in the New
England transcendentalism of the first half of the nineteenth
century. The foremost exponent of this was Emerson, whose writings
affirm the integrity of the individual mind in harmony with a
benevolent, impersonal, remote but all seeing God, regulated by the
order and finality of moral law as it is found in the evidences of
natural law.[39] In common with puritanism, his beliefs rested firmly
on the notion of the self in relation to God, without the intermediary
of institutions. But Emerson's self aspires to unite with nature and
thus God, yet retain individuality. Thus in contradiction to
puritanism a fusion was sought between idealism and sensual-
ism. The rejection of pre-defined forms, the emphasis on the
potential for every individual to attain knowledge independently,
together with the moral seriousness of the philosophy, made such
beliefs attractive to women seeking sanction to develop beyond the
self-abnegation of more 'social' Christianity. The intellectual links
with democratic ideals, expansionism and belief in a meritocracy[40]
harmonised the use of the American girl as a sign of both national
and moral individualism. In his book *The New England Girl*, P. J.
Eakin identifies a native tradition of a girl endowed with moral
idealism and belief in self-culture, yet also with the Christian and
feminine belief in self-renunciation. Eakin recognises the contradictions when he sums up the tradition he has been examining in Stowe,
Hawthorne, Howells and James:

> Their fiction offers an anatomy of puritanism and of the reaction
> against it, the flood of romantic individualism and the flowering
> of transcendental idealism. The redirection of moral energy
> previously contained in the Calvinist formulation was signalled in
> their novels by the emergence of new heroines to replace the once
> and former queen. In the succession the crown passed from the
> puritan maiden to the romantic rebel and finally to the American
> girl . . . The touted freedom and originality of this new dynasty
> proved illusory, however; the paradoxical power of the girl's

'audacious innocence' was revealed at the last as an improbable crossing of earlier lines of descent, an unstable synthesis of the rebel's dangerous pursuit of self-culture and the maiden's indulgence in morbid renunciations.[41]

The pursuit of self-culture was dangerous indeed to the status of woman as defined by social structures. Margaret Fuller, another prominent transcendentalist, editor of *The Dial* from 1840–3, wrote in *Woman in the Nineteenth Century*:

> It is not the transient breath of poetic incense that women want; each can receive that from a lover. It is not life long sway; it needs but to become a coquette, a shrew, or a good cook, to be sure of that. It is not money, nor notoriety, nor the badges of authority which men have appropriated to themselves . . . it is for that which is the birthright of every being capable of receiving it, – the freedom, the religious, the intelligent freedom of the universe to use its means, to learn its secret, as far as Nature has enabled them, with God alone for their guide and judge.[42]

It was thus not only the growing social freedom of the American girl, to enjoy herself, challenge European convention, appear alone and unchaperoned, talk openly with 'gentlemen', but the growing challenge of the right to self-culture, self-guidence for the development of one's *self* which made her both a vital sign of her emerging nation and a rebellious contradiction to the function of sign itself.

In the guise of American ignorance, innocence and fresh youth the subordination of her qualities in marriage was unproblematic. But as freedom and individualism, it was a different matter. The very qualities themselves appeared meaningless when subordinated totally and effectively in marriage. Of course, this subordination was only the inescapable manifestation of what was in any case present – the freedom of the American girl existed fundamentally for others, and not for herself. Her status as sign remained unchanged; as Harriet Martineau remarked, despite much indulgence the position of American women was really no better than in England. But it was the very obvious legal, social, and personal contradictions of the total submission of self in marriage for women that focussed the attention of those interested in the position of women at that time. Thus marriage becomes a paradigm for the relinquishing of the illusion of free subjecthood and for submission to social existence as other, as woman.

As material for study of these aspects of American and English nineteenth century culture, the novel has a particular suitability, in that it frequently took women and their sphere as its subject matter. Particularly in America, the popular fiction was written by and for women, but many English and American writers of novels which we identify as 'literature' (written by men and women) drew on the tradition of love, personal life and morality as material. W. D. Howells, in his *Heroines of Fiction*, uses as his defence of the novel (against the charge of frivolousness and artistic triviality) its potential for moral education, and lauds the influence of Austen, Edgeworth and Burney:

> The most beautiful, the most consoling of all the arts owes its universal acceptance among us, its opportunity of pleasing and helping readers of every age and sex, to this group of high souled women. They forever dedicated it to decency; as women they were faithful to their charge of the chaste mind; and as artists they taught the reading world to be in love with the sort of heroines who knew how not only to win the wandering hearts of men but to keep their homes pure and inviolable. They imagined the heroine who was above all a Nice Girl; who still remains the ideal of our fiction, to whom it returns with a final constancy.[43]

Howells cherishes an ideal of the 'Ever-Womanly', and judges the 'heroines of fiction' according to their participation in this category. Of all Hawthorne's heroines he prefers Zenobia because: 'She is a very woman-soul; what she does and suffers is by the very law of her womanhood.'[44]

However, not all English and American nineteenth century novelists dealing in primarily 'feminine' material were simply reflecting the prevailing significations of womanhood – some were engaged in exploring the nature of woman's position, even in challenging and questioning it. To some degree, all texts necessarily contain a mixture of conscious and unconscious challenge and conformity. In his essay *Woman and the Literary Text*, John Goode outlines some distinctions between the kinds of writing on women being produced:

> Insofar as we become conscious not of an ideology trapped secretly 'inside' the text, but of the sense of ideology itself, motivating and shaping the representation, we are in the presence

of a fictional coherence. On the other hand, insofar as the representation remains untransformed, unexposed, familiarized, we are in the presence of an ideological coherence.[45]

The demand for coherence and consistency which will inevitably dominate any writing with a specific ideological programme, will ensure that it either asks no questions, or represses some of them. Thus a straightforward assertion, whether of woman as subject *or* object, can deny the contradictions and questions raised in confronting the position of woman as both subject *and* sign.

In a novel like Grant Allen's *The Woman Who Did*, the overt programme – a championing of women's political, social and ethical rights – is undermined by the conventional ideological coherence of the language. Herminia, the heroine, is 'maidenly', 'womanly', the 'eternal woman'. She conforms utterly to the notions of submission, martyrdom and, above all, the function of woman first, person second:

> Herminia let him lead her. She was woman enough by nature to like being led. Only, it must be the right man who led her, and he must lead her along the path that her conscience approved of.[46]

> Alan thought as he looked at her he had never before seen anybody who appeared at all points so nearly to approach his ideal of womanhood. She was at once so high in type, so serene, so tranquil, and yet so purely womanly.[47]

At the end: 'Herminia Barton's stainless soul had ceased to exist for ever.'[48]

In Meredith's novels such as *Diana of the Crossways* and *The Egoist*, on the other hand, the realisation is fictional, yet still the realisation of an ideological programme. Woman is asserted as subject struggling against those who attempt to treat her as object. In *The Egoist*, for example, Meredith recognises and expands the transformation by the male 'egoist' of women into 'market produce':

> The devouring male Egoist prefers them as inanimate overwrought polished pure metal precious vessels, fresh from the hands of the artificer, for him to walk away with hugging.[49]

Yet Clara's resistance to this appropriation is the resistance of a separate subject, aware of the tendency of the world to treat her as other (and of the tendency of women to offer themselves as other) but in no way constituted by it. She copes by employing a familiar alienation from her object self:

> He fondled her hand, and to that she grew accustomed; her hand was at a distance. And what is a hand? Leaving it where it was, she treated it as a link between herself and dutiful goodness.[50]

Yet the extent to which Clara is irrevocably sign, and the extent to which she would have to dislocate herself from social existence to resist this, is repressed. The appropriation of the marriage institution is resolved through the illusions of individual freedom of both men and women to make a free and equal marriage. In this, the resolution of *The Egoist* is similar to that of *Middlemarch*, where sexual energy is finally correlated with social order and harmony. Writers like Gissing, Hardy and James himself recognised the inevitable danger of sexual passion and love, for women. Outside the bounds of marriage, it offered social and economic ruin. When pursued legitimately, it could offer only the limitations implicit for women in acquiescing to the social order embodied in marriage – even the 'exceptional' man of fiction would always have the power to withdraw, as well as extend, the partnership of equals. So an attempt to resist the actual position of women by asserting them as subject, will repress the contradictions of their state, whether expressed with fictional coherence (as in Meredith's work) or undermined with internal ideology (as in Grant Allen's). One apparent coherence (woman as object) is replaced with another (woman as subject).[51] A quotation from a discussion of the problems of women writers in France in the 1970s seems relevant here:

> In spite of our concern with creating a new, more suitable means of expression for women, many of us are still caught in the old analytic modes of thought in which ideological postures harden and rigidify. Intellectual women walk a tightrope trying to learn the dominant philosophical discourse in order to bring its assumptions into question.[52]

The texts which most fruitfully expose the contradictions of woman as sign and person are therefore those in which questions rather than answers are articulated. As John Goode expresses it, the texts in which:

the woman is summoned to be the subject of her experience in order that she can be revealed as subject to it; the true subject of her experience, in other words, is that of being the object of another's knowledge . . . it articulates the relationship between role and status in such a way that the programme itself makes the break with patriarchal ideology.[53]

Goode is primarily interested in exploring these ideas in relation to Hardy, here *Tess of the d'Urbervilles*. We witness, in reading *Tess*, her objectification, acted out, yet also mediations which give a developing substance to her subject experience. The contradictions (or the double process that Goode refers to) increase rather than decrease. Tess's final assertion of herself as subject, by killing Alec d'Urberville, is also the moment when she makes herself most object of retaliation:

> The 'human' Tess and the non-human forces that motivate her make of her a subject whose subjection is at war with its subjectivity. And we see Tess not as in a flat picture masquerading as depth, but from all the angles that are possible. And that is why, whatever Hardy's own ideological commitment, no frame will hold his novel in place.[54]

This seems to me to be an important point about the way James's novels work (despite the obvious and enormous differences between him and Hardy). Whatever his 'ideological commitment', James's novels develop chronologically into a process of exposing questions and contradictions. He does not start with a programme but a *donnée*, and then turns it inside out by probing, shifting and rearranging.

Meredith's *Diana of the Crossways*, Grant Allen's *The Woman Who Did*, Gissing's *The Odd Women*, Hardy's *Jude The Obscure* – all these novels to some degree explore the notion of the 'New Woman', the middle class woman who demanded education and financial independence, and who challenged the subservience of women in marriage. English fiction in the second half of the nineteenth century was definitely influenced by contemporary feminism,[55] and writers such as these took as a conscious project a response to feminist demands. That the New Woman often became simply a further sign was inevitable, but it meant nonetheless that argument and process centred round the woman as individual – even if only to demonstrate finally her essential womanliness, as Grant Allen does despite himself.

American novelists of the same period deal less directly and intellectually with the New Woman, but it is interesting how those who employed the American girl encountered similar problems – the difficulty of adequately resolving such a figure into a conventionally happy marriage. I would be cautious about making claims for the specific 'American-ness' of the 'American novel', heavily influenced as it was by the English and European novelistic tradition. The most clearly defined American tradition is that of the novels which eschewed the kind of subject matter – domestic, feminine, social – that I have been outlining, i.e. the works of Melville, Cooper, and Twain, Philip Rahv's 'redskins'.[56] However, in the area of the feminine as well as the specific character of the American girl, some writers have suggested a peculiarly American attitude to sex and female sexuality. Leslie Fiedler, perhaps the best known exponent of this theory, suggests a failure of the 'American psyche' (presumably the male psyche) to find a satisfactory adult to adult heterosexual relationship, and that instead there is a retreat into male comradeship, with women being either evil and sexually threatening or so palely virtuous that they die or go mad.[57] Similarly Milton Rugoff, in *Prudery and Passion: Sexuality in Victorian America*, concludes in his chapter on literature:

> We come away from such a survey of nineteenth century literature, and especially fiction, with a disturbing sense of the reluctance of the young heroes of novels to cope maturely with young women.[58]

Of course English fiction also contains its virtuous 'too good for this world' heroines – one has only to look at Dickens. But if the solution in fulfilling marriage is less common in American fiction, it may have to do, as Fiedler and others suggest, with the orientation of the male American psyche towards flight, escape from social responsibility, and childhood, in which woman signifies all that is being escaped from. It may also link up to the moral idealism and individualism which I touched on earlier. William Wasserstrom suggests that the relative unimportance of organised religion for the male American had a lot to do with the structuring of the relations between the sexes, and specifically American significations of the feminine.

The clergy, and most early novelists, hoped to frighten society back to church . . . Americans preferred to remain away and to compose a new secular dogma which would make passion unobtrusive, orthodox, orderly: they created the idea of the Secular Manly. Practical men who were occupied with the problems of settling and operating a new society . . . later simplified the whole matter by adopting an easy convention: good women embodied a living victory of the spirit over the flesh. Conviction of this sort did not require attendance at church; America itself became a cathedral. Womanliness came to mean sexlessness and in the 1840s and later fiction relied on this conviction whenever it presented an ideal woman.[59]

This is rather a generalisation, but it does describe a certain strain of American writing. What is interesting is that at the point where American writers might be seen to be utilising a particularly repressive signification of woman – as sexless and as moral representative – lie also the germs of her potential assertion as self. Sexlessness – or celibacy – could also mean resistance to absorption into marriage, or even just male passion, and morality in trans-cendentalist terms could mean the serious and high minded freedom to think for oneself in precisely the way that more traditional religion never allowed. Or, to combine the two, moral independence *had* to remain celibate. Novelists' attempts to explore the independence and essential 'goodness' of the American girl tend to find it difficult to resolve the story in a happy marriage.

In *Woman's Fiction: A Guide to Novels By and About Women in America, 1820–1870*,[60] Nina Baym sets out to describe how the deployment of conventional significations of the feminine could nonetheless result in a 'moderate and pragmatic' attempt to assert the female as subject by making her perception of her experiences the central thread of the novel. In contrast, some of the novelists in the second half of the nineteenth century who employed the figure of the American girl were using new significations of the feminine which hinted at her as somehow not-sign (thinking for herself, independent, socially iconoclastic) and yet attempting to resolve them in socially conventional ways. The least problematic version of the American girl was that which stressed her youthful ignorance and innocence. Her spontaneity and freedom thus becomes that of a child. Edith Wharton, writing retrospectively about the period that engendered the American girl, displayed the paradox through which feminine innocence and openness depended on its existing in a society which was rigidly closed. In *The Age of Innocence*, Newland Archer gradually realises that his fiancée is the product of a protective and elaborate social system:

> The result of course was that the young girl who was at the centre of this elaborate system of mystification remained the more inscrutable for her very frankness and assurance. She was frank, poor darling, because she had nothing to conceal, assured because she knew of nothing to be on her guard against.[61]

Innocence and openness thus becomes the very essence of the idealist illusion of the untouched, blank materials of signification waiting to be shaped and formed by the external (male) subject; as James expresses in *The Reverberator* (1888):

> Don't you see that she's really of the softest, finest material that breathes, that she's a perfect flower of plasticity, that everything you may have an apprehension about will drop away from her like the dead leaves from a rose and that you may make of her any perfect and enchanting thing you yourself may have the wit to conceive (vol. 13, p. 206).

The problematic relationship of unorthodox or individual behaviour in a world of rigid structures thus becomes the problem of the subject onlooker – as I shall discuss in Chapter 3, in relation to *Daisy Miller*.

The contained oppositions of the feminine can all serve to 'fix' a narrative morally. If representation creates morality because it necessitates contemplation of meaning, then not only did the pale purity of the New England maiden signify the virtue of puritanism, but her contrasting counterpart – the sensual dark lady – also provoked a moral dilemma for the observer. The division that Fiedler identifies in the classic novels of American literature is between sexual attractiveness and 'pallid' moral virtue, and it is interesting that in Hawthorne, at least, moral purity equates with simplicity, whereas sexuality is linked to complexity – in Hester, Zenobia and Miriam. The contemplation of virtue resolves questions, whereas the contemplation of human weakness provokes them. The fact that the freedom of the American girl was in reality the freedom to behave well of her own accord rather than by compulsion, is present in the New England morality signified by such women (in contrast, the sensual women were often European or Oriental in association and characteristic, again like Hester and Miriam). The embodiment of individual conscience rather than established religious custom was a more sophisticated form of restriction, and one which Howells characteristically expressed as a moral freedom for woman:

> Women owe our continent a double debt of fidelity. It's the paradise of Women, it's their Promised Land where they've been led up out of the Egyptian bondage of Europe. It's the home of their freedom. It is recognised in America that women have consciences and souls.[62]

But the addition of the signification of moral authority or intellectual independence renders the disposal of the American girl as sign more complex. Howells attempted various solutions in his early novels. Lydia Blood in *The Lady of the Aroostook* shames her lover Staniford into admiration of her individual and independent moral virtue, yet even this fairly conventional relationship of subject and moral arbiter can be sustained beyond courtship only by sending them to enjoy their married life out West – far and strange enough for the imagination to conceive some kind of moral equality in marriage which will not be too consistently undermined by the existence of woman as object in marriage. In *A Chance Acquaintance* Kitty Ellison has to reject her suitor altogether in order to maintain the consistency of her criticism – as sign of democracy – of his old fashioned snobbery – a criticism that would be impossible to reconcile with her role as representative of him in marriage unless he underwent the sort of geographical as well as moral sea change that Staniford does. And in *A Foregone Conclusion* he attempts to retain Florida Vervain's qualities of pride and independence in marriage by redirecting them towards her children, which can suitably be objects to her as she is now to her husband. Henry Adams runs into the same kind of problem in his two novels *Esther* (1884) and *Democracy* (1880). His two heroines are endowed with an essentially American morality, one which actively criticises the society around it rather than simply maintaining the Christian standards which justify the society without revealing its contradictions. In an article entitled *The Prison of Womanhood*, Elizabeth Sabiston discusses the line of heroines which emerges in the nineteenth century, which she classifies as that of the 'imaginative, provincial, heroine'. Citing

Austen's Emma Woodhouse, Flaubert's Emma Bovary, Eliot's Dorothea Brooke and James's Isabel Archer as examples, she focusses on the tensions between these heroines and their societies:

> The basic component in all four of these variations on the provincial theme would seem to be a society which imposes even more severe limitations upon women than upon men; and, as the protagonist, an imaginative heroine, nourished upon books rather than upon life and given to flights of fancy.[63]

Despite the social comedy (and implicit criticism) which Emma Woodhouse engenders, there is never any doubt that she is intrinsically part of (and reconciled to) her society, and the same can be said of Dorothea's more specifically Christian virtue. James's novel, on the other hand, triggers off a far more fundamental conflict between individual women and social structures. The 'irritable moral consciousness' which he found so characteristically American is not dedicated to preserving the *status quo*. Adams's two heroines run up hard against the essential contradictions of their existence – in exercising their independence of mind, they can be faced only with social displacement as women:

> Women must take their chance. It is what they are for. Marriage makes no real difference in their lot. All the contented women are fools, and all the discontented ones want to be men. Women are a blunder in the creation and must take the consequences.[64]

Both *Esther* and *Democracy* pivot around the progress of their heroines towards marriage, ultimately made impossible by its conflict with their assertion of subjecthood:

> The more confidently Hazard told her to leave everything to him, the less it occurred to her to do so . . . The moment he was out of sight she forgot that he was to be the keeper of her conscience, and without a thought of her dependence she resumed the charge of her own affairs.[65]

Both Esther and Madeleine retreat and renounce, both novels are strangely static, in the end one could say that nothing has happened. The full signification of the American girl results in fixity for her as individual heroine.

P. J. Eakin, in *The New England Girl*, states in his introduction to James that:

I take the Americanness of the fiction of Henry James, perennially a subject of dispute, to reside in certain qualities of moral consciousness, especially evident in his portraits of young women.[66]

He then goes on to define his approach to this:

The drama of the *hero's relationship to the American girl* in these tales lies in the disparity between his interpretation of her and the reality which she represents. (my emphasis).[67]

I am interested in the point at which the drama shifts to the American girl's *own* sense of the disparity between her hero's interpretation of her, and what she herself feels and perceives of, and for, herself.

2 *The Scarlet Letter*

Before discussing the novels of James, I want to clarify the notion of 'woman as sign in the literary text', by looking briefly at a work which confronts this idea in a form more clear cut and insistent than James was to use: Hawthorne's *The Scarlet Letter*.

> This rag of scarlet cloth, – for time, and wear, and a sacriligious moth, had reduced it to little other than a rag, – on careful examination, assumed the shape of a letter. It was the capital letter A. By an accurate measurement, each limb proved to be precisely three inches and a quarter in length. It had been intended, there could be no doubt, as an ornamental article of dress; but how it was to be worn, or what rank, honor, and dignity, in by-past times, were signified by it, was a riddle which (so evanescent are the fashions of the world in these particulars) I saw little hope of solving. And yet it strangely interested me. My eyes fastened themselves upon the old scarlet letter, and would not be turned aside. Certainly, there was some deep meaning in it, most worthy of interpretation, and which, as it were, streamed forth from the mystic symbol, subtly communicating itself to my sensibilities, but evading the analysis of my mind.[1]

In the introductory section to *The Scarlet Letter*, the section called The Custom-House, Hawthorne describes the discovery of the scarlet letter of cloth that we are to encounter throughout the novel on Hester Prynne's dress. The scarlet letter is a sign, *any* sign or symbol, and what it stands *for* is not particularly important. The letter, and Hester's relation to it – especially the question of her being both oppressed by it and made socially functional by it – seem to me paradigmatic of the questions I shall be discussing in relation to James's novels.

Hawthorne introduces the letter as mysterious, provocative of thought, and intrinsically calling for interpretation. The letter has a tangible, physical reality – he can measure it 'precisely'. It can be recognised as having had a specific social function, though its remoteness in time obscures that function: 'how it was to be worn, or what rank, honor, and dignity, in by-past times, were signified by it, was a riddle which . . . I saw little hope of solving'. Yet beyond this physical reality and the precise historical signification of social place, the letter suggests a 'deep meaning'. The speaker does not infer this meaning from any specific connection or correlation with experience, but 'senses' it. The instinctive level of this recognition of symbolism and significance is intensified in the next paragraph, when he places the letter on his breast and experiences 'a sensation not altogether physical, yet almost so, as of burning heat; as if the letter were not of red cloth, but red-hot iron'.[2]

The power of the letter, a power not accessible to analysis or logic, is firmly established. The introduction seems to promise some explanation of the letter, some demonstration of the 'deep meaning' streaming from it. Yet in fact the story which follows intensifies the mystery, and diversifies the possible ways and means of interpretation. The letter has an existence in cloth on Hester's dress, it appears as lightning in the sky, it is seen imprinted on Dimmesdale's flesh. In all its manifestations, it can be explained; physically, psychologically, religiously, superstitiously. In the same way, the meanings taken from the A multiply and change – Adultery, Art, Angel, Able – the meanings are sought both by the community surrounding Hester, and by the reader of the novel. No one explanation is finally favoured.

What I am suggesting is that Hawthorne is focussing on, at the centre of *The Scarlet Letter*, the *process* of symbolism, the search for meaning and order, the compulsion to signify, to connect and generalise, to interpret. The raw community on the edge of the wilderness brings with it from England not only the prison as a fundamental social structure, but the more ineradicable one of symbolism. The process of signification that Hawthorne shows at work, shaping and dominating the lives of the tiny community, is inextricably linked to Hester, she makes it visible and vivid. This showing forth is her social function, and her function within the novel as well:

> Throughout them all, giving up her individuality, she would become the general symbol at which the preacher and moralist might point, and in which they might vivify and embody their images of woman's frailty and sinful passion.[3]

As far as commitment to, and interpretation of, the social codes embodied in the A goes, the story revolves *around* Hester, but *concerns* Dimmesdale and Chillingworth, both of whom are struggling to destroy or survive within the social mechanisms they make use of. As James said:

> The story, indeed, is in a secondary degree that of Hester Prynne; she becomes, really, after the first scene, an accessory figure . . . The story goes on, for the most part, between the lover and the husband.[4]

However Hester's relationship to the A is interesting; she and the letter are shown as physically ('really') separable, yet functionally inseparable. She accepts the letter, her social existence is dependent on it, then she transforms and embroiders it. Her alienation from her society, caused by her sin, is never complete, and is mediated as well as expressed by the presence of the letter. Although her cottage is 'out of that sphere of social activity'[5] it is still visible, still linked to the village. Her child, Pearl, is as strange, vivid and impenetrable as the letter – she cries out for interpretation and understanding, yet Hester, whose child she is, cannot understand her. The signifying activity is produced by Hester, to some extent controlled by her, yet she is also alienated from it – perhaps because it does not take place for her benefit, it is not really hers. Though we see Hester develop as subject and range in thought far beyond her society, we also see that this development cannot be communicated outwards because it has no name, no recognition in the social world. Hester's subjectivity is peripheral to the society she inhabits, and to a large degree left untouched as long as she functions through signifying. Her refusal to abandon this function, even when she could, by taking the letter off her dress for ever, suggests the way her identity is bound up with being recognisable as a sign. But her insistence also suggests control, a point at which she will signify whether they like it or not, an assertion. The embroidery of the letter prefigures the way in which Hester can transform her socially functional alienation and impose her own values on it. And through this alienation and the growing awareness of her position within society, Hester gains a resisting, conscious subjecthood. She does not, perhaps cannot, reject her function as sign, but she can use it, even insist upon it:

> She had returned, therefore, and resumed, – of her own free will, for not the sternest magistrate of that iron period would have

imposed it, – resumed the symbol of which we have related so dark a tale. Never afterwards did it quit her bosom. But, in the lapse of the toilsome, thoughtful, and self-devoted years that made up Hester's life, the scarlet letter ceased to be a stigma which attracted the world's scorn and bitterness, and became a type of something to be sorrowed over, and looked upon with awe, yet with reverence too.[6]

Hester commits herself, finally, to propagating the search for 'divine and mysterious truth'.[7]

There is a fine line between seeing Hester and seeing the scarlet letter, one potentially obscures the other in a reciprocal relation. By making the sign value of woman so tangible, as a cloth letter placed on her dress, Hawthorne allows us to see the puzzling nature of this function. We see it as artificial, constructed, temporally imposed. We see that the letter is more important than Hester, to the subjectivity of Dimmesdale, the village community, even the majority of Hawthorne's readers. Yet we also see her transforming and controlling the A, establishing a fragile social existence that is both forced on her and defined by her. Hester's return to New England to resume her penance states clearly the extent to which she can exist only within the society which defines and limits her. It is in resisting it that she becomes a free ranging, questioning subject, but those questions relate back to her society, she is formed by the world which makes her a 'general symbol'.

James found Hawthorne's symbolism too obvious and insistent, and certainly his own use of similar 'badges' or 'masks' does not usually involve the same literal separability of person from sign.[8] Yet the 'scarlet letter' is present, and in James's early work especially we see the letter more clearly than the woman, learn to recognise it and the various questions and interpretations it raises – is it America or Art?, Innocence or Individualism? It is in the later novels that the conscious woman, reflecting and internally questioning, positioned between the village and the wilderness, gradually emerges to be the subject of the text as much as the sign value she carries.

3 The Early Work

In Chapter 1, I suggested ways in which the qualities of the American Girl existed for others, rather than for herself. Henry James used 'American-ness', signified by men and women, to raise all kinds of questions in his fiction, and it might be argued that whether the dramatised American is male or female makes little real difference. So I begin by looking at two of his early novels, in both of which Americans come to Europe and fare badly – *The American* (1877), and *Daisy Miller* (1879).

I have chosen to compare these two works for three main reasons. The subject matter of both books forms the framework of material for much of James's later fiction. Even more to my purpose is the fact that in one the central American is male – Newman – and in the other female – Daisy. I hope to show that there is a difference in treatment, and through a comparison of the use of both Newman and Daisy as sign to show that this function is paramount and intrinsic for Daisy, while it is not for Newman. Finally, I believe that *Daisy Miller* 'leads on' to many of James's major novels in a more diverse and complex way than *The American*, and that this is to do with the different emphasis accorded the process of interpretation (of signs) and its implication for the individual (woman) thus defined.

Before making claims for the peculiar aptness of the American girl as a vehicle for James's novelistic concerns, it seems appropriate to give some outline of those concerns, and provide a framework for my concentration on the tension in his work between women as both signs and central consciousnesses.

Perhaps the critic most systematically to examine James's 'beliefs', and the moral and philosophical heritage he drew on, is Quentin Anderson who, in *The American Henry James*, speaks of 'the truly metaphysical status which James grants consciousness', and adds that: 'James is truer than William Blake to a vision of the world as wholly the product of the human imagination.'[1]

However, in a discussion of the differences between the elder

James and Emerson (a contrast which Anderson sees as significant in pinpointing the novelist's position), he also emphasises that, unlike Emerson, James's father stressed the importance of social institutions and the need to understand them. J. C. Rowe, in a comparison of Henry Adams and Henry James, endorses this approach, seeing the field of action as precisely the attempt to align the areas of perception and understanding, and of 'social' life:

> They explore scientific, literary, philosophical and sociopolitical realms trying to find a relation between public and private, to formulate a nexus between the *language* of consciousness and the *names* of society. (my emphasis).[2]

This nexus can be achieved only through available structures of signification, explored and restructured in the attempts to relate the individual consciousness to the material outside at moments of conflict and change. In James's fiction, patterns of conflict emerge, concerned again and again with the individual's attempt to establish some kind of relationship to her/his world. In the work which deals with the figure of the artist (usually male), the conflict may emerge in the shape of doubts concerning the correspondence of art and the reality it seeks to describe, the power of creative signification to distort and manipulate, and the challenge posed by the realisation that the 'outside' may be created only through such signification, and never objectively known.[3] In a similar way, the fascination with the past and with the supernatural lies in the suggestion of alternative realities, alternative relationships with the world in which the individual has both greater responsibility and greater power.[4] At the same time conflict arises out of the desire for control, the individual fears the reciprocal reaction of the outside world; James is all too well aware that the world is *not* 'wholly the product of the [individual] human imagination'. Much of his work is thus concerned with the fear of experience and interaction, often crystallised into the fear of love.[5] And this awareness of the need for reciprocity is also manifested in the exposition of the sterility of any too single minded an approach to experience. Full awareness of the place of the subject in a material world, to which it may be object, requires an awareness of the varied responses of others; pure intellect, pure morality, even pure passion deny the validity of the other. James's requirements for a productive relation between the individual and the world are thus not only intelligence, but imagination and irony.

The structures that James chose to explore these conflicts are many and varied. As an American, he felt himself the illusion of detachment, of being outside the artistic tradition, and the freedom that this conferred to select whatever came to hand, whatever seemed vivid and apposite:

> it seems to me that we are ahead of the European races in the fact that more than either of them we can deal freely with forms of civilisation not our own, can pick and choose and assimilate and in short (aesthetically, etc.) claim our property wherever we find it.[6]

Yet he was conscious of his nationality in the approach he was to bring to his subject matter, and continued his letter:

> We must have something of our own – something distinctive and homogeneous – and I take it that we shall find it in our moral consciousness, our unprecedented spiritual lightness and vigour.[7]

However, among the familiar patterns of courtship, marriage, childhood, the dilemma of the artist, the implications of wealth, the theme so early recognised as particularly James's own was the international one, and the expression of this theme pivoted around the figure of the American girl. James's contemporary W. D. Howells, credited James with being the inventor of the 'International American girl'.[8]

The American girl, as she appears in James's early stories and novels, has all the major characteristics identified and discussed in Chapter 1. She is independent, moral, free, innocent, and her attractiveness is either 'delicate' or of a pale and rather asexual kind.[9] In her less refined or serious form, she may be ignorant, brash or simply naive.[10] She is, of course, always unmarried. In using the American girl as central to his exploration of the interaction of American and European society, it was not at first in the girl herself that James placed the distinctive American moral consciousness, and when she was endowed with moral seriousness the conscious response to its clash with social convention was again, in the early work, usually located in a male onlooker. Her self-consciousness developed out of a line of American girls who were absorbed by Europe, withdrew from it, or were destroyed by it, and it is the reason for the destruction which suggests the need for an assertive self.

The patterns available to women, in James's work, fall into distinct categories – those of marriage which signifies social existence and all too often annihilation for the woman of any autonomous existence; of withdrawal from marriage and thus from a fruitful relationship with society; and of death. When talking about the constraints and limitations of being other and functioning as sign, it is important not to forget the parallel realities that James is well aware of, of the constraints of economic dependence and the lack of practical alternatives to marriage. At this level, men are never constrained to the same extent; even when given the disability of poverty, their social and economic potential is greater. And they are not dependent in the same way on their appearance or their value as objects to others – this value may exist without determining their fortunes in the same fundamental way, or even being in any sense universally recognised.

James for instance recognised that the sense, the understanding, of how one is seen by the world is fundamental to women. Their looks and dress determine their marriageability, on which in turn their economic survival depends. In marriage, their success depends on their existence in relation to husband and family. In the wider world success depends on a social, representational status. James's stories are full of women selling themselves, or being sold, on the marriage market. *The American Scene* is full of meditation on the extent to which American women are the visible part of their nation. James also recognised the extent to which, to perform this function adequately, women are ideally blanks which can signify whatever is required. In *The Modern Warning* (1888), a wife has to abandon her American identity and her relation to her American brother, in order to represent England and her English husband. The effort in this story kills her. The most intelligent of James's women survive by learning and understanding the world of social codes and forms, by using language – that primary means of signifying – with consummate skill. Their function becomes a semi-artistic one, enhanced by the fact that the best of them are not simply clever but imaginative as well, and have that moral relation to the world which James saw as indispensible to the most realistic of artists.

It is only in certain of his central female characters that James focusses on the conflict between female consciousness of self and existence as sign, defined socially and linguistically. The novels establish women as signs, both in their reflection of social reality and in their use of women as 'other', suggestive of interpretation, at the same time as they probe this sign function as problematic for the aware and conscious female individual. The heroines in whom this conflict is explored are young and usually unmarried, poised, as it were, on the threshold of social existence and limitation. Older women in James's work are often very much 'fixed' socially, and are linguistically and socially adept. Easily recognisable, they function both as social reference points and as interpreters of the social world to the subject of the novel's experience. Maintaining the social structures they inhabit, they encourage marriage and objectification of the hesitant young girl.

Much of the time, particularly in the stories, James uses women in a conventional way. However, he parodies the apparatus of domestic and romantic literature as well as using it.[11] In *Washington Square* (1880), in which the lack of European contrast takes the edge off the 'American-ness' of the characters, the conventional expectations of the feminine are exposed as repressive in their inaptness and banality. Catherine Sloper is not an inadequate American girl, but an inadequate romantic maiden, fairytale princess or heiress. Her insistence on loving romantically nonetheless means that she fails to signify even the plain honest virtues of domestic femininity. Inarticulate, almost dumb, in a world of linguistic adepts, Catherine contradicts the conventional significations, and thus loses any functional social identity except that of the quasi-comic old maid

In my comparison of Newman and Daisy, I shall suggest that Daisy is destroyed because she fails as sign. As a vivid signifier there is no clear indication of what is signified. Her salvation would be not in herself but only in the male subject's ability to trace some correspondence – an ability which emerges too late. Daisy signifies something, but what we are not sure. In *Washington Square*, however, the structures of signification are supplied by those around Catherine, but she does not fit into them. She is condemned to a trivial and meaningless existence because she does not appear to suggest any signified at all. There are meanings in plenty but she obstinately, yet passively, refuses to signify any of them adequately. She is neither the romantic heroine nor the sensible, obedient, practical girl who will accept the suitable offer for her hand. This miscorrespondence more than anything else exposes through the questions it raises the complete dependence of the girl on her fulfillment of a recognised structure of signification, and this dependence clashes with her possession in the text of the qualities of the independent, American individual.[12]

The starting point for the protagonist in *The American* is the same as for Daisy; the independent American individual arriving in the Old World. Christopher Newman comes to Europe as an American; the plot revolves around his potential marriage with a European. Such a marriage does not mean for him a representation of American values for Europe (unlike, for instance, Martha in *The Last of the Valerii*, or Bessie Alden in *An International Episode*), nor a being absorbed and fitted into European society. He seeks in marriage values to represent him, a tangible symbol of his successful existence to bear with him back to America.

In the opening chapters, Newman is described as 'a powerful specimen of an American' (p. 6), the 'great Western Barbarian stepping forth in his innocence and might, gazing a while at this poor effete Old World and then swooping down on it' (p. 34). He signifies the material wealth of America, its raw energy and individualism. R. W. Butterfield, in his essay on *The American* refers to the readings of the text which find Newman incredible and unreal as a specific and historical individual. He goes on to give a convincing discussion of the elements of nineteenth century Americanism incorporated in Newman: 'He is the American Protestant individualist displayed in his economic guise as the Capitalist.'[13] The conception of Newman is 'as much generic and allegorical as it is specific and realistic'. Yet within the text Newman's allegorical status is not a realisation of any other character's conception of individualism or capitalism; in fact to communicate his reality to an alien world, he searches for the means to represent himself and his qualities in an understandable form.

As the American individual, Newman confronts a formal, traditional aristocratic European society; yet there exists a second dichotomy which modifies Newman's existence as individual vulnerable to the response of the social world he encounters. In Chapter 1, I described how within America itself a division was seen to exist between men 'doing' and making money, and women 'representing' culture and thus the cultural products of money, functioning both as consumers and products. In *The American*, the money/culture split is defined partly as American/European, but also as male/female. Newman is first and foremost a doer and buyer. He watches, observes, sees and buys, and he is doing so in order to obtain some sign of his material success, some means whereby he will be interpreted and represented to the world. Newman is more appropriate as a rich American than as an innocent one, but even so the signification of his wealth remains at a literal level. The moral questions raised by wealth – the power, freedom, responsibility and potential for transcendence of the material that it brings – are not explored in the way that they are elsewhere in the rich girls who, through their indirect relationship to the sources of wealth, both represent it and present the illusion inherent in apparently going beyond its worldly base.

Newman's use of money is the straighforward one of acquisition. In the very first chapter he buys Noemie's painting, which is a travesty of the art of Europe. His inability to acquire European culture efficiently or successfully without some guidance is aided by the mediation of Mrs Tristram, to whom be expresses his previous obsession with action to the exclusion of feeling and reflection: 'The fact is I have never had time to feel things. I have had to *do* them' (p. 33).

Telling Mrs Tristram of his desire to marry, he explains that: 'To make it [his financial success] perfect, as I see it, there must be a beautiful woman perched on the pile, like a statue, on a monument' (p. 37) going on to say: 'I want to possess, in a word, the best article in the market' (p. 37).

As Newman goes off to view architectural culture in a tour of Europe, we are reminded that: 'The world to his sense, was a great bazaar, where one might stroll about and purchase handsome things' (p. 62), and that Newman doesn't want to take his purchases *too* seriously:

> an undue solicitude for 'culture' seemed a sort of silly dawdling at the station, a proceeding properly confined to women, foreigners, and other unpractical persons (p. 62).

On seeing Claire de Cintré, however, he recognises the 'culture' he has been looking for; embodied in a woman, it can be transformed for his purpose:

> he always came back to the feeling that when he should complete himself by taking a wife, that was the way he should like his wife to interpret him to the world (p. 113)

and continues to compare her always to his conception of his 'ideal wife'. At the engagement party given by the Bellegardes, the last moment in the novel before the machinery of the plot takes over, Newman reflects on his success:

> The lights, the flowers, the music, the crowd, the splendid women, the jewels, the strangeness even of the universal murmur of a clever foreign tongue, were all a *vivid symbol* and assurance of his *having grasped his purpose and forced along his groove* (p. 209). (my emphasis).

The action emphasised here is fundamental to Newman's function; he is not 'seen' as a passive object by observers, he initiates action and we are continually told how he hates leisure, cannot relax, and believes that: 'words were acts and acts were steps in life' (p. 315).

To free him for action, he needs his existence to be rendered intelligible by the structures of signification which European culture appears to hold out. Claire de Cintré, as woman, is, like Mrs Tristram, the instrument of mediation, the woman who, as sign, can signify to and for Newman, interpreting the world to him and him to the world.

Richard Poirier, in his discussion of the open and closed characters in *The American*,[14] describes how Claire is invested with certain American and open qualities, as for instance in this passage:

> Madame de Cintré's face had, to Newman's eye, a range of expression as delightfully vast as the wind-streaked, cloud-flecked distance on a Western Prairie (p. 125).

Newman can see in Claire the qualities he is looking for. Earlier, when he discusses her with her brother Valentin, Valentin says:

> You have seen her; you know what she is: tall, thin, light, imposing and gentle, half a grande dame and half an angel; a mixture of pride and humility, of the eagle and the dove. She looks like a statue which had failed as stone (p. 102).

The two follow it up with a bundle of labels: perfect, good, charitable, intelligent – which suggest that Claire is the ever-womanly repository of values and qualities which can represent the culture and nature of its possessor: the Bellegrades' 'grande dame' or Newman's 'Western Prairie', Madame de Bellegarde's 'woman of conventions and proprieties' or Newman's 'ideal wife'.

From the initial chapters in which Newman, as the great Western

Barbarian, swoops down on the society of Europe, the book develops in structure into a tug of war between American and European power over the spoils that Claire represents. The satire is fairly equally divided between the corrupt aristocracy, over-observant of form, and the brash materialism which tends to treat the world as a shop, people as articles and human potential as uninvested capital. Although Newman cannot protect himself from being rejected as 'American', the Bellegardes cannot actually manipulate him, they can only deny him what he wants, which denial is facilitated by his lack of understanding of form, his failure to see that he cannot buy culture without some understanding of what it is. In fact, James acknowledged later that the weakness of the book lay in the fact that the Bellegardes would *not* have rejected Newman's money – whatever they thought of America and commerce – and the only likelihood of their ditching him would have been in the appearance of a more valuable suitor.

The tension between Newman and the Bellegardes, played out initially as a comedy of manners, and later as rather unconvincing melodrama, is essentially a reciprocal one. The Bellegardes do not seek to absorb or acquire Americanness in Newman, merely to resist its potential to acquire from *them* – the object of acquisition being feminine and fundamentally exchangeable as sign rather than as fixed value. Newman's signification as American does not define him as primarily sign, merely as American, as a specific cultural type. As a man he is active and predatory – thwarted by the Bellegardes but not significantly affected by them. Whereas marriage for Bessie Alden, for instance, is the moment of choice at which she has to decide whether to relinquish her American self to Europe or not, Newman's freedom is not in question. That he is limited (as are all subjects) by the specific material and cultural facts of his existence is not developed into an exposure of his basic subjectivity residing in his object existence for others. Thus the Bellegardes' opinion of Newman is irrelevant to him, he is merely concerned with doing business with them and getting what he wants. The way they respond to his Americanness is relevant only up to this point, and not beyond it.

I am suggesting that Newman's function as the great Western Barbarian is modified by his function as an active, predatory individual with American qualities who is engaged in a hostile struggle with alien people with alien ideas. The comparison of European and American ideas is engendered through this struggle, yet not centred in an interpretation of Newman by an observing consciousness. That Newman is not a catalyst for another subject experience does not detract from his symbolic reverberation for the reader, but it does mean that we are not focussed on any sense of his existence as sign in relation to his world. He is finally only as 'American' to the Bellegardes as they are 'European' to him. Claire, representing the potential best in both, is portrayed as inexplicable and motiveless, and her powerlessness in relation to both Newman and the Bellegardes consistently levels the power balance between the two cultures to sets of different yet predatory impulses, with Claire as prey.

There seem to be two modes of subject experience, that of appropriation and that of interpretation. The first is a male preserve; women can aid, but not appropriate for themselves. Living, however, through their ability to be interpreted, women can construct their subjecthood not only through conscious awareness of themselves as sign to be read, but in the offer of a reading, an explanation. Newman is not so concerned with the interpretative side of life, indeed both Mrs Tristram and Claire appear to offer to take care of it for him; he is more concerned with acquisition and ownership as a means of establishing his existence in the world. In *Daisy Miller*, the accent is on the act of interpretation, of gazing, puzzling and riddling. The subject existence of Winterbourne is established through his attempts to 'read' Daisy. She is the paradigm of women as sign and 'nothing else', and the 'nothing else' is exposed as problematic (rather than concealed as inevitable) through her sudden death at the end of what has been a light, charming story.

When a friend attacked the story of *Daisy Miller*, saying:

> Those awful young women capering at the hotel door, they are the real Daisy Millers that were, whereas yours in the tale is such a one as – for pitch of the ingenuous, for quality of the artless – couldn't possibly have been at all.[15]

James defended his heroine with 'My supposedly typical little figure was of course pure poetry.'[16] Whereas the structure of *The American* is primarily that of the struggle between two cultures for some accepted respository of value and meaning, in *Daisy Miller* the question becomes not so much who will get the prize, but what it is. Daisy, like Newman, arrives in Europe visibly an American, and is related immediately and continually back to her Americanness. To

Winterbourne, she is always a representative of 'them':

> 'Here comes my sister . . . She's an American girl' (vol. 4, p. 144).

> 'How pretty they are!' thought Winterbourne, straightening himself in his seat as if he were prepared to rise (vol. 4, pp. 144–5).

Winterbourne is quickly puzzled by Daisy's behaviour, the apparent contradiction of her open, free behaviour in talking to a man she has not been introduced to, and the frankness and charm of her manner. He looks for an explanation of her behaviour by relating her back to her (national) femininity:

> Was she simply a pretty girl from New York State – were they all like that, the pretty girls who had a good deal of gentlemen's society? ·. . . He was inclined to think Miss Daisy Miller was a flirt, – a pretty American flirt . . . *Winterbourne was almost grateful for having found the formula that applied to Miss Daisy Miller* (vol. 4, p. 151). (my emphasis).

The assumption here is that there *is* a formula, or should be, if only Winterbourne could find it. He is going to find it by relating Daisy to her femininity, to her existence as potential sign.

In his discussion of *Jude the Obscure*, John Goode describes the major difference between Jude and Sue, in the demands they are subjected to both within the narrative, and without, by the interpreting reader. Sue is questioned by Jude over her illogical behaviour: is this typically feminine or not?

> What is more important is that this question should be asked; it poses for Sue only one of two possibilities – that the nature of her blindness to her own logic must be explained either by her 'peculiarity' or by her belonging to womanhood. Either way, she is committed to being an image, and it is this which pervades the novel. Nobody ever confronts Jude with the choice between being a man or being peculiar. The essential thing is that Sue must be available to understanding.[17]

Similarly, one can look at *Daisy Miller*, at the vagaries of Winterbourne's behaviour, and see that as male subject he is not expected to be, above all, consistent and comprehensible. We identify with him as subject, and thus as complex and changing. It is Daisy who must be understood, who must make sense.

Goode goes on to say that Sue is destructive because she 'utters herself', whereas 'in the ideology of sexism, the woman is an image to be uttered'.[18] In the later novels of James, when he returns to interpretation as a major theme, I shall examine how the woman as subject learns to 'utter herself', either destructively, like Sue, or in an acceptable, consistent form as image, but mysterious and complex image. Daisy, however, is not destroyed through her own assertion of subjectivity and articulacy. She is destroyed because Winterbourne cannot fathom her, cannot come to terms with what she signifies.

The immense popularity of *Daisy Miller* when it was published, and the extent to which it was discussed and argued about, focussed on the nature of what Daisy was and how she was portrayed.[19] As an American girl she was a recognisable figure, the question was the evaluation and composition of the American girl. Winterbourne is the consciousness through which the story is told, the onlooker within the text that *The American* lacks. He is an American himself, one who has lived in Europe and understands its conventions and language. In much of James's work involving the international element, it is the American who learns his or her way round the social world embodied in Europe, who is potentially most fully conscious of the interactions between individuals and the defining and limiting factors of social existence. The American individual, once fully aware of the world entered, is most free to 'pick and choose and assimilate'. Yet the Europeanised American may also be more corrupt, more consciously manipulative and condemnatory of fellow American innocents than the Europeans themselves. Desire to be socially functional and acceptable can lead to hostility to those who appear to be unconventional or independent. Thus the developing awareness of an Isabel Archer, Lambert Strether or Milly Theale is juxtaposed with the rigidity of the convert in the deeply conventional Gilbert Osmond, Madame Merle or Charlotte Stant.

Winterbourne is somewhere between the two, indeed *Daisy Miller* can be read as the dramatisation of his choice. P. J. Eakin sees the story as one of James's 'fables of redemptive courtship',[20] a courtship which in this case is not brought to fruition. Eakin sees Daisy as Winterbourne's chance to embrace an American reality, its freshness and vitality along with its brashness and crudity. His failure to do so is a rejection of these national characteristics.

This is in accordance with Cristof Wegelin's more general statement that:

> It is a striking fact that while the promise of unencumbered American vitality is in James almost invariably symbolised by the young American girl, the questions which it raises and the threats which it contains are usually dramatised in American men.[21]

Winterbourne is, however, not so much agonising over the relative attractions and merits of European and American values (as Roderick Hudson is, for instance, in his position between Christina Light and Mary Garland), nor is he simply weighing up the balance of good and bad in America, as represented in Daisy's prettiness, freshness, spontaneity, ignorance and crudity. He is faced with the problem of interpreting signs, of trying to decide *what* Daisy (or America) signifies, rather than simply the value of the signified. He attempts through Daisy both to decide what American girls are really signifying and, by referring Daisy back to this class, to place her as an American girl. Puzzled by Daisy's behaviour, he retreats again and again to generalisation, seeking to find a clue to her in a given social interpretation. Yet the very newness and lack of orthodoxy of the American girl presents its own problems:

> Some people had told him that, after all, American girls were exceedingly innocent; and others had told him that, after all, they were not (vol. 4, p. 151).

The fact that Winterbourne bothers to expend energy on interpreting Daisy makes him active and conscious in relation to the rest of his society who 'read' Daisy simplistically, and condemn her against their own codes of womanhood and the ladylike. Mrs Costello can simply declare 'They are hopelessly vulgar' (vol. 4, p. 172), but Winterbourne seeks to make out another layer of meaning in Daisy which will reconcile the fact that ' "Common", she was, as Mrs Costello had pronounced her; yet it was a wonder to Winterbourne that, with her commonness, she had a singularly delicate grace' (vol. 4, p. 161).

We are given very few clues to Daisy's own response to events; we are given very little of her consciousness, and this is emphasised by the vision of her as socially unselfconscious, unaware of the potential response of others to her until she is brought face to face with it. As far as we are concerned, Daisy is presented as a surface to look at:

> Daisy stopped and looked at him, without a sign of troubled consciousness in her face; with nothing but the presence of her charming eyes and her happy dimples (vol. 4, p. 180).

This surface being puzzling, Winterbourne, and by identification the reader, seeks for meaning 'behind' it, thus somehow bypassing the reality of Daisy herself. In *Decoding Advertisements*, Judith Williamson discusses how the use of jokes, puzzles, humour and understatement in advertisements directs the subjects' response to a channelled interpretation of the 'meaning' of the joke, etc., rather than to a questioning of the basic relationship of sign and the external reality it refers to:

> The motion of the mask . . . illustrates perfectly the overlooking of the materiality of the signifier in the hermeneutic pursuit of the signified, and apex 'behind' it . . . A crucial part of this is the advertisement's built in *concealment* of it, by referring to a 'reality' or 'meaning' behind its surface: the 'mask' conceals nothing but itself.[22]

Herself engaged in no conscious process of interpretation or self-presentation, Daisy is entirely an object of the experience of Winterbourne, and the reader. If she fails to provide an adequate correspondence between her 'appearance' and the meaning she is expected to point to, she has no adequate reality.

James deliberately isolates Daisy as a person, which serves both to intensify her social freedom as an American, and her vulnerability as sign. Daisy is unconstrained by her mother, her absent father, or her own sense of what is or is not socially acceptable or apposite. She does what she likes, responds to what she likes. To the world around her she is a young girl, an American girl, she represents a society and a sex. She is expected to be what she appears – whether that is an innocent girl or a fallen woman. The mechanisms of society simply expel Daisy when her behaviour no longer conforms – she is cut dead at a party, and no longer invited out in respectable society. Yet Winterbourne still attempts to correlate Daisy's behaviour with what she is, to read her as a sign and make sense of her. If he could succeed, Daisy would be saved, but his success, finally aided by another man, comes too late.

It is interesting that when Winterbourne comes upon Daisy at the Colosseum at night and thinks that he finally understands her, what he responds to instinctively is not the nature of that understanding but the fact that the process of interpretation can now cease:

> Winterbourne stopped, with a sort of horror; and, it must be added, with a sort of relief. It was as if a sudden illumination had been flashed upon the ambiguity of Daisy's behaviour and the riddle had become easy to read. She was a young lady whom a gentleman need no longer be at pains to respect . . . He felt angry with himself that he had bothered so much about the right way of regarding Miss Daisy Miller (vol. 4, p. 202).

One of the significations of the American in Europe is the demand of the individual to be responded to individually. Conversance with social codes and conventions gives a shorthand for placing people, the arrival of the American disrupts this procedure, demanding a new approach to an individual who does not apparently fit the existing structures. Each new individual has both to take account of the society surrounding and responding to him or her, and to be taken account of by it. Existing values and correspondence may have to be adjusted accordingly. The juxtaposition of Europe and America continually shows up each in a new light. But this process is demanding and time consuming; what is more, it demands that the conscious subject attempting it risk his own, secure, social identity. So Winterbourne is glad to be spared the trouble, to retreat into the stiff formality of 'She was a young lady whom a gentleman need no longer be at pains to respect'.

That he is wrong in his judgement does not so much locate the questions raised by the tale in the final valuation of American qualities (in a sense, they are taken care of by Giovanelli), more it raises the question of Daisy's vulnerability to a wrong judgement, the implications of her subsequent death. Daisy is an inscrutable mixture of 'audacity and innocence', she appears wonderfully independent, subject to no restraints. Judith Fryer, in *The Faces of Eve*, identifies self-reliance as her major trait.[23] But Daisy's final vulnerability and destruction go beyond the fictional realisation that each individual is in fact created through social existence, and cannot live in disregard of it. For Daisy does not die *only* through exposure to the fever-ridden air of the Colosseum, the sterility of a hostile, decaying society. She shrivels at the mis-interpretation of Winterbourne, his failure to validate her by continuing to see her and read her. Her other consistent value, as well as her independence, is, after all, her blankness, literalness, superficiality, innocence – in short, her existence as observed other rather than a reflective self. As Winterbourne probes her chatter for nuance and import, he realises that 'in her bright, sweet, superficial little visage there was no mockery, no irony' (vol. 4, p. 14). Daisy is what Winterbourne sees, it is up to him, the conscious subject, to accord Daisy some social place, some function as sign. Our attention is inevitably directed towards the tension between Daisy's signification as free and active, and her passive dependency on a subject, masculine response. Her freedom is not merely limited, like Newman's, it is denied by a society which decrees that young girls do not exist for themselves, and by a fictional presentation as a blank surface, a reflection for the consciousness of Winterbourne.

In *Communities of Honor and Love in Henry James*, Manfred Mackenzie describes Daisy's death as a kind of suicidal self-rejection in response to the shame of public condemnation – in the Colosseum itself – that Winterbourne exposes her to.[24] I don't think Daisy's sense of self is really developed enough for this interpretation to be convincing. The dramatic picture of the American individual, and the individual *consciousness* of self, are divided between Daisy and Winterbourne, so that Winterbourne rejects Daisy as object at the same time as he ceases to bother about re-examining social assumptions. Daisy dies because she cannot be fitted into any European scheme of things, and because her very existence as American girl depends on her continuing to be seen within that scheme. Once she is cut dead by everyone, she ceases to exist. Paradoxically, the representative of unconventional individuality is thus totally dependent on external recognition – Daisy as self exists only as an objectification of selfhood for those already occupying a social position, and catalyses a re-examination of that position, from within.

Daisy's failure is thus not as an individual woman who may, or may not, be innocent, but in failing to be a satisfactory other to Winterbourne's subject meditation on experience. The fact that the process of *Daisy Miller* is the process of interpretation suggests that Daisy sinks under the pressure of study, of being an object of observation finally discarded as unsatisfactory.

The questions raised by the story are those of the confinement and ultimate destruction of the individual by the projected interpretations and objectifications of the external world. The process is, however, inevitable, Winterbourne occupies the middle position – both defined himself, and practising definition on Daisy. For Daisy herself there appears to be no reciprocal relation, she functions in the text only as the object of Winterbourne's experience. Winterbourne can attempt to define himself in relation to what Daisy signifies; can, as subject, make demands on the other to represent experience for him. In the same way Newman, though himself representative to the Bellegardes of the raw American, can demand to be 'interpreted to the world'. But as sign, and only sign, Daisy cannot be subject, she gets no reflection, makes no demands of European society. Endowed with freedom, she cannot use it for herself. Her only value is in her representative status, if that is unclear she is the passive prey to a host of misinterpretations.

As we are led to look at Daisy as self-reliant and individual, her death poses questions as to the possibility of the girl who signifies independence and freedom actually being free herself. Once discarded by her male interpreter, she sinks fast. Newman after all merely runs up against a wall of defiance and denial, he can't get what he wants from society, as an individual he has to recognise limitations. Daisy meets a negation of what she is – she is what Winterbourne might want to get, and as such she is rejected. If the social structures of power turn individuals into predators and prey, possessors and possessions, subjects and objects, then the possessor denied a possession has only to look elsewhere. The possession, on the other hand, if rejected as such, loses all value altogether. That the American girl can apparently never realise her freedom and independence for herself but must submit it to another, is intrinsic to the position of existence as sign, or other, functioning for an observing consciousness.

The problem of Daisy's death is still a problem for Winterbourne, or by implication for the reader. Her limitation as sign is not presented as a source of conflict for Daisy herself. Any real exploration of the conflict between the girl being defined through her sign status, and her own consciousness of her individual freedom, needs the presentation of the heroine as an 'object of study' to be balanced by the presentation of her attempts to be the subject of her own experience. In *The Portrait of a Lady*, the false nature of the freedom of the individual girl is confronted not simply by the observers for whom, as feminine, she is automatically confined, but by the girl herself. In *Daisy Miller*, the fictional presentation of Daisy is as 'one of them'. Daisy's existence within the text is limited to her feminine status as an American girl. With Isabel Archer, James attempted to go beyond this and present an American girl who is a person.

4 *The Portrait of a Lady*

Isabel Archer, the young American heroine of *The Portrait of a Lady* (1881), is recognised by all who meet her as possessing potential – potential for action, for meaning, for giving a value to experience. In a predatory world, she is not faced with interpretation, like Daisy Miller, so much as appropriation (or, by those more passive or benevolent' observation). Isabel is appropriated as sign, to be given fixed meaning by the man who succeeds in possessing her.

The Portrait of a Lady poses confrontation with a complex European society whose codes and customs are performed and manipulated both by its native products, and by those who have integrated themselves till they are more native than the natives – the opening scene displays Americans having the most English possible of afternoon teas. Exactly who, or what, confronts this society in the person of Isabel Archer it is less easy to be sure. The individual potential for freedom from social restraint, the rootless and restless American, is certainly present in Isabel, yet the progress of the novel suggests that this freedom is somehow aimless and insubstantial compared with the highly motivated and specific activities of the social characters. As Arnold Kettle says:

> *The Portrait of a Lady* is one of the most profound expressions in literature of the illusion that freedom is an abstract quality inherent in the individual soul.[1]

The world of *The Portrait of a Lady* is very much a world of labels, categories and theories. The language of society seeks to define people in terms of their quantifiable value, and the relationships between them become appropriative in terms of that value. The 'abstract theories' that Isabel is addicted to in her search for *moral* worth or value are still part of the process of limiting and defining which also encompasses the dry appearances of social price – and the interplay between the two is one of the constant themes of the novel. Fluid notions of personal worth, the visual impressions, harden into correspondences of social position, wealth and conventional aestheticism, the rigid two-dimensional portraits. And this process of designation operates in a masculine culture where the appropriators are male and the signs of value to be acquired or disposed of are female. Like Christopher Newman, Isabel surveys the Old World as a field of potential action and choice. But her freedom to act is not simply limited by the need for reciprocity inherent in any social behaviour. Her choices seem inevitably to narrow down into the choices of marriage which mean rendering herself up as value. The exposure of her illusionary faith that she can create a marriage for herself in which the nature of her life will be partly shaped and directed by herself does not simply trace her entry into social, limited existence, but into social existence as a woman.

In the language of *The Portrait of a Lady*, the more powerful subjects are those who watch, observe and spectate. The pictures and impressions and *objets d'art* are the values and meanings which can be appreciated and appropriated. Isabel's desire to remain a spectator suggests her instinctive recognition that once she engages fully in life she will become a spectacle and be defined through her appearance. Not challenging this basic pattern, she hopes to transcend it by engaging at levels of high cultural and moral value, but the process of appropriation is basically the same, and the material intrinsically linked to, indeed facilitating, the spiritual or aesthetic. Believing in the ideals of her world without understanding how they are maintained in reality, Isabel cannot really challenge the process of signification which demands that she, as woman, becomes portrait rather than painter or spectator. Unequipped to recognise fully the appropriation of her self as a range of values by those around her, Isabel's freedom is indeed an illusion.

As an American girl, Isabel is the perfect victim of such an illusion – the illusion being both hers and society's – which labels her as a sign of surrogate freedom to be observed by those already anchored in their ways and places. The great novelty in James's approach to this sign is pinpointed by him in the Preface to the New York edition of the novel. He first quotes George Eliot's description of the young girls of fiction: 'In these frail vessels is borne onward through the ages the treasure of human affection', and then goes on:

The frail vessel, that charged with George Eliot's 'treasure', and thereby of such importance to those who curiously approach it, has likewise *possibilities of importance to itself*, possibilities which permit of treatment and in fact peculiarly require it from the moment they are considered at all. (my emphasis).[2]

In an article on James's work, W. D. Howells skirts around the same point in a comparison of *The Portrait of a Lady* and Eliot's *Middlemarch*:

> I do not know just how it should be stated of two such noble and generous types of character as Dorothea and Isabel Archer, but I think that we sympathise with the former in grand aims that chiefly concern others, and with the latter in beautiful dreams that primarily concern herself.[3]

Howells isolates without comment the special nature of Isabel as heroine – her self-motivated idealism – but by comparing it to Dorothea's more traditional feminine self-negation, he implies the important point about *The Portrait of a Lady* which James had stressed; that this kind of self-discovery is centred on a young *girl*. That the central figure as female, rather than as American or individual, was the dominant impression is evident in most contemporary reviews. These, while often condemning James's lack of religion and his unsatisfactory ending to the book, seem to recognise it as important, and recognise the strangeness of its significance. To explain this, Isabel is interpreted as 'Mr James in domino'[4] as one of many characters who don't behave like real people[5] or more specifically as an example of the real weakness women can display when they attempt to act independently. Edgar Fawcett, in *The Princeton Review*, excuses her on the grounds of her 'femininity' – she makes a 'pitiable error', but 'she makes it in all womanly faith and sincerity'.[6] H.E. Scudder, in *The Atlantic Monthly*, goes further and explains how Isabel epitomises the dilemma of womanhood in nineteenth century America:

> [Isabel is] representative of womanly life today. The fine purpose of her freedom, the resolution with which she seeks to be the maker of her destiny, the *subtle weakness* into which all this *betrays* her, the apparent *helplessness* of her ultimate position, the conjectured *escape* only through *patient forbearance* – what are all these, if not attributes of womanly life expended under current conditions? (my emphasis).[7]

The language of victim (helplessness, escape, forbearance) is piled on to Isabel's image so that her situation is presented as acting on her, as passive receptor, rather than being created and finally comprehended by her as an active process. The nature of Isabel's 'ultimate position' is thus seen as something created by external forces – the implication that Isabel herself is involved in development and growth which both leads into and out of such situations, is avoided. Of course it would be equally one sided to view the events of *The Portrait of a Lady* as being totally controlled by Isabel as to say that they simply act on her as feminine victim deluded into attempts at autonomy. From the beginning, we see how in attempting to observe the world we can do so only equipped with the vision created by the experience of society, or its abstract culture (Isabel's world of books).

So Isabel looks at the world in terms of its potential for herself, but her vision has as its frame of reference the social structure which not only tends to convert others into objects of certain value, but to treat women as other to the extent of rendering them functional as signs of a range of values, referring them back to their femininity rather than to their individual value. Isabel sees herself and others as objects, too. Objects of fine and noble theories, perhaps, whereas the world around her deftly manipulates these theoretical labels as expediency demands. Equipped with an imperfect sense of the rules of the system and her place as woman within it, Isabel fails either to work it successfully or submit to it resignedly. This failure leads to the development of her consciousness of self in opposition to an appropriative masculine world. The function in the text of the manipulation of the woman as sign is no longer in the evaluation of the signified by a male onlooker, or even in a recognition of the manipulative process by a male onlooker. The recognition takes place in the suffering of Isabel as she realises her existence as the 'portrait of a lady'.

The importance of the point James was making in his Preface, and which he reiterates there, is that of the woman as sign, manipulated for the purposes of others, 'mattering' to herself and therefore, by implication, to us. It was a theme he had opened up in the book written the year before, *Washington Square*. Catherine Sloper is ruthlessly manipulated by those around her. She does not actively fight back, and merely continues to exist. Nothing very dramatic happens, there are no moral triumphs or reprisals. The point, almost the whole point, seems to be the fact that, although no character within the book realises or much cares, all this matters intensely to Catherine herself – her understanding of her manipulation and her dull, strong resistance to it. So in reading and analysing *The Portrait of a Lady*, the implied criticism and failure of Isabel is always tempered by James's initial impulse – that things matter for her, they are important in their significance for her, and it is from this angle that they are important to the reader.

In the opening chapter of *The Portrait of a Lady*, the constituent elements of the novel are established. Tea on the lawn at Gardencourt is made a vivid picture, yet at the same time we are made to feel how nothing here is 'simply' pictorial. The timeless late afternoon links the old house with old Mr Touchett, who loves the house and is aware of its past. A sense of social continuity is introduced into which Mr Touchett, while retaining some detatchment, knows where to slot. The sense of continuity is made present by a light-hearted discussion between the old man, Ralph and Lord Warburton, of impending social and political change. Mr Touchett adds that social and political change, the fabric of day to day life, won't affect the 'ladies', at least not those who really are ladies: 'The ladies will save us,' said the old man; 'that is the best of them will – for I make a difference between them' (vol. 3, p. 11)

The best of the ladies, the most purely 'lady' like of them, are not affected by the day to day adjustments of active participation in life – better than this, and immutable, they exist for the active participants in society as fixed reference points outside the expediency of a world which requires ideals at a safe distance. The extent to which this particular status for the ladies may be idealised or merely representative of worldly qualities is suggested in the discussion of the American girl that Mrs Touchett has mentioned in her telegram. She has hinted at her being independent – the response of the tea party is to wonder whether it is financial or moral independence that is to be surveyed in this new arrival.

When Isabel arrives, her difference is quickly marked out by her prime activity – while they, and we, are surveying her, she is surveying everything. She has an 'eye that denoted clear perception', her face is 'intelligent and excited' with 'a comprehensiveness of observation', her 'perceptions were numerous'. Isabel is looking at everything, and as we look at her through Ralph's eyes we see:

> her white hands, in her lap, were folded upon her black dress; her head was erect, her eye lighted, her flexible figure turned itself

easily this way and that, in sympathy with the alertness with which she evidently caught impressions (vol. 3, p. 21).

The extent to which perception at this stage in the novel equates with static pictures and impressions is evident both in others' sense of Isabel and in Isabel's sense of them and of herself. Awareness of appearances is primary, and exists long before the understanding of such appearances. In *Ways of Seeing*, John Berger analyses the way in which men, as spectators of women as pictures, turn women into spectators of themselves, in order to monitor their existence for the external world, to try and gain some 'self' control from inside the system that controls them: 'Men survey women before treating them. Consequently how a woman appears to a man can determine how she will be treated.'[8]

Isabel instinctively interiorises the process of being seen as an attempt at control, and tries to present herself (and to see others) in a very fine abstract way. She is concerned with her appearance as feminine – we are told that she doesn't want to be thought 'bookish' but 'clever', and that she is aware of the importance of prettiness (vol. 3, p. 45). But this awareness of her feminine self is carried over into a sense of a transcendent femininity, a moral harmony of appearance. Isabel determines then that 'Her life should always be in harmony with the most pleasing impression she should produce' (vol. 3, p. 69). It is in expectation of a judgement on her moral character as well as her appearance that she desires to 'look very well' (vol. 3, p. 69).

By projecting an active, spiritual appearance to the world, Isabel apparently hopes to keep her options open. Though she herself sees others as types, they are often types expressive of wide ideas – Lord Warburton as the English social system, Henrietta as American democracy – and if she projects herself as a general enough range of significations her chances of appropriation might be less. For she is afraid of the 'ruinous expenditure' of giving herself to another person.

Unfortunately in a world of appearances not necessarily high-lighted by a qualitative perception, others may see one in a more limiting way. This is not necessarily a product of malice; we are told of Mr Touchett, who is very fond of Isabel, that she: 'amused him more than she suspected – the effect she produced on people was often different from what she supposed' (vol. 3, p. 74).

This concept of entertainment, of watching Isabel to see what will happen, of seeing her as a series of images from which amusement can be derived, is present in all the Touchetts. Their fondness for Isabel, and willingness to help, their restraint from actual manipulation, disguises the shortcomings of this approach. And in comparison to the more specific appropriation practised by other characters, this spectatorship is not so harmful. Nonetheless it turns Isabel into a performer, and heightens the sense of her as an image of free womanhood, as a principle in action. Ralph is exonerated in a sense by having the role of spectator forced on him by ill health. He, like Warburton and Goodwood, would be willing to involve himself with Isabel rather than just watch her, if he only could. However, confined to watching, he does so very thoroughly. He views Isabel as 'occupation enough for a succession of days' (vol. 3, p. 54), and considers that 'she was better worth looking at than most works of art' (vol. 3, p. 61).

This tendency to aestheticise the personal, so marked an indication of sterility in Osmond, is present as a warning note to our view of many of the characters, and Ralph sounds it often with regard to Isabel. Sometimes jokingly, as when he calls her Columbia:

He drew a caricature of her in which she was represented as a very pretty young woman dressed, on the lines of the prevailing fashion, in the folds of the national banner (vol. 3, p. 83).

The idea of the young girl as the spirit of America is assumed to be such a commonplace that it can be taken for granted, laughed at and seen as inadequate for a view of Isabel. However, Ralph does not at first really discard a taste for images. He persists in viewing her self as a kind of idealised product on display, superior to other aesthetic objects in its capacity for life. He thinks to himself that:

A character like that . . . a real little passionate force to see at play is the finest thing in nature. It's finer than the finest work of art – than a Greek bas-relief, than a great Titian, than a Gothic cathedral (vol. 3, p. 86).

However, Ralph's most important response to Isabel is the recognition that she might be able to act *for* herself, he does not expect her to function simply as an object for others. He has notions of her 'doing' something. If he unwittingly limits her existence in the world by regarding her as a spectacle, he does at least acknowledge her as an extraordinary spectacle – a woman who goes further in her suggestion than the static and tired Columbia role:

> Most women did with themselves nothing at all; they waited, in attitudes more or less gracefully passive, for a man to come that way and furnish them with a destiny. Isabel's originality was that she gave one an impression of having intentions of her own. 'Whenever she executes them,' said Ralph, 'may I be there to see!' (vol. 3, p. 87).

In this sense, at least, Ralph attempts to see beyond the obvious labels which attach to Isabel – 'pretty', 'American', 'innocent', 'free' – to the potential within her, the possibility of dynamism. He persists in regarding the whole thing as an experiment, with Isabel as specimen. This highlights the peculiarity of Isabel being what she is (full of intentions, and so on) *and* a woman. Or to use Mrs Touchett's simile, when Ralph asks her what she intends to do with Isabel: 'Do with her? You talk as if she were a yard of calico' (vol. 3, p. 59).

However, Isabel's fate is precipitated not only by the vision imposed on her by others but also by the culturally conditioned vision which she brings to her own experience. A woman in a male society, Isabel adopts the masculine mode of viewing the world as signifying meaning and value for her as subject, yet fails to see that she is being appropriated as sign in a far more fundamental way. For whereas Isabel takes people as examples of various theories, *she* is taken as potential signifier of any number of signifieds, depending on the male subject communicating through her. Her husband would determine her function; his value is intrinsic, hers linked to his. Isabel thus looks at what the men and women around her appear to signify, in simplistic terms, searching for people who will fit her ideals nearly enough for her to link herself to them. She fails to see that the real threat to her freedom comes from the way she is seen and fitted into social structures of signification – she assumes herself as subject to be external to them, and thus unthreatened and unplaced. The length of time it takes her to understand the interaction between herself and the world appears to be linked to her rather abstract and theoretical vision, which can shield her from unpleasant realities.

Isabel's impressions are too theoretical to survive in the real world, and are also too consciously divorced from any practical perception. It is suggested that this lack of vision based on direct experience is linked to an addiction for theory – a sense of the idiosyncracies, even of the trivia, of the surrounding world is necessary for any attempt at judgement. So when we have first seen Isabel, tall and slim in the doorway at Gardencourt, we are taken back to her early years at Albany. Here she was largely self-taught, having rejected school, which gave her 'the elation of liberty and the pain of exclusion' (vol. 3, p. 29). Already she is different, an outsider. The female who attempts to be independent of society gains liberty at the expense of company, and even identity. To a certain extent, Isabel is afraid of the attempt of that society to give her identity and of its limitations of opportunity. She never opens the locked door on to the street because what she imagines there is bound to be more interesting. Characteristically, when Isabel does venture out into the world it is not into the familiar Albany world which might prove so disappointing to the imagination, but into the new Old World offered by her aunt. Absurdly for one of her age and experience, but suitably as what she represents – New World freedom – she has 'a desire to leave the past behind her and . . . to begin afresh' (vol. 3, p. 41). The limitations of her imagination, fed on literature rather than experience, are spelled out 'she paid the penalty of having given undue encouragement to the faculty of seeing without judging' (vol. 3, p. 42).

The provincial heroine, socially narrow yet nourished on wide ranging flights of fancy[9] is indeed ill-equipped to face the cosmopolitan society that her aunt so boldly carries her off to. It is interesting to observe Mrs Touchett's certainty about meddling in Isabel's life. She herself has rejected any real involvement with life and has separated herself emotionally from her husband and son. She is perhaps what Isabel might become if she avoids emotional commitment successfully enough. Yet we are told that she 'enjoyed the consciousness of making an impression on a candid and susceptible mind' (vol. 3, p. 36). Mrs Touchett would enjoy moulding Isabel – she operates in the social terms of control and manipulation that she has rejected for herself. It is plain that her kind of retreat from interaction has been no solution to the existing structures, she has evolved no alternative types of process. As Isabel asserts her independence in England, Mrs Touchett loses the secondary kind of control that she could assert over her, and fades into the background.

Even on coming over to Europe, Isabel is determined to exercise a control over her experience, and to be selective. Talking to Ralph about the Gardencourt ghost that can be seen only by those who have suffered and can therefore not be seen by her she comments: 'I think people suffer too easily . . . Well . . . that's what I came to Europe for, to be as happy as possible' (vol. 3, p. 65). She projects this personal plan on to her surroundings, 'she had a fixed determination to regard the world as a place of brightness, of free expansion, of irresistible action' (vol. 3, p. 68).

There is a disparity, or rather a gap, between the independence with which Isabel observes and categorises the world in the first part of the novel, and the potential in her for action which Ralph recognises. The 'act' seems to clash irrevocably with the independence – for reasons which involve not just her personal failure of judgement, or a particular plot by Osmond and Madame Merle, but a whole sense of the way the world takes Isabel, and the illusion of the independence it allows her as an American girl. Once Isabel does anything, she engages with the world in which she does it, and her existence for that world as communicable sign will shape her actions and their consequences beyond her control.

As Isabel finds her feet in England, James introduces the world of people that are to provide her medium, and plays out her approach to life gleaned in the library at Albany. She theorises with Ralph, and asks questions about English forms, desiring to see English 'specimens'. Meeting Lord Warburton, she sees him as 'a hero of romance' (vol. 3, p. 91), and his house 'affected the young visitor as a castle in a legend' (vol. 3, p. 108). On a serious level, she still sees Warburton as an 'example' of something she knows very little about: 'What she felt was that a territorial, a political, a social magnate had conceived the design of drawing her into the system' (vol. 3, p. 144). Lord Warburton accuses her 'You judge only from the outside – you don't care' (vol. 3, p. 112).

This is evident in the rather glib exchange that Isabel has with her aunt over the issue of the propriety of her sitting up late along with the gentlemen. When Mrs Touchett accuses her of being 'too fond of your own ways', she replies "Yes, I think I'm very fond of them. But I always want to know the things one shouldn't do." "So as to do them?" asked her aunt. "So as to choose," said Isabel' (vol. 3, p. 93).

This is a theoretical definition of moral freedom, but it becomes increasingly obvious, as we follow Isabel's career, that it is meaningless unless accompanied by some understanding of what the available choices really involve and mean. Also present is the hint that between what one should or shouldn't do very little choice is open. Marriage in one form or another hounds Isabel from the start – the choice of suitable or unsuitable, socially acceptable or unacceptable marriage is another form of the illusion of choice. Even among the intellectual choices of principle Isabel finds it hard to choose, to commit herself, saying 'So long as I look at the Misses Molyneux they seem to me to answer a kind of ideal. Then Henrietta presents herself, and I'm straight away convinced by her' (vol. 3, p. 130).

Isabel is facing a choice of sign function rather than of exploration and action. Unlike Christopher Newman, she is not looking for someone to express *her*, but for an ideal to which she can submit her independence in a form of moral action. The reality of such submission takes the shape of a husband – once again marriage is the paradigm for the young girl's absorption into social, representative existence. What happens continually from birth is displayed in the text as taking place at the moment of adult commitment.

No wonder then that faced with the pressure to make a concrete, physical choice, Isabel recoils. As Lord Warburton approaches her in the garden she is reading Caspar Goodwood's letter, she 'seated herself on a garden-bench . . . where, in a white dress ornamented with black ribbons, she formed among the flickering shadows a graceful and harmonious image' (vol. 3, p. 140).

As these two men close in on her freedom, we see her for a moment as a pleasing picture, as what they desire to possess. Isabel has equally little sense of them as personalities, Lord Warburton is very remote from her sense of reality, so that she can muse 'She had received a strong impression of his being a "personage", and she had occupied herself in examining the image so conveyed' (vol. 3, p. 143). Isabel is apprehensive that her very fear of committing herself to the system isolates her from the norm, she knows she is expected to be 'different', but can find no way of justifying this difference in alternative action. Rejecting Lord Warburton, she is 'really frightened at herself' (vol. 3, p. 157), because she doesn't want what 'nineteen women out of twenty' (vol. 3, p. 157) would have wanted. Once again, her independence (taken past a certain static sense of it) clashes with her role as woman, we are reminded of the pain of exclusion she suffered in Albany.

Her sense of Caspar is equally remote. He figures in her imagination in martial imagery in the same way as Lord Warburton does in social imagery:

She saw the different fitted parts of him as she had seen, in museums and portraits, the different fitted parts of armoured warriors – in plates of steel handsomely inlaid with gold (vol. 3, p. 165).

What she is aware of with both of them is the extent of their desire to possess her. By the time she is faced with rejecting Caspar, she has worked out the answer she could not quite formulate for Warburton, it is 'part of a system, a theory, that she had lately embraced' and she says to him 'I don't wish to be a mere sheep in the flock; I wish to choose my fate and know something of human affairs beyond what other people think it compatible with propriety to tell me' (vol. 3, p. 229).

Caspar's attitude is the practical one 'An unmarried woman – a girl of your age – isn't independent. There are all sorts of things she can't do' (vol. 3, p. 228).

There is great irony in the 'unmarried' qualification. The greater 'social' freedom that marriage allows women involves acceptance of precisely the sort of rigid role that Isabel fears. The catch in Isabel's situation is already becoming clear: how can she know anything of human affairs without committing herself to them in a world where that committal will inevitably pin her down like a specimen butterfly? At this stage, her function is largely a suggestive one, and thus fluid and capable of change. The others are still watching her to see what she will do.

Surrounded by people fundamentally well disposed to her Isabel, up to this point, has retained some control. A naive, theoretic control, perhaps, but she remains poised on the edge of action, successfully avoiding the advances of the world. Having rejected Caspar, she goes back to Gardencourt to a mood of new seriousness as Mr Touchett lies dying. In this changed tone, she encounters Madame Merle.

James allows us an inside glance at Madame Merle that is denied to Isabel. We are shown that 'Her grey eyes were small but full of light and incapable of stupidity – incapable, according to some people, even of tears' (vol. 3, p. 249). Isabel sees 'a Bust . . . a Juno or a Niobe' (vol. 3, p. 249) and, strikingly, 'Experience' (vol. 3, p. 250). We watch Isabel being manipulated by Madame Merle, by the apotheosis of the social world which labels, not naively or enthusiastically, but deliberately, according to usefulness and practical value. The worldliness of Madame Merle is continually stressed, even Isabel is aware that her new friend is hardly 'natural':

> She was in a word too perfectly the social animal that man and woman are supposed to have been intended to be . . . Isabel found it difficult to think of her in any detachment or privacy, she existed only in her relations, direct or indirect, with her fellow mortals (vol. 3, p. 274).

This constant theme of James, the extent to which we are defined by our existence for others and our relations with the social world (explicitly contrasted with the solitary artist role in *The Private Life* (1882)), is given weight here by the sense that Isabel, proponent of individual existence apart from social relations, cannot prevent herself being seen by the world in a certain way. When she and Madame Merle have the famous argument about whether the 'shell' – the friends, house, clothes, of one's life – determine you, or whether you are yourself expressed by nothing else, Isabel's own tendency to view other people as representative of theories exposes her naivety in expecting to get away without being similarly pinned down herself. And when she protests: 'Certainly the clothes which, as you say, I choose to wear, don't express me; and heaven forbid they should!' (vol. 3, p. 288), Madame Merle's reply 'You dress very well' (vol. 3, p. 288) is in one way unanswerable. Isabel cannot stop the people around her reaching the conclusion that she dresses very well. And the answer she does make in fact supports Madame Merle's proposition more than she realises:

> Possibly; but I don't care to be judged by that. My clothes may express the dressmaker, but they don't express me. To begin with, it's not my own choice that I wear them; they're imposed upon me by society (vol. 3, p. 288).

But of course if Isabel's identity resides partly in what she looks like, and how she can be interpreted from that, then this identity has also been imposed upon her by society, and without it she would have no place at all. Not only is she expressed by her physical and material circumstances, she is given substance by the acts of observation and interpretation which establish her as feminine and identifiable, either as a cultural sign or as specifically representative of a particular man.

With the death of Mr Touchett and Isabel's inheritance, enough money 'to meet the requirements of . . . [her] imagination' (vol. 3, p. 261), the novel changes. Hitherto, in keeping with Isabel's own self, it has been largely theoretical. Isabel has been seen in conjunction with a gallery of different people, a lot of theoretical discussions have taken place. Now, while Isabel still ponders on the possibilities opening up to her, practical schemes are erected around her.

Isabel becomes aware of the pressure of the potential that her inheritance carries with it. She feels 'that to be rich was a virtue because it was to be able to *do*' (vol. 3, p. 301). The need to go beyond the acceptance of the passive female identity is accentuated by the new horizons opening up. Money, she concludes:

> was the graceful contrary of the stupid side of weakness – especially the feminine variety. To be weak was, for a delicate young person, rather graceful, but, after all, as Isabel said to herself, there was a larger grace than that (vol. 3, p. 301).

Money is a source of power and a potential for action, it makes tangible the spiritual potential that Isabel has signified. Given the economic base to her ideals, Isabel is finally brought face to face with the irresistible need to do something, and the nature of the available choices, and the extent to which her imagination is limited and defined by them, is fully exposed. Isabel cannot imagine a course of action which has no existence, in, or relation to, a society where women live through and for their husbands, fathers and sons.

Crossing the channel to Italy suggests the continuation of the journey into the world that Isabel began when she ventured out of her room in Albany. The first two chapters set in Italy act in direct contrast to one another, a contrast that is central to the direction of Isabel's journey. In the first, Ralph and Isabel have a friendly discussion about how Isabel can now act, about the need for her to 'live' and to be strong. It all sounds very convincing. In the second, we pan in on a picture as deliberately composed and as laden with implication as our opening picture of tea on the lawn at Gardencourt. Osmond's villas has windows which 'seemed less to offer communication with the world than to defy the world to look in' (vol. 3, p. 326).

Yet we do look in, on a room full of beautiful objects of which Osmond's daughter Pansy. is the most valuable and significant.

Madame Merle and Osmond's discussion of Pansy is an overt acknowledgement of the manipulation of the feminine that they practice on Isabel in a more sophisticated form. In the smooth-running machinery of the world as it is, the female is acted upon, like Pansy, or serves the male by acting upon, by offering up its sisters and daughters in the way that Madame Merle serves Osmond. Pansy is 'a passive spectator of the operation of her fate' and 'impregnated with idea of submission' (vol. 3, pp. 337–8). She is the arch-feminine, child in the adult world. As the betrayal of Isabel takes its course, this female principle, embodied in Pansy, is to become the bone of contention between Osmond, Madame Merle – the woman who sacrifices the principle to the man – and Isabel, who struggles to invest it with some dignity and autonomy. However, at this stage, Pansy is not contended over, but calmly allotted to everyone's satisfaction.

Madame Merle and Osmond then discuss Isabel's attributes, especially her fortune. While she and Ralph are building spiritual castles, her money and her beauty are being weighed up against Osmond's capacity for boredom.

Isabel recognises the contrivance of everything that surrounds Osmond; 'even Mr Osmond's diminutive daughter had a kind of finish that was not entirely artless' (vol. 3, p. 367). Yet she cannot place the man himself in any one category 'Her mind contained no class offering a natural place to Mr Osmond – he was a specimen apart' (vol. 3, p. 376). This seems to be part of his appeal for Isabel, he has the charm of the mysterious and also he does not suggest any system or scheme of demands that would engulf her. The aesthetic basis of collecting and admiring is one which maintains a distance, which suggests a certain untouchable quality. Earlier we have been told that there is something 'pure and proud' (vol. 3, p. 71) that holds her back from intimacy; but the intimacy of a totally defined and static relationship and one which Isabel feels she is helping to create through her money, is a more acceptable proposition – at least she will not have to become part of a pre-existing system, but can make her own. The unwillingness to commit herself is balanced by the desire to do something that she has controlled by the deliberation of her assent to it. Thus when Osmond proposes 'she answered with an intensity that expressed the dread of having, in this case too, to choose and decide' (vol. 4, p. 18). Yet when Osmond then stresses her importance to him 'Isabel looked at herself in this character – looked intently, thinking she filled it with a certain grace' (vol. 4, p. 19). Isabel is struck with Pansy's helplessness, her dependence on the benevolence of those around her and her lack of will to act on her own behalf 'She would have no will, no power to resist, no sense of her own importance' (vol. 4, p. 27).

Unable to perceive that she has been seen and placed in the same kind of way as she sees Pansy, Isabel assumes that she is making a free choice. As marriage and the assumption of a life in relation to a man seems to be the only mode of action, she attempts to control it by defining her position within her action. There is stress at this point on Isabel's seriousness, her literal reading of the world, which inevitably causes a degree of moral blindness. Osmond calls to this side of her, and the narrowness that lack of humour can cause is later revealed to her, in a horrifying recognition of how 'He took himself so seriously; it was something appalling' (vol. 4, p. 196).

It is made quite plain how Osmond objectifies Isabel, how he is prepared to subordinate her to his requirements. Thus he judges her as to whether she will enhance his status and position. He likes her having rejected Lord Warburton, 'he perceived a new attraction in the idea of taking to himself a young lady who had qualified herself to figure in his collection of choice objects by declining so noble a hand' (vol. 4, p. 9). And he prepares now to refine her very imagination as a process of amusing himself; her intelligence 'was to be a silver plate . . . that he might heap up with ripe fruits, to which it would give a decorative value, so that talk might become for him a sort of served dessert' (vol. 4, p. 79). And he is prepared to 'tap her imagination with his knuckle and make it ring' (vol. 4, p. 79). He talks to Isabel about the attempt to make life into a work of art. She takes this as a process which they will create together. He takes her as a part of his pattern, she is to be certain things and not others, and he is quite prepared to sacrifice those of her ideas that he doesn't like. It is Osmond's apparent disregard for society that encourages Isabel to feel she will be free from externally imposed values – she thinks that her active step has been the perception of Osmond's fineness, despite all social disapproval. As Caspar Goodwood shrewdly says to her: 'And you don't mean in the least that he's a perfect nonentity. You think he's grand, you think he's great, though no-one else thinks so' (vol. 4, p. 47). And Isabel's response to Ralph's truth-telling is also revealing: 'You're going to be put in a cage'. 'If I like my cage that needn't trouble you' (vol. 4, p. 65). By building her own picture frame, she feels she retains control over the picture, over how she is for herself and the world, but she builds it with far too little understanding of what will make up the cage, and how it will confine her.

Just before the marriage, the final warning is sounded, we are shown Pansy again, Pansy whose 'good manners are paramount' (vol. 4, p. 84). She behaves so perfectly that one can only wonder 'what penalties for non-performance she dreaded!' (vol. 4, p. 86).

There is a time lapse, and we return to the marriage already a few years old. From this point onward, the situation of Pansy is in the foreground. She becomes the point over which Isabel and Osmond confront each other. The world of abstract theories and choices has hardened into a specific relationship of owner and owned, subject and object. The power accruing to the owner, the wealthy, the man in control of resources can render the less powerful culturally other or momentarily feminine. Thus Ned Rosier, though generally existing as a man and thus as subject in relation to women, can be rendered object in relation to Osmond. He regards Pansy as a – beloved – object: 'He thought of her in amorous meditation a good deal as he might have thought of a Dresden-china shepherdess' (vol. 4, p. 90). When he approaches Osmond, he puts himself in the 'Pansy' position, saying 'I'm afraid that for Mr Osmond I'm not – well, a real collector's piece' (vol. 4, p. 92).

The process of looking is specifically linked now to that of assessment and manipulation, when Rosier goes to Roccanera to see Osmond 'he had never in his life felt himself so efficiently looked at' (vol. 4, p. 104).

Isabel looked without judging, either in the worldly sense or in the moral – which would have needed an awareness of the worldly. Now her own glances have been stilled, she no longer signifies potential, she has assumed a static, masklike quality. Her first appearance after her marriage is counterpointed to her initial one in Gardencourt. Now, as then, she is in black:

> The years had touched her only to enrich her; the flower of her youth had not faded, it only hung more quietly on its stem. She had lost something of that quick eagerness to which her husband had privately taken exception – she had more the air of being able to wait. Now, at all events, framed in the gilded doorway, she struck our young man as the picture of a gracious lady (vol. 4, p. 105).

Isabel is at once more opaque and more public. We look at her for some time before we are shown her feelings again. As for us, so it is now for Ralph; for whom Isabel is now inscrutable:

> if she wore a mask it completely covered her face. There was something fixed and mechanical in the serenity painted on it; this was not an expression, Ralph said – it was a representation, it was even an advertisement (vol. 4, p. 142).

As a specific representation or sign, Isabel is now part of a system of understood communication and action; whereas before she suggested possibilities, she now suggests a static aesthetic and social value. The potential for a reciprocal action, for her effecting change as well as being looked at as a 'given', for her existing for her own vision as well as for others, has, for the time, been lost. She is more public, just as Madame Merle (at one end of the scale) and Pansy (at the other) are public.

Because Isabel appears so different to Ralph and her other friends, and because it is not merely a quantitative but a qualitative difference – she is an opaque representation – we see the constructed nature of her existence now, and the aspects of herself that it represses:

> The novel is not merely the conservative response to womanhood, nor the realization of a gracious lady, but a realization of her picture. What we see in the frame alerts us to the excluded space outside it. The adorable object is not 'nature', but a specific product within a specific system.[10]

It is the presentation of Isabel within the picture frame, in contrast to her presented previous hopes and present suffering, which provokes questions. Pansy, for instance, is presented as the passive, well-behaved little girl. Our sense of her restriction as image, as 'a specific product within a specific system' comes from Isabel's response to her as the feminine principle which was appropriated in herself. In growing consciousness of her self as object for the world, in Osmond, Isabel has to build up her subject identity in acceptance and recognition of the portrait, the gracious wife that she has become. Yet this kind of conscious alienation cannot protect her from increasing perception and increasing unhappiness in response to her conflicting existence as self and other. Repression of this probing unhappiness results in passivity, which, in turn, exacerbates her position as feminine and powerless. Isabel attempts merely to be what she appears, imitating Madame Merle's 'firm and bright' (vol. 4, p. 156) qualities. Yet she is aware of the limits of such patient repression; faced with Lord Warburton, who has given himself a new sense of purpose with his involvement in politics, she 'gave an envious thought to the happier lot of men, who are always free to plunge into the healing waters of action' (vol. 4, p. 130). Action is precisely what Isabel thought herself capable of. Now, it appears, she knows better. Yet she instinctively recognises that passivity and repression of self precipitates suffering, once it is self-conscious. She simply cannot envisage a mode of action now, but she 'could never rid herself of the sense that unhappiness was a state of disease – of suffering as opposed to doing. To 'do' – it hardly mattered what – would therefore be an escape' (vol. 4, p. 174).

Isabel has not just stayed beautiful, she has lost her sense of flux, of potential. Ralph muses that 'The free, keen girl had become quite another person; what he saw was the fine lady who was supposed to represent something' (vol. 4, p. 143). The only action and change open to Isabel now is that of comprehension of the processes of signification, and her place within them. Through understanding her manipulation as sign, she will be equipped to build up some sense of herself in relation to the world, and perhaps some idea of how to control her function in that relation. But as yet Isabel cannot open herself to understanding how completely she has been objectified, her sense of identity still needs some illusion of subjective control. So she views her situation as self-determined, as a failure of judgement, she cannot yet see the way she has been manipulated. That would involve a recognition of the real extent of social imposition, going far beyond the need for correct clothing. Even on seeing Madame Merle and Osmond together, on catching a glimpse of their relation to one another, she represses its implications. Her sense is mainly one of suffocation and darkness 'as if Osmond deliberately, almost malignantly, had put the lights out one by one' (vol. 4, p. 190). And her only energies lie in the resistance to Osmond's and Madame Merle's plans for Pansy. If Isabel knows that Osmond is not what she thought, she also realises that she is not what he expected:

> There were times when she almost pitied him; for if she had not deceived him in intention she understood how completely she

must have done so in fact . . . she had made herself small, pretending there was less of her than there really was (vol. 4, p. 191).

Her honesty is internal now, kept for this sort of fireside meditation. In front of others she dissimulates, for various reasons – if she presented only a certain image of herself when Osmond was courting her, it was a deceptive process engendered by him which now extends to her relationship to the whole world. She pretends to them all.

The issue of Pansy's marriage becomes an arena in which Osmond determines to force Isabel to act against her will. She refuses to surrender her integrity, to comply in the conscious and heartless disposal of the submissive and self-denying girl. It is as though Isabel is being asked to admit the lack of self-existence of the young girl she herself once was, to compound her own guilt in having wanted anything for herself by denying Pansy's right to any honest emotion of her own. Appearances still matter to Isabel, she still feels some retention of control over her existence if she can sustain them, and thus the moral imperative to resist Osmond's plans for Pansy (and his attitude towards her seeking her old friends) involves her in a struggle more painful than that of simply admitting her own conflict with Osmond to him: 'To break with Osmond once would be to break for ever; any open acknowledgement of irreconcilable needs would be an admission that their whole attempt had proved a failure' (vol. 4, p. 246). The 'whole attempt' includes, after all, Isabel's engagement with the world in an active sense.

Understanding and consciousness, and with them a relaxation of mask and image, finally work through Isabel. She starts to mistrust Madame Merle without knowing why; she feels a 'consciousness of respite' (vol. 4, p. 278) when that lady is away from Rome. When Henrietta arrives, she is able to admit to her that she is sad. In Isabel's changed circumstances, the other characters have been thrown into a kind of moral relief by their response to her. The laughable and decadent Countess at least recognises Isabel's worth, and Henrietta would do anything she could to help her. Neither of them see Isabel so much as the situation she is in, their vision is less rigid than that of the world which sees her simply as the gracious portrait. When Caspar comes to see Isabel before leaving Rome and says to her what Ralph had privately thought, that she is 'so still, so smooth, so hard. You're completely changed. You conceal everything' (vol. 4, p. 318), she admits to him as well that she is sad, that he may pity her.

When Isabel finally understands just how she has been used, it is as though she seemed 'to wake from a long pernicious dream' (vol. 4, p. 323). As she begins to perceive, to see within and beyond the images and appearances, her feeling and understanding become active and living rather than theoretic or repressed. The language is of movement: 'It had come over her like a high surging wave' (vol. 4, p. 327). Whereas Madame Merle can say to Osmond 'You've not only dried up my tears; you've dried up my soul' (vol. 4, p. 334); when Isabel finally learns Pansy's true parentage, she can weep for Madame Merle, her first tears for a long time.

Recognising the appropriation incarnate in Osmond, Madame Merle has subordinated herself to it as a woman, and in his interests has sacrificed another woman. By resisting this pattern, Isabel retains her ability to weep, to respond generously. At an internal level, she refuses to become totally a victim of the structure which makes her object, neither is she prepared to try and exploit it. She insists on her consciousness as independent subject.

As Osmond loses his grip on Isabel, he tightens it on Pansy. Pansy's attempts at passive resistance can be easily crushed, not least because she is materially as well as ideologically a helpless person. Not equipped with any of the economic necessities for autonomy that made Isabel's dilemma seem a real one, she can go only where she is put. When we first saw Pansy she was straight from the convent in much the same way as Isabel was straight from her pure, isolated little world in Albany. The repression overtly displayed in sending Pansy back to the convent suggests the kind of repression that Osmond practices in a more sophisticated and less successful form on Isabel – by trying to isolate her from her old friends. Isabel's capacity to resist is strengthened by her growing consciousness of the unacceptable nature of what Osmond does; the only alternative to resistance would be a retreat into passive innocence again. Once awake, whether to understanding or, like poor Pansy, to love, it is meaningless (and Pansy finds almost unbearable) to go back out of the world again. Pansy can gain a reprieve by promising to play according to the rules by denying the self-discovery she has made. Isabel is not prepared to do that, her powers of resistance are stronger, her situation less easy to force. Images continue to break and move, her consciousness is described as a sea. Isabel now sees the connections, the organic nature of things. Her world is no longer controlled by categories which stand fixed and immutable. She made static functions for herself and others, and seeing how the same has been done to her, the language of static image breaks down. Seeing Madame Merle in the convent she notes that 'The effect was strange . . . her appearance in the flesh was like suddenly, and rather awfully, seeing a painted picture move' (vol. 4, p. 375). Isabel is now 'far afloat on a sea of wonder and pain' (vol. 4, p. 376).

Isabel's innocent interpretations of the world, although engendered by that same world's tendency to interpret reality through the control of signification, never involved a desire to use the people so docketed, more a desire to control how she was seen by ordering what she saw. Now she sees how such designation can render a person secondary to their usefulness as sign, they become simply a thing – and not even an abstract, idealised thing but a minimised reduced object to be utilised. She sees 'the dry staring fact that she had been an applied handled hung-up tool, as senseless and convenient as mere shaped wood and iron' (vol. 4, p. 379).

The fear of being used and confined spreads to an awareness of the potential for this not simply, specifically, in Osmond and Madame Merle, but in the way the world works, in the weight of social institution. The convent confining Pansy is an expression of this as much as it is an expression of Osmond's will. Suddenly things connect and inter-relate in a way that Isabel has never allowed them to before:

> Now that she was in the secret, now that she knew something which so much concerned her and the eclipse of which had made life resemble an attempt to play whist with an imperfect pack of cards, the truth of things, their mutual relations, their meaning, and for the most part their horror, rose before her with a kind of architectural vastness (vol. 4, pp. 390–1).

In recognising the relations and structures of events, Isabel recognises the *process* of signification in which the existence of a sign communicated between subjects fixes that sign as secondary, as functioning for another, regardless of the nobility or meanness of what is signified. Isabel's developing consciousness is aided by a period of withdrawal from the world, which takes place in a journey away from Italy and back to England. Here she meditates and confronts what has happened. Yet there is no sense for a moment of any kind of complete withdrawal. Her fear of the 'surrender of a personality' (vol. 4, p. 382), that she felt on Pansy's behalf when faced by the convent, is equally strong for herself. Though she recognises the pull of the temptation that Pansy had succumbed to in the end, that of ceasing to resist, and she envies Ralph dying, yet 'Deep in her soul . . . was the sense that life would be her business for a long time to come' (vol. 4, p. 392). Painfully Isabel relinquishes both the blankness of surrender and the illusion of total freedom. Everyone is subject to the 'mutual relations' of things, even Henrietta, who, in deciding to marry 'had confessed herself human and feminine. Henrietta whom she had hitherto regarded as a light, keen flame, a disembodied voice' (vol. 4, p. 400).

Significantly Henrietta now also announces her determination to 'grapple in earnest with England' (vol. 4, p. 401). Commitment, even at this comic level, must be both internal and external, personal and social. Freedom means a denial of the feminine, for the feminine is not free, and Henrietta, whatever Osmond thinks, is as inescapably feminine as Isabel.

Returning to Gardencourt, Isabel's sense of human existence is now in direct contrast to its setting and its possessions; her new sense of flux is something she is only beginning to come to terms with. We are told that 'She envied the security of valuable "pieces" which change by no hair's breadth, only grow in value, while their owners lose inch by inch youth, happiness, beauty' (vol. 4, p. 403). The sterility of attempting to experience life as an object in an artistic collection is exposed by implication as self-delusion. Similarly Mrs Touchett, who has been successful in fending off human experience, is now exposed as empty. She has had to deny human relations in order to avoid personal and specific control of herself as sign, so now she will be 'an old woman without memories' (vol. 4, p. 407).

As Ralph and Isabel finally acknowledge the truth between them, and abandon all looking at each other for a mutual looking at the truth together, it is Ralph who comes down on the side of the world as having ultimately used Isabel more than she used it or herself. He recognises the extent to which she could never have seen properly in a world which would not admit that kind of independent sight, and says to her 'You wanted to look at life for yourself – but you were not allowed; you were punished for your wish. You were ground in the very mill of the conventional!' (vol. 4, p. 415).

Isabel's existence as conscious subject, asserted out of her recognition of her social manipulation as other, gains substance through being communicated externally to Ralph. His death forestalls any possibility of the two presenting any real challenge to existing structures.

As Isabel remains in Gardencourt for Ralph's funeral, the ends running through from her first experiences there are tied up by a sort of re-experiencing of them with much greater clarity. She recognises what is of value, 'the beauty of the day, the splendour of nature, the sweetness of the old English churchyard, the bowed heads of good friends' (vol. 4, p. 420). And she finally confronts the last temptation, and the strongest, to surrender the painful burden of consciousness. When Caspar meets her for the last time in the garden the violence of his passion is openly met by a violence of surrender in her. The flux which has been an opening up of her perception has also resulted in a confusion which is precipitated by the sexuality, the abandonment of the social world of appearances, that Caspar represents. As he says, 'It's too late to play a part' (vol. 4, p. 432). The imagery is totally physical – of desert winds and white lightning – yet this sense of deluge is internal, confusions are 'in her own swimming head' (vol. 4, p. 436). Surrender to the physical world would be a denial of consciousness, of all she has learned concerning the social shell, of the relation of appearances to reality. She knows that submission to Caspar, to passion, would be 'the next best thing to her dying', yet also, like dying, it would be a blacking out of the vision she has so lately won. Here the female surrender to sexuality is precisely that – surrender. It involves loss of self, just as being a spiritualised feminine sign does. Just as the nineteenth century feminists often reacted against ideas of sexual freedom because they saw them as encroaching on their personal and intellectual autonomy by imposing their 'sex' on them too strongly, so it is as a part of the same retention of self, of a self-perceived being, that Isabel rejects Caspar. She goes back to Europe, back to the field of experience, resistance and continuing life.

It is her imagination which differentiates Isabel from Daisy Miller. Daisy is watched and observed as a function of Winterbourne's experience. Before the potential meaning of the feminine as sign can be used and directed by the female herself, as a function of her experience, she must comprehend the process of watching and manipulation that is imposed on her, and which helps to create her. Two kinds of development are offered in *The Portrait of a Lady*. One is the exposure of the specific, appropriative and selfish use made by the world of the moral and aesthetic values signified by the feminine. The American girl symbolises a freedom and spontaneity that can never be realised in the structures of power and manipulation that make up the social world. As her values are possessed and her significations limited, so is the girl who functions as sign.

The other development is the attempt of the American girl to live and function for herself, and to realise her own freedom. Her failure exposes the extent of her manipulation, both internal and external. The extent to which the female self is both sign and yet more than sign (and thus can never be reduced simply to sign status without limiting and denying its other aspects), is developed on from this in texts where the young girl quite consciously contradicts the limitations of her signification as innocent and ignorant. The assertion of a subjecthood which may extend beyond the specifics of the feminine renders the girl vulnerable to ostracism, yet at least aware of her position in the world – fully conscious. Thus this aspect of Isabel Archer's emergence into social existence, and consciousness of her place in such existence, leads on into the bids for social happiness made by Maisie and Nanda in *What Maisie Knew* and *The Awkward Age*.

The failure of idealistic and absolute values to direct social existence, and the appropriation of them in the figure of the young girl – as America or as Art – is explored in *The Bostonians* and *The Tragic Muse*, where the woman as sign is explored in terms of exploitation, rather than in terms of the values she signifies. Isabel Archer undermines the 'face value' of Daisy Miller by exposing her vulnerability and ultimate confinement. Verena Tarrant lacks Isabel's powers of resistance, but also Daisy's quality of 'pure poetry': she is finally appropriated less as America or social freedom than as feminine prey in a world of predators. Miriam Rooth resists appropriation in order to retain her powers of wider, self-controlled signification. She controls her appearance as woman by professionalising it as actress – the professional equivalent of feminine signification that prostitution is of marriage. Both Verena and Miriam operate in specific social worlds where money and employment intrude – before returning to the mystery and power of interpretation and meaning played out in the later novels, James described a world where the structures are less of interpretation than of straightforward possession and commitment.

5 Women in the Public World: *The Bostonians*, *The Princess Casamassima* and *The Tragic Muse*

At the end of *The Portrait of a Lady*, we recognise a disparity between the limitless opportunities presented as being open to Isabel Archer and the actual choices she has been offered in the course of the narrative; a disparity which suggests a fundamental failure in the conception of the freedom of the American girl. Despite her desire to act and be free, Isabel fails to understand what the world is doing *to* her – in the guise of Osmond, Madame Merle, the Touchetts and her other suitors – how it defines her as lady, and uses her. Only by understanding her existence as sign, as carrier of potential meaning, could Isabel begin to make any real 'choice' at all. As it is, she accepts others' image of her and can therefore experiment only within the limitations of that image. All the indications are that she does not really want to marry, and that she finds the prospect alarming and potentially engulfing to her as an individual. Unable to think of any alternative she chooses, disastrously, the marriage she thinks she will be most able to control and least engulfed by.

Despite the disillusionment inherent in the presentation of Isabel's fate, the submersion of idealism and innocence and the manipulation of the feminine, *The Portrait of a Lady* does put forward values and ideals which retain their impact alongside the irony with which they are sometimes treated. Isabel's independence and desire for moral freedom and knowledge may be vulnerable and naive but a positive, even protective response to them is legitimated by the language of emotional seriousness which surrounds her loss and imprisonment.

In the three long novels of the 1880s which followed – *The Bostonians* (1886), *The Princess Casamassima* (1886), and *The Tragic Muse* (1890) – James presents worlds which are more specific in sense of place, economic necessity, means of employment and class conflict, in which these concrete details have as much reality as the symbolic oppositions they may suggest. This may be due, in part, to James's interest in naturalism during this period, influenced somewhat by French contemporaries.[1] Those of his critics interested in the more symbolic and philosophical side of James's work tend not to treat these novels at all.[2] I think one can generalise about these novels to the extent that there is an apparent breakdown of the spiritual individualism embodied with some seriousness in characters like Christopher Newman and Isabel Archer – even Daisy Miller. Though these characters may be destroyed or disillusioned in the course of the novel's events, that they are in existence at *all* presents the values they carry for examination.

The Bostonians is in part a final reduction of the way in which society manipulates and appropriates the female as sign, so that each and every active, voracious individual can re-interpret and claim the American girl for his own. Verena can be anything for anyone, she no longer even has the autonomy and clarity of signifying anything clear cut, perhaps only 'potential', potential meaning. The possibility of her standing apart from her function as sign is never really raised at all, she *is* what she is seen to be. As sign, she does, however, have a firm status within the structures of her society. The desire to discover and possess some absolute value or meaning is portrayed as a pattern leading to the exchange and manipulation of such as Verena, the mythifying of the Princess and the professional existence of Miriam, as material characters in a material world. They do not possess the same freedom from material considerations that facilitates the abstraction of Daisy to an 'American girl', or Isabel to a free 'individual'. Verena has two awful parents and no money, Miriam has one awful mother and the need to earn her own living. The Princess is pursued and defined by husband and lovers, by possessions and her dependence on them. The power structures of society are exposed openly, as a matter of course, whether in Verena's being sold by her parents, Hyacinth being unable to transcend his poverty and illegitimacy, or British political and diplomatic life attempting to buy off the artists in *The Tragic Muse*.

In discussing these novels, F. W. Dupee seizes on their changed mood, and its expression, as he sees it, in the similarly changed nature of the female characters:

> a mood that may be described as an inverted idealism since it was so far from being a settled despair or even a reasoned scepticism.

Types of human perversity now almost fill the picture, the chief
sign of the prevalent evil being the corruption of the feminine
principle . . . Olive Chancellor, the Princess Casamassima, and
in a different way Lady Dormer and Julia Dallow, are all
wonderful studies of women in whom the will to power has
supplanted the wisdom, as James conceived it, of suffering and
understanding.[3]

The values assumed here are conventional; the realisation of the
feminine principle lies in 'suffering and understanding' – an assumption rather unfairly laid at James's door. Two other things are worth
noting: it is probably no accident that Dupee sees the 'inverted
idealism' manifesting itself in the feminine principle and not the
masculine. Male characters are not related back to the masculine
principle, that is not the primary means of their identification. The
second is an assumption of a continuity in James's work of absolute
values (including, presumably' those of the 'feminine principle').
We look for the same meaning, but presented more or less negatively
or positively in a range of examples.

I think that James is exploring in these works, among other things,
the validity of this notion of absolute values against which behaviour
and relationships can be measured. Certainly the desire to see a
principle embodied in a female figurehead – corrupt or otherwise –
is one James exploits in these novels. Unlike *Daisy Miller* or *The
Portrait of a Lady*, where the relationship between the young girl and
what she signifies is more or less complete (Isabel and Daisy *are*
primarily youthful, innocent, attractive, vivacious, etc.), in the
novels under discussion here the signifieds attached to the women
seem more specifically imposed by society. For instance, in *The
Princess Casamassima* and *The Tragic Muse*, we have two books which
are concerned with their main characters' confrontation with the
idea suggested in the title – social status and beauty in one case, and
the potentially tragic demands of art in the other. At the same time,
the books contain women characters of the same 'name' as the titles,
who have suggested the ideas that form the bulk of the subject matter
for the heroes, and who are present in the background functioning in
a rather different way from that their names would suggest. The
dislocation between the woman as sign and the woman as subject of
her own experience is implied by making one character perform
both functions. The Princess as conscious subject only indirectly

comes into the narrative, and the same goes for Miriam. The lack of freedom involved in acquiescence to the sign function is implicit in the confrontations between the two functions that are present in the narratives. Hyacinth's attempts to form a permanent relationship with the Princess based on what he first sees her to be would fix her forever in Medley, Peter's desire to marry Miriam would bar her from her profession.

James does not, however, suggest that the two aspects of the women's existence are not linked, or are not both integral and incomplete. Miriam and the Princess are defined partly through their value as signs for their society; even though this visible signification may be inadequate or misleading as a total expression of them, it is the available means for women to communicate with the world. *The Tragic Muse* is largely concerned with this need to communicate, to name, to make visible through action and performance. However limited and misdirected the interpretation foisted on the Princess by Hyacinth, or on Miriam by Nick and Peter, their social existence as women – and thus their sense of their own identity – is dependent on this process. Its inadequacy precipitates the conflict for the women, who are actually more complex than any naming of them as signifying absolute values might suggest.

The Bostonians, even more than *The Tragic Muse*, seems to me to be concerned with the appropriation of the 'feminine principle' as a desire to maintain a belief in such a thing, a desire to harmonise or salvage the materialism and corruption of the public, commercial world. This appropriation takes place regardless of the specific reality of the qualities present in the girl concerned. Verena Tarrant apparently signifies so much to the people around her that she really signifies very little at all except, as her function in the text, the blank passivity of the (any) feminine principle. The world present in *The Bostonians* suggests certain simple things: that Verena is bound to be preyed on; that Olive is bound to lose her in the struggle with Ransom; that these two inevitables represent the way of a world which is not a particularly pleasant, moral or happy one. The apparent polarity of North and South, as represented by Olive and Ransom, suggests conflict as a process rather than a clear division of bad and good. Ransom adopts the values of the North, seeking financial success and public acclaim. Whatever the name of the battle – North against South, European against American – there will be territory to be gained and spoils to be won. Verena will always be the spoils. That she is fought over primarily here by a man and a woman, rather than by two men, is surely significant, and it is here that the values of the reader assert themselves in the assessment of its significance.

In *The Resisting Reader*, Judith Fetterley surveys the criticism of *The Bostonians*, and shows how there are repeated, in diverse critics, the assumptions that Ransom embodies the positive values of the novel, that his appropriation of Verena is a good thing and the best thing for her, and that Olive is perverse and depraved.[4] The desire to see heterosexual union and masculinity vindicated by James is so strong that it can lead to rebuking the author for not treating his own characters in the way he 'should':

> More serious than these equations between the combatants, which after all might be attributed to evaluative sophistication, is a stream of jokes at Basil's expense that is gratuitous, if not downright silly.[5]

Fetterley compares the criticism of *The Bostonians* with the comments James made about it in the *Notebooks*, comments which define Olive and Verena's relationship as 'a study of onè of those friendships between women which are so common in New England'.[6] As she says:

> Much is made of the impact on the writing of *The Bostonians* of James's visits to America in 1881–82 and 1882–83 . . . Yet, not one critic whom I have read, with the exception of Leon Edel, has mentioned what would seem to be an obvious familial influence and one of potentially far more importance to *The Bostonians* than the parental deaths – namely Henry's sister, Alice James, who was herself involved in one of those friendships which the brother saw as so common to New England soil.[7]

James was close to his sister, and elsewhere spoke with admiration and understanding of her close friendship with Katherine Loring.[8] Although I don't think this makes a case for any specific championing of Olive and Verena's relationship I agree with Judith Fetterley that it helps to counterbalance the notion that in dealing with such a relationship James was confronting a threatening and dangerous perversity, and will also suggest that the satire directed at Olive (which no character in the novel escapes) is very much tempered by the sense of her ultimate powerlessness, even in so-called 'feminised' Boston, to combat the *status quo* of marriage, family and heterosexual love. I think that in this novel, as in so many of James's novels, sexuality is an expression of a desire for dominance and a threat to personal integrity for the woman. This is emphasised by the repetition of this pattern in a relationship between two women, set as it is in the context of a world where sexual relationships are visible between men and women and where the woman is dominated, the man the captor:

> But are we then to assume that the love of Verena and Basil is 'really' personal in some sense? – heterosexual being better than lesbian, in spite of its grotesque variants in the book . . . Eventually it comes to the question of the nature of the relationship, the union. And uncertainties and forebodings about that do not spring from the novel's grim last sentence alone . . . If this is the most substantial relationship in the book (although one would have to say that the Olive–Verena is the more subtle, also involving as it does a rationale of free union), it is because it takes up and confirms what all other 'unions' point to: dominance for one partner, defeat for the other. That is the force of sexuality in the novel.[9]

At the beginning of *The Bostonians*, the polarities seem clearly established. Confident sexuality, provincial conservatism and old-style masculinity confront the nervous intensity opposed to the established order that prevails in the woman-dominated world of Boston. Although the threat to Ransom of this world is in its power to 'feminise' society, the women who inhabit it are attempting to deny or transform their femininity, to act as subjects. This denial is presented to a certain extent in James's portrayal of them not as wives and mothers, beauty or innocence, but as a strange assortment of caricatural eccentrics. But this process of caricature is applied to men and women alike, just as the modes of subject behaviour available, of appropriation and possession, are not transformed by these women but adopted, albeit in a narrow, privileged sphere. Olive Chancellor is defined in the wider world as a failure as a woman, as an old maid – yet within the framework of Boston her status as appropriator and buyer (of Verena) rather than as feminine goods, and Ransom's recognition of her as an adversary, makes her culturally an active subject.

Confronted with Olive, Ransom muses:

The women he had hitherto known had been mainly of his own
soft clime, and it was not often they exhibited the tendency he
detected (and cursorily deplored) in Mrs Luna's sister. That was
the way he liked them – not to think too much, not to feel any
responsibility for the government of the world, such as he was sure
Miss Chancellor felt. If they would only be private and passive,
and have no feeling but for that, and would leave publicity to the
sex of tougher hide! Ransom was pleased with the vision of that
remedy; it must be repeated that he was very provincial (p. 11).

The division of male and female is made by Ransom into one of the
private and the public – male control over the existence of women is
easier to maintain on a private, individual basis. Women fixed
specifically as representative and interpreter of one particular man
are less free to change or to extend what they signify. Just as in *The
Tragic Muse*, Peter's attempt to marry Miriam and confine her
acting to the enhancement and representation of his own career is
inevitably an attempt to limit her, so Ransom feels more able to
control Verena by removing her from the public sphere. Yet this is
not to suggest any necessary vindication of the public sphere as the
arena for women's fight for freedom – the reduction here of women
to surrogate men with all the same faults can, in fact, be seen as
paving the way to the need for the personal, individually reasoned
struggle for autonomy of consciousness that takes place in the
heroines of the later novels.

    The Bostonians can be divided into six distinct sections. The first,
located in Boston, introduces the characters of Boston juxtaposed
with that of Basil Ransom, an implicit conflict into whose midst is
plunged the figure of Verena Tarrant. In the second, the developing
and intense relationship of Verena and Olive is portrayed, bounded
still by Boston and Cambridge. In the third, a brief sortie into New
York brings Ransom back into the Boston world where he begins his
counter-relationship with Verena – a conscious move against Olive.
In the fourth, the battle takes on real seriousness and is pitched in the
harsher and less familiar ground of New York. Flight and chase take
the protagonists to the failing sanctuary of Marmion, where the
gentle Miss Birdseye relinquishes *her* struggle, in the fifth. Finally
Basil wins the war in the newly public world of the Boston Music
Hall. Seen in terms of this analysis, the pulls and strains of the book

are very much between Olive and Ransom. Whoever gains final possession of Verena will somehow have vindicated their beliefs and feelings.

Olive has searched for some time for emotional verification of her beliefs about women and their independence, and has failed in her attempts to 'take up' some working class girl;

> She took them more tragically than they took themselves; they couldn't make out what she wanted them to do, and they always ended by being odiously mixed up with Charlie. Charlie was a young man in a white overcoat and a paper collar; it was for him, in the last analysis, that they cared much the most. They cared far more about Charlie than about the ballot (pp. 34–5).

The pull between what one feels and believes in a general way and what one, as an individual actually *does*, so eloquently expressed by Isabel Archer:

> You talk about one's soaring and sailing, but if one marries at all one touches the earth. One has human feelings and needs, one has a heart in one's bosom, and one must marry a particular individual (vol. 4, p. 74).

is here satirised, brought out of the realm of the transcendental dilemma and firmly or to the plane of external conflict between Olive's intensity, 'tragically' concerned with the ballot, and the girls' predictable following of a pattern deliberately rendered commonplace by 'paper collars' and 'Charlie'. For Olive to retain Verena within her circle of intensity and tragedy would be a victory over the inevitable ways of girls and young men in paper collars.

Similarly Ransom, certain of the ways and places of men and women in his mind, and confident of the pull of 'natural' sexuality over Olive's 'morbid intensity', seeks to establish this sense of an ordered universe which is threatened by his failing career and by the female-dominated society he finds himself in, by submerging Verena in his personality and physical presence. Again a comparison with *The Portrait of a Lady* is instructive. Caspar Goodwood's final encounter with Isabel is the most concrete expression of a sexuality that has been hinted at in all his appearances. Its effect on Isabel is described in a series of natural images:

this was the hot wind of the desert, at the approach of which the others dropped dead, like mere sweet airs of the garden! (vol. 4, p. 434).

The world, in truth, had never seemed so large; it seemed to open out, all round her, to take the form of a mighty sea, where she floated in fathomless waters. (vol. 4, p. 435).

His kiss was like white lightning, a flash that spread, and spread again, and stayed (vol. 4, p. 436).

Ransom's sensuality in *The Bostonians* is not expressed in such universal images, but in particular commonplaces – he drinks beer, he has a friend in a variety actress, and he has a vision of a rather banal domestic harmony while sitting with Mrs Luna who is immensely attracted to him. Just as the open-ended language of Isabel's drama, her 'soaring and sailing' is rendered into the hard specificity of Olive's concern for the ballot and her battle against white overcoats, so the opposing forces of physical abandon are no longer reverberating symbols of lightning and water, but found out in routine encounters of flirtation and beer drinking.

Both Ransom and Olive want Verena as a love-object, an emotional concretion of their status in their worlds and their sense of themselves. Verena's fitness for this resides in her qualities of empathy, response to others and openness to external demands and pressures. Her existence for others is endorsed by her lack of introspection: 'She had no particular feeling about herself; she only cared, as yet, for outside things' (p. 77).

Near the end of the novel we are told in the narrative voice that Verena's 'essence' does not reside in any particular knowledge or commitment:

What *was* part of her essence was the extraordinary generosity with which she would expose herself, give herself away, turn herself inside out, for the satisfaction of a person who made demands of her (p. 380).

Olive recognises this in Verena when she longs for a 'union of soul':

It took a double consent to make a friendship, but it was not possible that this intensely sympathetic girl would refuse. Olive had the penetration to discover in a moment that she was a creature of unlimited generosity. (p. 80).

Verena's inability to refuse what is demanded of her is the consequence of her being a medium, a reflection, kindled into life by another's touch. Her own pleasure resides in pleasing. Her existence is defined by the recognition of her as a signifier – regardless, Basil Ransom considers, of what she signifies:

> For the necessity of her nature was not to make converts to a ridiculous cause, but to emit those charming notes of her voice, to stand in those free young attitudes, to shake her braided locks like a naiad rising from the waves, to please everyone who came near her, and to be happy that she pleased (p. 61).

Verena is not subjected to the careful moral interpretation that Daisy Miller receives at the hands of Winterbourne and his society. In the world of *The Bostonians*, the young girl as sign is a devalued commodity, able to be manipulated by anyone who can gain control over her and direct what she signifies. There are no 'real' values or meanings, only those assigned by the expediency of the moment. Mrs Farrinder is observed by Ransom to see Verena's possible value to her as quite divorced from any intrinsic worth:

> It was none of his business whether in her heart she thought Verena a parrot or a genius; it was perceptible to him that she saw she would be effective, would help the cause (p. 65).

After Verena's first speech, Matthias Pardon expresses the same feeling even more bluntly: 'There's money for someone in that girl; you see if she don't have quite a run' (p. 63).

Other forms of possession abound. Mrs Burrage wants Verena to keep her son happy, and Mrs Tarrant hopes to use her to re-enter a social world that she has lost through her marriage. But the keynote is financial, and its climax is the selling of Verena by her father to Olive. This defines Verena, the feminine principle, as clearly and unequivocally a thing, an object with a currency value. This stark presentation of her as an object with no autonomous status – either in the world she inhabits or the structure of the novel itself – seems connected to the overall change of tone that I have pointed out between this book and *The Portrait of a Lady*. As ideals and principles fail in the face of actual behaviour and motivation, the saving grace of meaningful or moral representation is stripped from the justification of the feminine as sign, leaving simple currency used expediently between individuals or groups. The more feminine the woman, the more she exists as object for others, the more she will be submerged as subject. Verena appears vivid enough now, but what is Miss Birdseye but a very much older Verena without her beauty?

> She had never, in her long, unrewarded, weary life, had a thought or an impulse for herself. She had been consumed by the passion of sympathy; it had crumpled her into as many creases as an old glazed, distended glove (p. 37).

In either private or public world, the choice seems to narrow down here to buying and manipulating others or giving oneself up to others. The basic structures of possession are unchallenged in the specific lives and activities of the people who are conceptually devoted to, or opposed to, a cause – here femininism, in *The Princess Casamassima* anarchism. Though the cause may attempt to oppose oppression or limitation of expression, it functions more as a catalyst for personal needs. Where Daisy Miller provoked some kind of general reflection on the clashes between custom and freedom, appearance and essence, America and Europe, even while also raising the problem of her passivity and vulnerability as sign, the position of 'women', exemplified in Verena serves more to expose the particular motivations of the individuals around her – Mrs Farrinder's search for fame and power, Pardon's desire for money, her mother's desire for a new social world.

Verena is a medium in the public world, a conveyor of others' messages, just as she will be in the private, as Ransom's wife. Having very little subject self to assert, no signifieds of her own to project and make visible, she is simply prey to the demands of others. Her performance, unlike Miriam's, is directed and manipulated by others, and she has no control over it. She retreats rapidly from her larger role. She can do her 'piece' but cannot cope with the multiple demands it elicits:

> Verena heaved a thin, private sigh, expressive of some helplessness, as she thought what a big, complicated world it was, and how it evidently contained a little of everything (p. 290).

Her progress is very much from the public world, which she cannot order and which wishes to sell her as completely as she will sell, into the private world in which she will be lost, but lost in accordance with her nature.

When Americans are viewed in a European setting, or in juxtaposition with visiting Europeans, they appear rootless and timeless because of their lack of an established culture or custom. Here the setting *is* America, and it is rendered very particularly – the streets of Boston, the contrast of the Back Bay to the bustling world of New York, and the rural seclusion of Marmion. The world of money and publicity is firmly located in New York, and the two sorts of provincials – Ransom, the Southerner, and Olive, who is sick of the Back Bay – seek to widen their horizons by moving into that world. New York is the first step into 'life', in its corrupt, cosmopolitan sense. In part it is provincialism that motivates them. Verena is the American in America – she really comes from nowhere and no-one, or from such a strange, mixed, itinerant past that it amounts to such: 'A girl without a setting, or too many settings . . . cannot be that symbolic. Nothing American can be that symbolic.'[10]

Or perhaps she is too symbolic: in a world where one is moving from Boston to New York and then fleeing to Marmion, a wider Americanism in the earlier, transcendent sense is simply not applicable. Whereas in *The Portrait of a Lady*, places suggested states of mind and character – houses such as Gardencourt and Roccanera represented stages of Isabel's experience – in *The Bostonians*, despite a basic sense of territory according to which Olive belongs to Boston, Ransom to the South, and New York is more or less neutral ground, the overriding sense of place is in its local reality: New York is first and foremost New York. This suggests a focus of importance on the signifier, in the terms of the novel, on the specific realities which may or may not engender meaning or function as signs. Such a focus serves to underline the dependency of Verena on the sign function. Unlike New York, she cannot simply 'be' Verena, she has to please, to intrigue, to offer something in communication with someone.

Indeed Verena's charm, her sweetness, lies in her indiscriminate desire to please everyone. As she retreats into the smaller, local world, she relinquishes this range and becomes one person who can please only one person – she is going to make speeches on Ransom's dining table in the privacy of his dining room.

Brian Lee voices a fairly frequent critical judgement on the ending of *The Bostonians* when he concludes that:

The whole tenor of the book suggests that Verena Tarrant gained her freedom by marrying Basil Ransom at the expense of equality, and that this freedom is ultimately the more valuable.[11]

Certainly Verena – on an emotional and physical level – is more attracted to Basil than to Olive, but there seems to me a false equation between attraction and freedom (it is dangerous to use one novel to substantiate reference points in another, but the final scene of *The Portrait of a Lady* seems relevant here). James bases the entire action of *The Bostonians* around battles for which the prize is Verena Tarrant – a prize which can be bought or carried off as spoils of war. Indeed, the final scene is one of abduction. Verena is a Helen for whom Ransom storms the city of Troy – or, in this case, the Boston Music Hall:

> 'Olive, Olive!' Verena suddenly shrieked; and her piercing cry might have reached the front. But Ransom had already, by muscular force, wrenched her away, and was hurrying her out . . . Ransom, as he went, thrust the hood of Verena's long cloak over her head, *to conceal her face and her identity* . . . Ransom, palpitating with his victory, felt now a little sorry for her [Olive] (pp. 448–9). (my emphasis).

The only freedom for Verena will be the traditional female freedom from choice or responsibility.

The Bostonians is a novel without a critical or reflective observer to make anything of the possibilities suggested by Verena's 'desire to please', her intimations of life – nor is this creativity located within Verena herself. Without this interpretation she recedes into the lives of others, first Olive's and finally Ransom's. Verena does not perceive what is happening to her, her existence remains defined by her function for other people. Her potential to signify is linked to the desire for generalities and abstract solutions and their failure to harmonise or clarify the actual and specific. The woman as sign neither makes social existence meaningful (for instance as virtue, innocence or freedom), nor comprehends her existence as sign in order to take control of the signifying process herself.

The Bostonians is a problematic novel because it appears to oppose female Boston to male Ransom, but in fact opposes the two to the placeless and limitless sense of 'life' that Verena suggests. It becomes almost an opposition of actual to abstract, with different elements of the actual fighting for possession of the abstract feminine values which get swamped in the process. The apparent male/female opposition in the 'actual' fabric of the novel is a deceptive one, as Pardon and Selah Tarrant are struggling against Ransom, and Mrs Farrinder is struggling against Olive. Possession of Verena would facilitate social existence in some way for each of them, whether it would be the establishment of an emotional or a financial possession. A relationship to society, to the external world, can be made through a woman, the recognised and visible carrier of meaning.

Verena acquiesces to being possessable (even if she struggles against actual possession), but the conflict arising when the woman is elusive, enigmatic or simply more complex and self-motivated than Verena, once again exposes the illusionary nature of looking for absolutes. The Princess Casamassima is such a woman. In *The Princess Casamassima*, the total world of the novel is glimpsed through Hyacinth Robinson – hardly uninvolved, yet above all a spectator. One of the central images of the work is evoked by the Princess's sympathy for Hyacinth for being:

> Constituted as you're constituted, to be conscious of the capacity you must feel, and yet to look at the good things of life only through the glass of the pastrycook's window (vol. 6, p. 61).

In a crowded, poverty-stricken world in which people jostle each other to survive, the 'good things of life' are available only to a few. Those who enjoy them form a select group by dint not only of money and class but also of consciousness and understanding. Internal conflicts, rather melodramatically symbolised in Hyacinth's mixed parentage and lurid origins, prevent membership for Hyacinth either of the 'understanding' group or of the supposedly unconscious mass. He is the archetypal outsider, whose desire for identity (denied him due to his suppressed background and its contradictory elements) leads him to attach himself to causes. Within a cause he searches for the 'real thing' – a fixed value which he can believe in, and to which he can ally himself. He thinks he has found it in anarchism, Paul Muniment's friendship, Millicent Henning's vitality, and most intensely in the Princess herself.

All the other characters, with the exception of Hyacinth and the Princess, are social 'insiders' – they know what they are, where they live, what they are doing. Hyacinth and the Princess are outsiders through their awareness of (and dissatisfaction with) their social identity – the one as poor and uneducated, the other as a beautiful woman. Where Hyacinth can look only through windows, however, the Princess can walk in and buy. She has access to various groups and walks of life through her wealth and her rank, but above all through her visibility as a beautiful woman. Though she rejects the specific functions of being the Prince's wife, she carries her recognisable femininity with her as a quality which crosses barriers of class and place. This quality gives her a social identity of the kind that Hyacinth lacks, and renders her vulnerable to recognition and appropriation *as* a beautiful woman, as a carrier of meaning and value, whether she likes it or not. The world seeks to render her static, to fix her, because as a woman this is how she functions, as a sign to be interpreted, one way or the other. Hyacinth himself seeks to establish a new, less bleak relationship to the world, through fixing the Princess as a value. Though he is also made use of, it is for what he can do, what he can offer – he is not possessed or defined as object in order to create the reality of another subject.

Both at odds with the social order, Hyacinth and the Princess struggle with different processes. Ultimately Hyacinth is at home nowhere and the Princess everywhere; he fails to forge an identity for himself where she cannot escape the ones given to her, the ones which have constructed her.

In terms of social place (in both senses) the bulk of the characters in *The Princess Casamassima* are static and provide reference points for the progress of Hyacinth and the Princess. Miss Pynsent belongs to Pentonville and so does Mr Vetch – though his feeling of having moved 'down' accentuates the poverty of Lomax Place. Paul and Rose Muniment belong to Camberwell, and despite Paul's revolutionary activities his personal aspirations stretch no farther than Blackheath. Lady Aurora is firmly located in Belgrave Square, her situation there as an 'eccentric gentlewoman' is vital to her freedom to make sorties into other parts of London, but there is no question of her moving *herself*, she moves only continually for others. It is Belgrave Square that she brings to others, though she may not like the fact, and it is that they want from her. Millicent Henning belongs to the whole, bustling, diffuse world of London – she moves freely there, but more than anyone else we cannot imagine her outside the city.

The progress of this long novel is a geographical as well as an internal one. Hyacinth moves by a series of external pressures and accidents. Starting in Lomax Place he encounters new possibilities in Camberwell, across the river, and finds here the bridge that leads him to Belgrave Square and Mayfair. In Book Three and the beginning of Book Four, the literal centre of the work, he moves to the twin pinnacles of Medley and Paris. Leaving London, he is most potentially free himself but he can leave only at the behest and aid of others. Back in London, the arc he describes curves down via the dreary suburbia of Paddington to his death in Westminster.

The Princess moves with Hyacinth in part of this arc as she guides him from Mayfair to Medley, and then down to Paddington. She, however, moves of her own free will, as and when she pleases. There is an impression of continual flux as we glimpse a distant past covering most of Europe.

In *What Maisie Knew*, there is a sentence directly evocative of Hyacinth at the pastrycook's window: 'She [Maisie] was to feel henceforth as if she were flattening her nose upon the hard windowpane of the sweet-shop of knowledge' (vol. 11, p. 137). And Hyacinth, too, is not simply excluded from the 'good things' but from the knowledge of how they are to be enjoyed: 'It was not so much that he wanted to enjoy as that he wanted to know; his desire wasn't to be pampered but to be initiated' (vol. 5, p. 169).

He sees them as things which he could and can appreciate, but cannot relate beauty to the oppositions surrounding it. As a passive receptor of sensations, an innocent vision who looks for the first time on whole areas of life during the course of the book, Hyacinth's activity takes the form *not* of attempting to partake or to change (despite his vow to Hoffendahl) but of trying to sort out, label and define his impressions. He is impotent because he will commit himself only to a discovered absolute, to the 'real thing'. The mixed nature of society and of the individuals who make up society finally defeat this attempt at total purism.

His response to the people he meets, for instance, is to categorise, to think in terms of types and fixed references. When Lady Aurora is talking to Hyacinth he attempts to discover a swan beneath the ugly duckling, her moral beauty enables him to convert her into: 'a true heroine, a creature of a noble ideal' (vol. 5, p. 274).

Reflecting on Millicent Henning from the safe distance of Paris, Hyacinth veers between perceptions of her as of a various 'type' or 'specimen' or 'shopgirl' or 'chieftainess' (vol. 6, pp. 131–3). Finally he concludes that she is 'a loudbreathing feminine fact' of some description. His response to complexity is to simplify.

The whole of Book One not only creates the gallery of Hyacinth's society, it builds up to a production of the sharpest impression of all, his first meeting with the Princess. His encounters with Poupin and Paul and Millicent have been important, but have remained reciprocal encounters; the first sight of the Princess is a 'vision', and is described in suitable pictorial language:

> She was fair, shining, slender, with an effortless majesty. Her beauty had an air of perfection; it astonished and lifted one up, the sight of it seemed a privilege, a reward (vol. 5, p. 207).

Hyacinth is 'dazzled', and immediately relates this experience to far off beautiful objects he has seen through glass. 'That head . . . suggested to Hyacinth something antique and celebrated . . . in a statue, in a picture, in a museum' (vol. 5, p. 207).

Hyacinth is transported by the very static unreality of his situation, the sense of having arrived at a fixed point:

> so pleasant was it to be enthroned with fine ladies in a dusky, spacious receptacle which framed the bright picture of the stage and made one's own situation seem a play within the play (vol. 5, p. 208).

In fact, the Princess's humanity and reciprocal subjectivity is made immediately evident, although Hyacinth fails to comprehend at this stage:

> He might at that instant have guessed what he discoverd later – that among this lady's faults (he was destined to learn they were numerous) not the least eminent was an exaggerated fear of the commonplace (vol. 5, p. 209).

Also made evident is the Princess's tact, she is able to respond to Hyacinth and to his responses:

> He was conscious he looked frightened, and he was conscious the moment afterwards that the Princess noticed it. This was apparently what made her say: 'If you've lost so much of the play I ought to tell you what has happened' (vol. 5, p. 212).

and again:

> At these last words Hyacinth flinched a hair's breadth; the
> movement was shown by his dropping his eyes . . . The Princess
> doubtless guessed it as well, for she quickly added: 'At the same
> time I can see you're remarkable enough' (vol. 5, p. 217).

Hyacinth is very susceptible to appearances – he thinks of Millicent
that: 'If she had been ugly he couldn't have listened to her' (vol. 5, p.
165). He has been pestering Paul for some tangible evidence of the
reality and potency of the anarchist cause: 'If you'll show me the
thing itself I shall have no more occasion to mind the newspapers'
(vol. 5, p. 149). Now in front of him he has an intense visual
revelation of beauty, taste and knowledge – knowledge of a world
that he knows nothing of:

> Her manner of speaking was in fact altogether new to her listener,
> for whom the pronunciation of her words and the very punctu-
> ation of her sentences were the revelation of what he supposed to
> be society – the very society to the destruction of which he was
> dedicated (vol. 5, p. 216).

In short, Hyacinth takes the Princess as the feminine principle of
beauty and harmony, incarnate. This is clear from the intensity of
language of his first encounter with her, and from the intensity with
which he continues to respond to anything to do with her as their
relationship develops. He also displays a tendency to associate her
with beautiful objects – the ones she possesses and those which he
wishes to render homage with, superbly bound books. He is relieved
to discover that her most beautiful things have not been finally
disposed of on the move to Paddington, but only put in store. To a
certain extent, the Princess is defined for Hyacinth by her association with art-objects, and it is one of the reasons he finds it so
difficult to adjust to her changing circumstances (although he does
find it easier to attempt a domestic relationship with her on this
score). What is equally clear is that the Princess is also self-
motivated, restless and changeable. Hyacinth fails to come to terms
with this conflict, even as he slowly becomes aware of the volatile
element in her as a person. In their final meeting, when his
disillusionment is at its highest, he cannot relinquish his desire to

objectify her, to make of her a special remote 'thing' – true to her*self* she can only be impatient with this, and Hyacinth *yet* manages to make this response a magnificent one:

> 'Why am I so sacrosanct and so precious?'
> 'Simply because there's no-one in the world and has never been anyone in the world like you.'
> 'Oh thank you,' said the Princess impatiently. And she turned from him as with a beat of great white wings that raised her straight out of the bad air of the personal (vol. 6, p. 406).

The obvious dislocation between what Hyacinth would like the Princess to be and what she *is* gives rise to a critical tendency to condemn her – apparently because she is not what Hyacinth first hopes. F. W. Dupee concludes:

> we see her at last as a rather futile woman whose surrender of her feminine and aristocratic status has left her with nothing but an insatiable appetite for adventure and for men.[12]

The Princess's surrender of her feminine status is apparently an affront to the reader as well as to poor, deluded Hyacinth.

Maxwell Geismar also sees this kind of reduction of the Princess as an accurate picture: 'She is a rather good portrait of a discontented, bored, neurotic and empty society woman struggling to amuse herself.'[13]

There seem to me to be several elements in the novel which suggest a larger view of the Princess, a need to take her in a way more complex than Hyacinth's, or that of the critical approach outlined. One that I have already mentioned is her structural function in terms of environmental and geographic movement. Both she and Hyacinth are rootless. Both move among a web of people who are fixed, delineated by their origins and acting according to them. Both seem aware of a larger dimension to life. Their means of approach are very different. Quentin Anderson suggests that the Princess is trying to obliterate her personal self, her rank as well – that she seeks to deny inner conflict.[14] But it is precisely her personal self she clings on to, her rank, everything that suggests her *public* self she seeks to destroy. The comedy to a certain extent lies in her allegiance to a lot of what that public self represents, and thus the play acting of her abandoning beautiful things to live in an ugly, suburban villa. But the impulse springs from precisely that impatience that she displays to Hyacinth – impatience with the external perception of her that limits her from so much active experience. When she first meets Hyacinth, she says to him:

> I wanted to know something, to learn something, to ascertain what really is going on; and for a woman everything of that sort's so difficult, especially for a woman in my position, who's tiresomely known (vol. 5, pp. 15–16).

Not only does social position prevent the Princess from anonymity, but her status as a woman ensures that she is taken in a certain way, certain things are understood by her, expected of her and these things prevent her from coming close to issues and problems that are not encompassed by her expected sphere. One of the things she envies in Hyacinth is his invisibility, his ability to go anywhere and to observe and respond and reflect without a similar process being imposed *upon* him. Hyacinth, in reverse, longs to be more solid, more defined, because he suffers from a lack of delineation. One of the attractions of women for him is their continuous presence in the world as women, recognised as such and somehow common property as such. Walking in London with Millicent, he is struck with the difference in their reality for the external world:

> In the midst of this his sense was vivid that he belonged to the class whom the 'bloated' as they passed didn't so much as rest their eyes on for a quarter of a second. They looked at Millicent who was safe to be looked at anywhere (vol. 5, p. 170).

Although Millicent belongs to exactly the same class as Hyacinth, sexual division is more fundamental than any other. The Princess's conscious and deliberate lack of any defining accent or manner implies a half realised attempt to escape categorisation that extends towards an escape of femininity as well:

> My husband's a foreigner, a South Italian. We don't live always together. I haven't the manners of this country – not of any class, have I, eh? (vol. 5, p. 222).

The inescapable fact about the Princess, reiterated throughout the book and never denied by anybody, is her beauty. This ineradicable mark of her as feminine is recognised by her as incompatible with herself as a changeable person, active and continually searching for a sense of purpose outside this passive role of 'art-object'. She gains pleasure from showing beauty to Hyacinth for the first time at Medley. On hearing that he's never seen 'a park nor a garden' before, she exclaims:

> I'm so glad – I'm so glad! I've never been able to show anyone anything new and have always felt I should like it – especially with a fine sensitive mind (vol. 6, p. 15).

The beauty of Medley *is* a fixed thing. While the Princess does not object to Hyacinth's initial pleasure in her as beautiful she is aware that because she is not, cannot, be a fixed quantity, 'safe to be looked at anywhere' that he is bound to be let down in the end. When he first visits her in Mayfair, they discuss the possibility of meeting again and Hyacinth remarks that despite the incredible fact of experiencing such pleasure twice, he has seen her in the theatre:

> 'And yet here I am!'
> 'Yes, there you are,' said the Princess thoughtfully – as if this might be a still graver and more embarrassing fact than she had supposed it. 'I take it there's nothing essentially inconceivable in my seeing you again; but it may very well be that you'll never again find it so pleasant' (vol. 5, pp. 296–7).

Hyacinth is warned from the very beginning by Madame Grandoni that the Princess is not 'reliable' or 'stable' – he cannot rely on her being there. Because there is never any hint of a sexual relationship, this can be taken beyond a hint of female fickleness and applied to his perception of her as the 'real thing'. If she were, she would be immutable and inspirational. Yet her effect *is* undeniable. Talking to Hyacinth, Lady Aurora comments admiringly on the Princess's 'caring' for the poor:

> 'You really care – so why is she more remarkable than you?' Hyacinth demanded. 'Oh, it's very different – she's so wonderfully attractive' Lady Aurora replied (vol. 6, p. 192).

The difference is on two counts. One is that the Princess is so admirably suited to fill a more feminine function, to be a crown to any society she chooses, that her decision to reject this role and engage with a hostile, suspicious world, even if it is partly motivated by boredom, is one that requires more sacrifice than Lady Aurora's. The other is that because she is so 'attractive' anything she does takes on the quality of being in a spotlight, it is doubly effective. James continually uses the language of the theatre to describe the Princess – because she is always being watched and she knows she is being watched. Beauty is effective, and it gives an intensity to experience that Hyacinth is almost drunk from after the combined experiences of Medley and Paris:

> A hundred confused reverberations of the recent past crowded on him and he saw that he had lived more intensely in the previous six months than in all the rest of his time (vol. 6, p. 126).

In an essay on *The Tragic Muse* by D. J. Gordon and John Stokes, the following parallel is drawn between Verena Tarrant and Hyacinth Robinson:

> Hyacinth Robinson . . . and Verena Tarrant are . . . examples of a rare potential for experience admired and pursued by those eager to possess them.[15]

This aligns Hyacinth with Verena as a representative of life, to be appropriated, whereas I have been suggesting parallels between the Princess and Verena, in as far as they are both objects which are viewed by spectators. Hyacinth's vulnerability to manipulation (rather than to possession) comes from his poverty, not his gender, and while it can make him the object of another's wishes it does not make him a generally visible sign. Unlike the Princess or Millicent Henning, at their opposite ends of the class scale, he remains anonymous, existing as an observing subject, receptor of sensation and impression rather than generator of them. Yet the Princess differs from Verena, too, her energy and attractiveness do catalyse experience for others (as Verena's do) yet they also function for herself. She suggests a more active and self-directed energy.

Returning to the dreariness of London from Paris, Hyacinth visits the Princess and: 'was struck more than ever with the fund of life that was in her, the energy of feeling, the high free reckless spirit' (vol. 6, p. 177). The Princess seizes on life with strength and enthusiasm, but she disdains to look too far towards the consequences for others.

Rejection of a static existence as beautiful madonna and/or society lady seems to involve a rejection of responsibility towards her 'audience'. With those such as Sholto this is harmless enough, he can take care of himself. With Hyacinth, she is treading on more dangerous ground because she is radically altering the balance of his life. Madame Grandoni recognises the danger of this: 'It's too terrible to spoil him for his station,' the old lady went on. 'How can he ever go back?' (vol. 6, p. 79). When the Princess becomes absorbed in Paul, and ceases to concern herself with Hyacinth on a regular basis Madame Grandoni finally condemns her and leaves. Yet the very theme of the work – the futility of the search for absolutes and the need to recognise and integrate the commonplace and the beautiful, permeates the presentation of the characters. The Princess is not 'heartless' any more than she is, as Hyacinth first perceives her, the apotheosis of luminous charity. She is genuinely fond of Hyacinth, and when she realises that he is in danger it is she who runs after him and who is the first to mourn for him. Richard Poirier makes a distinction between the psychological and the moral in James's work[16] and although there are moral elements in *The Princess Casamassima* there are no villains as there are in *The Portrait of a Lady* or other, later works. Both the humorous treatment and the concept of human paradox struggling against limiting definition and imposed stasis militate against too rigid a moral interpretation.

The life and fertility implicit in the Princess's energy and beauty (stressed so often in the book that it is difficult not to stress it here) are also endorsed by their opposition to the alternative 'real thing' – the vow taken, under Paul's initiation, by Hyacinth to Hoffendahl. When telling the Princess of it, Hyacinth uses familiar language: 'Pardieu, I've had a vision!' (vol. 6, p. 50).

But the vision is not shared with the reader, we are never given a direct description of Hyacinth's encounter with the great anarchist. What we do see is that Hyacinth's commitment to this vow begins to fail almost as soon as he has taken it – as he realises the destructive nature of the principles on which it is based. Hyacinth's real animation in life has a personal basis, and however much the Princess may seem to fail him on this level she does have *some* real feeling for him. Just as the beauty she has shown him in Medley has a more lasting effect than the vision of murder given by Hoffendahl, so her affection is a more warming legacy to his memory than the chill indifference of Muniment. Muniment knows that Hyacinth is motivated by friendship and love – when the Princess talks to him about Hyacinth's opinions he replies. 'His opinions? He never had any opinions' (vol. 6, p. 230). Yet he allows Hyacinth to delude himself as to the friendship between them:

> He [Hyacinth] merged himself, resting happy for the time, in the consciousness that Paul was a grand person, that friendship was a purer feeling than love and that there was an immense deal of affection between them. He didn't even observe at that moment that it was preponderantly on his own side (vol. 6, p. 218).

Whatever mistakes Hyacinth makes in the Princess, then, his being attracted by her and all she suggests is certainly more positive than his adulation of Muniment.

In finally recognising the complexity of the Princess, he sees the impossibility of either taking her as a religion, or of condemning her as selfish and flighty:

> To ask himself if she were in earnest was now an old story to him, and indeed the conviction he might arrive at on this head had ceased to have any high importance. It was just as she was, superficial or profound, that she held him, and she was at any rate sufficiently animated by a purpose for her doings to have consequences, actual and possible (vol. 6, pp. 259–60).

In this, Hyacinth is wiser than the critic who condemns her as simply bored and insincere. She is recognised here not only as an individual who, in rejecting traditional role and occupation, is in danger of diffusing aimless or harmful energy, but also as the possessor of vibrant qualities of beauty and life. This is for others – the impact of all this on the Princess herself is presented very obliquely. We really only 'view' her, the novel is not concerned with her perceptions except indirectly. She is a function of Hyacinth's experience, expected by him (and by the reader in most cases) to provide some consistent reference points to the dilemmas and events of the novel. As in her earlier appearance as Christina Light in *Roderick Hudson*, we see the Princess as an actress, a performer – more independent and self-motivated than Verena, yet aimless. It is a performance without real substance, as the Princess can never really decide what she wants to do, how she wants to appear. Her self is, after all, created through being observed, through reflection and response, as well as through a dissatisfaction with this and a desire to act as independent subject. Hyacinth does come to glimpse this complexity, and to realise that a woman may act for herself rather than for other people:

> The Princess . . . was not a system; and her behaviour, after all, was more addressed to relieving herself than to relieving others (vol. 6, pp. 260–1).

Despite this understanding, the craving for some absolute, some fixed point, is too strong for Hyacinth. And he seeks it in a woman. At the last, he turns back to Millicent, who he now senses is not only the 'vulgar' life of London, but the capacious life of the reassuringly familiar world he sprang from. He attempts to formulate his mistake with the Princess as being simply one of having aimed too high:

> He [Hyacinth] had been provided with the best opportunities for choosing between the beauty of the original and the beauty of the conventional (vol. 6, p. 329).

But his mistake with the Princess was a larger failure of perception, of taking human complexity with all its suggestive possibilities for something as aesthetic and static as Medley itself. Similarly Millicent is not just a 'type', a 'nymph of the wilderness of Middlesex' who represents London's 'immense vulgarities and curiosities, its brutality and its knowingness, its good nature and its impudence' (vol. 5, p. 61), she is an individual whose life continues when Hyacinth is no longer present, and who is not always available for such an abstract choice as that between the 'beauty of the original and the beauty of the conventional'.

The beauty which is certainly present lacks direction, so that it cannot give meaning to the events of the story, but can pervade it. The limitations imposed by society and environment – so vividly called up by the endless walks from one part of London to another – are mirrored by the limitations imposed by femininity. Attempting to eschew both, the Princess carries her sign status with her and thus, although lacking coherence and consistency, retains effectiveness.

In order to retain her freedom, however, the Princess has to remain dislocated from society, to remain rootless and exceptional. Isabel's dilemma of what to 'do' could, in the terms of reference of *The Portrait of a Lady*, be met in the language of growth and understanding. In the more concrete practical world of the novels being discussed here, the terms of reference are those of physical life and action, and the solution for the female individual is left hanging in movement and play acting and impatience.

The world of all three of these novels is very much the public world, especially in comparison to other novels of James, and the woman attempting to resist appropriation as sign in the way that Verena is appropriated is not resisting within the domestic arena of personal communication and perception. Asserting herself through action in a wider world, the problem of what to 'do' becomes practical as well as psychological. Performance is foisted on the woman as a public mode of signification, and where Verena's performance takes her over as a passive medium, and that of the Princess is insubstantial and half-serious (like the voluntary work of the gentlewoman), Miriam Rooth works hard and professionally at her performance as an actress, as an increasingly conscious choice over the limitations of domestic femininity. Suitably enough, as an actress, we have to see her professionalism, her work and her rejection of private appropriation, as an objective performance. Rather than sharing the deliberations of her consciousness we observe her as vivid, iconic, even as she chooses and works at the nature of her performance. Miriam, like the Princess, is presented as feminine, visible and suggestive of meaning – a bearer of the letter A – even as she is also displayed as puzzling, inconsistent and directed toward experiencing as subject rather than clarifying and harmonising experience for others.

> What has become in that imperfect order, accordingly, of the famous centre of one's subject? It is surely not in Nick's consciousness – since why, if it be, are we treated to such an intolerable dose of Sherringham's? It can't be in Sherringham's – we have for that altogether an excess of Nick's. How on the other hand can it be in Miriam's, given that we have no direct exhibition of hers whatever, that we get it all inferentially and inductively, seeing it only through a more or less bewildered interpretation of it by others . . . Miriam *is* central then to analysis, in spite of being objective; central in virtue of the fact that the whole thing has visibly . . . to get itself done in dramatic, or at least in scenic conditions.[17]

It is curious that in *The Tragic Muse*, a book so didactic, so full of academic discussion, our interest is held and judgements made on the basis of what people actually do. And not on any idealised sense of moral action, but on the question of active commitment – for James is here dealing with the profession he understood, that of the artist, and he expands from this centre to define his other characters in terms of their active social roles, of diplomat or politician. Our sense of people is gained not solely by getting at the roots of their feelings or beliefs but by seeing which way they jump – 'existence' is defined by commitment and limitation rather than by expanded possibilities.

James decided to use the stage as a central motif for this novel, which is concerned with the various relations between art and experience, art and the other professions, and indeed various theoretical debates about the practices and priorities of any art form. Gabriel Nash and Nick Dormer debate the tensions between simply being and experiencing, and attempting to create and communicate. The importance of style is placed against that of content; the freedom of silence against the commitment of speech. On a literal plane, the use of the theatre precipitates dialogue about the nature of dramatic art, of actors (and therefore artists) as professional people, and particularly raises the debate over whether art is inspirational or a product of work – a debate encapsulated in the differences between the English and the French stage. The theatre also raises another series of questions about the nature of art and the function of the artist, concerning which I think it is significant that of the two artists in the book Miriam Rooth is an actress and Nick Dormer is a painter. The very commitment and limitation involved in producing or creating that Nash shies away from lies in the need to communicate with the external world through a recognisable medium. Nick, as a painter, attempts to communicate through a created product separate from himself – he relates himself to the world through an object which expresses him. Miriam, as an actress, communicates through a series of presentations of herself. This raises all kinds of questions about Miriam's reality as a conscious subject when she is not being interpreted, located in Peter Sherringham's uneasiness as to what she 'is' when she is offstage. Unlike Christina Light/Casamassima, whose performing self is both at war with, and inseparable from, her self as subject, Miriam suggests a kind of professional and creative control over her appearance, a subjective awareness of how she will be taken, and a readiness to command this rather than to escape it.

I have centred on Miriam in order to emphasise her importance to the metaphors and themes of *The Tragic Muse*. She is not only the symbol of art which titles the work, she is the artist at work throughout, subject to various attempts to render her status as artist subordinate to her status as feminine. Criticism of *The Tragic Muse* tends to go for the evidence of consciousness, and focus on the dilemmas of Nick Dormer and Peter Sherringham.

The problem of being defined in terms of what you do rather than what you are is played out by Nick and Peter in action, whereas Miriam is seen to have made her choice when the book begins. It is the environment, the society that encroaches on her off stage that seeks to reverse her decision, that of 'that oddest of animals the artist who happens to have been born a woman' (vol. 7, p. 232).

The issue of definition encompasses not only what you do, which is limiting in the sense that you can do only one thing rather than another and therefore have to make a choice, but what you are, in a public, social sense – names and categories also limit and differentiate. D. J. Gordon and John Stokes analyse the artistic battle in *The Tragic Muse* in these linguistic terms, and identify the clash between Nick and Nash as that between the process of art as 'naming' and the maintenance of style, which is personal and can be generalised and therefore vulgarised only if it is deliberately attempted as communication:

> In this society [that of *The Tragic Muse*] it is proposed that a man in his metier (which is his way of making his fortune) is subject to judgement, not in terms of the effort involved but of his success: which is a social cohesion and depends on the relationship with audience. Nash can deny this but politician, actress or portrait painter cannot.[18]

The act of communication must limit, because it involves a response which may be partial or even hostile. On the other hand, a rejection of communication, of naming and being named, implies a possible, literal disappearance. Nash cannot survive being painted by Nick, and chooses the alternative invisibility. Part of the emphasis in this period of James's work on a more concrete social reality – an attempt to render streets, shops, pubs, jobs, all kinds of people (however successful or unsuccessful you may consider it) – springs from this awareness of the need to act on and in an 'audience'. One's existence and one's creations must be recognised as being such by others before they can have any meaning. In *The Princess Casamassima*, a woman attempting to act freely or unconventionally in a society that allows her very little scope in real terms for this is condemned to be dislocated from this society, to be an outsider.

The princess does not become invisible or a surrogate man, her sign status as a woman, her suggestion of beauty and culture simply militate against her attempts to observe and participate at other levels. By entering a profession which exploits and extends the representation which is an intrinsic part of femininity, Miriam does not reject the process of signification but adopts it deliberately. This conscious adoption, assumption of choice over what is signified and how, and the stasis it rejects by choosing many performances over one, is a threat to the masculine *status quo* because it resists control. Not only this, but it assumes a status of its own, a social place wider than that of being defined through a relationship to a particular man. Through becoming an artist, a worker – even though this work employs the feminine functions of representation and appearance – Miriam can assume an independent, subject importance. Also, very importantly, she acquires the economic freedom to back it up. Arguing with Peter, Miriam offers a logical reversal of roles:

'I thought you liked the stage so,' Miriam artfully added.
'Don't you want me to be a great swell?'
'And don't you want *me* to be?'
'You *will* be – you'll share my glory.'
'So will you share mine.'
'The husband of an actress? Yes, I see myself that!' Peter cried with a frank ring of disgust.
'It's a silly position, no doubt. But if you're too good for it why talk about it? Don't you think I'm important?' (vol. 7, p. 373).

Having made her point, she doesn't push it, but sweetly appeals to friendship, in a manner explicitly likened to one of her performances on stage. But the point remains, and the basic relation between the sexes involving the reflection of one by the other, remains weighted in the balance of the man. By comparison Julia Dallow attempts to manipulate Nick, but by offering herself as a representation of him as politician – if he will only become one.

The limits placed on each and every individual, on women through their function as signs, on men and women through their class, wealth, environment and so on, is a specific part of the structure of *The Tragic Muse* as it is of *The Princess Casamassima*.

There I suggested how the bulk of the characters are located geographically; they do not move, only Hyacinth and the Princess do that. In the same way in *The Tragic Muse*, within a framework of static characters placed in Harsh, Beauclere, London and Paris, a few characters are seen to move – Nick, Miriam and Nash. Peter Sherringham attempts the mobility of these three, but ends by rejecting it in favour of a more fixed social position. The private houses are arenas for socially predictable encounters and confrontations concerning conventional social behaviour. The theatre and Nick's studio are more fluid areas where people meet who otherwise might not, and things happen which are unplanned and unforeseen. Some of the more abstract or challenging discussions between Nick and Nash, or Peter and Nash, take place as they wander through the streets of London and Paris, or drive through them in taxi-cabs.

The desire to escape the limitation of conventional social names, to exist outside recognised structures, is opposed by the recognition that one exists within a social world, that sense of self is created through recognition by others and recognition of others. Nash, in his refusal to translate his idiosyncratic sense of self and existence into something communicable (and thus limited or defining) ends by simply not being recognised or seen at all. He literally disappears. Nick and Miriam, as artists, attempt to replace through artistic creation, to use and transform existing structures. Though both reject conventional lifestyles and identities they are also dependent on a recognition – Nick of his painting, Miriam of herself.

Structurally, *The Tragic Muse* is the clumsiest of the three novels under discussion here, and its attempts to follow through three individual cases rather than two inter-connected ones are largely responsible for this. For although Peter is connected with Miriam, he is also connected with Biddy and Nick, and the whole Julia Dallow and Lady Agnes element has nothing to do with either Peter or Miriam, except very indirectly. The attempt to give the book unity by using Nick as a lynchpin and connecting him with Miriam, both symbolically as being his muse, and personally as being in love with him, accounts for concentration on Nick as the core of the book. It also accounts for the book's stodginess. Dupee sees *The Tragic Muse* as full of virtuosity, but killed by the deadness of Sherringham and Dormer[19] and Geismar recognises Miriam as giving the book its 'only vital interest'[20] (it is interesting how qualitative judgements catch on Miriam, while thematic judgements ignore her). This 'deadness' in the two 'conscious' characters is something James himself was aware of, particularly with regard to Nick, whom he felt he had failed to make sufficiently interesting. He isolates the dual function of Miriam as giving her a greater weight than the other two:

> I never 'go behind' Miriam; only poor Sherringham goes, a great deal, and Nick Dormer goes a little, and the author, while they so waste wonderment, goes behind *them*: but none the less she is as thoroughly symbolic, as functional for illustration of the idea, as either of them, while her image had seemed susceptible of a livelier and 'prettier' concretion.[21]

It is the fact that Miriam is a 'prettier' concretion – that at its simplest she is an attractive and unusual woman – that strikes first. It is simpler for Nick or Peter to see her as a muse than as an artist, because that way they look and re-interpret as they will (Biddy as muse is more self-effacing and finally more effective because of this). As an actress, Miriam's roles bewilder because they suggest a fluidity of signification that could extend to all areas of life. Peter considers this with a certain horror.

> It struck him abruptly that a woman whose only being was to 'make-believe', to make believe she had any and every being you might like and that would serve a purpose and produce a certain effect, and whose identity resided in the continuity of her personations, so that she had no moral privacy, as he phrased it to himself, but lived in a high wind of exhibition – such a woman was a kind of monster (vol. 7, p. 189).

One has only to look back at the Princess Casamassima, to Verena Tarrant, or even to the puzzling lack of consciousness of Daisy Miller, to know that this question is not simply a product of Miriam as an actress. The assumption that there is always a conscious subject behind the interpreted sign, a sentient woman behind the scarlet letter, is challenged by the suggestion that the woman is constructed through, and only through 'the continuity of her personations'. But again it is the multiplicity and autonomy of these personations that really worries Peter. In 'rescuing' Verena from public life, Basil Ransom is really snatching her from other contenders who control her representations just as he wishes to control them as his wife. Verena's father gives her the power to speak, Olive re-shapes that speech and Pardon facilitates its public appearance. Miriam, however, is going a long way towards controlling her own performances. Peter would like her to play a private role for him for life, if he could choose the appearances and limit them he could control what Miriam represents, whereas now the interpretations are all hers. When he proposes to her for the second time, she accuses him of trying to stifle her as an artist. He responds: 'The artist is irrepressible, eternal; she'll be in everything you are and everything you do' (vol. 8, p. 339). Miriam knows this is not true, that her being as an artist is a specific 'job' that she works at, and she refers to her tricks of her trade: 'Without my share of them I should be a dull empty third-rate woman' (vol. 8, p. 341). Sherringham, desperate to convince her that she *is* woman and that is where her genius lies, says:

> What I ask you to give up is the dusty boards of the playhouse and the flaring footlights, but not the very essence of your being. Your 'gift', your genius, is yourself (vol. 8, p. 341).

Now Sherringham knows that this is untrue. Miriam has talent but it was (and is) nothing without the hard work, technique and professional setting she has enlarged it with. James makes a great point of the fact that Miriam's art is not inspirational, that she is not a passive medium overtaken by the breath of genius. When we first see her perform at Madame le Carré's she is atrociously bad. It is sheer effort and dedicated labour that has produced her artistry, and it is as a working artist on stage that she is consummate. In fact, despite his frequent off stage contact with her, it is after watching her perform in the theatre that Sherringham is moved to propose, on two occasions.

Moreover there is a suggestion that her working life – and the word 'work' accompanies Miriam almost as that of 'beauty' accompanies the Princess – has freed Miriam from the limitations of a static signification, that she has permanently moved on from the function of being named and keeping that name for life. She pours scorn on the life she would lead and the person she would be as Peter's wife:

> A nasty prim 'official' woman who's perched on her little local pedestal and thinks she's queen for ever because she's ridiculous for an hour . . . I've seen them abroad – the dreariest females –

and could imitate them here. I could do one for you on the spot if I weren't so tired (vol. 8, p. 347).

Her harshness, which she tempers with affection before she leaves Peter, is justified in that Peter is not only trying to woo her from her work but is betraying his real feeling for the theatrical art he had professed to admire above all. His refusal to act for what he believes in, to commit himself to the theatre with Miriam, in the terms of reference of this novel alienates him from any real connection with art at all.

In the first real picture of Miriam that we get at Madame le Carré's, when her identity as an artist and a professional is still embryonic, Miriam is presented in a series of symbols and visual 'snaps'. She is a 'rich type', a 'priestess on the tripod', the 'Tragic muse', she has a 'disposition for the statuesque' (vol. 7, pp. 126–7). In her final scene with Peter she is a complex person who argues with and humours him – his engagement with her is no longer that of spectator to visual object but of reasoning and argued communication in which he comes off worst; a risk all aspiring Pygmalions run. The passage in which he claims that he will let the artist in her loose on everyday life is very reminiscent of the one in which Basil Ransom says that Verena's gifts will enhance their private lives.

However, as I suggested in *The Bostonians*, the fact that the attempts of Ransom, the Prince or Peter Sherringham to rescue, or wrest, their loved ones from the larger public world are not vindicated or endorsed within the novels, does not necessarily mean that the public world as an arena for assertion of freedom is endorsed either. The world of these novels is a public one, where reality is described as a product of specific physical details as much as of personal feelings, where the identity imposed by society is a product of a general practical consensus rather than the imposition of one consciousness on another. The possibility of being a free unlimited individual is barely present, except as satire in the figure of Gabriel Nash. Freedom appears only to exist in the making of specific choices and commitments, not so much in psychological perception and evaluation but in conscious communication of oneself and one's actions with the external world. We do not see the struggle of a conscious subject to gain awareness of its place within the structures of society, as we do with Isabel Archer. The characters of these novels are all more or less contructed from the beginning – we wait to see what they will do.

Within this framework, the woman as sign is either publicly or privately appropriated. Verena displays no resistance to either. Her innocent enthusiasm and capacity for life exist, in the end, only for others. In a concrete, practical world her suggestion of a wider, poetic significance is limited to the provision of reassurance and love for Ransom. Neither Verena nor Miriam and the Princess are predicated either as total object (like Daisy Miller) or as total subject (as Isabel Archer initially is). While clearly existing as object for the world of each novel, each woman also has a subject response to the perception of this, though in Verena's case this is hinted at only as a vague conflict and confusion and does not suggest any active resistance.

The Princess and Miriam, however, are themselves more practical, more conscious of their existence for the world as beautiful or vivid women, and more specifically self-directed. Within the larger world, this self-direction is problematic. The assertion of self *as* self has to find recognition in an audience, and on this general scale appears doomed to misapprehension, for the Princess at least. The solution of the artistic life resolves Miriam's dilemma in one sense, though not in another. She has to relinquish any real personal communication, although she retains control over her actions and the interpretations given to her. She becomes: 'that oddest of animals, the artist who happens to have been born a woman'.

The similarity of Miriam's particular brand of art, however – an interpretative one, interpreted through the medium of self rather than through an object – the similarity of this to the social construction of women as signifiers and interpreters, in private and public life, suggests a parallel course of action for the woman *not* born an artist. The attempt as woman (rather than actress) to control and direct her appearance for the world, to assert her own value, takes place in full knowledge of herself as sign (as Miriam knows herself an actress). But it also takes place in a different framework, in the more private, shifting and indefinable world of ambiguous personal communication that emerged in James's later novels, separated from these by a gap of some seven years.

6 The Novels of the 1890s

The years between *The Tragic Muse* and the production of James's next novels were filled with the writing of stories and reviews, but also with his great attempt at writing for the stage. The story of this attempt and failure is well documented,[1] and there has been speculation as to the effect this period had on the subsequent novels. Looking broadly at the three novels which followed – *The Spoils of Poynton* (1897), *What Maisie Knew* (1897), and *The Awkward Age* (1899) – there seems to me to emerge a general shift in framework and direction from the novels discussed in Chapter 5. The world portrayed is no longer a public but a private one, and along with this there is no longer a sense of a general, public consensus as to the nature of events or realities. Perhaps this shift away from a large many-faceted public world was in part due to a failure of confidence after the dismal reception afforded his drama; but the changing premises of the novels opened up the possibility of a greater weight being given to the individual vision. Part of the same development is the loss of the 'omniscient narrator', the voice speaking over and above the characters, convincing the reader of some certainty as to what 'really' happened. Each novel still contains a society which has rules and structures, but the possibility of a personal view of all of this, even of a re-naming and re-structuring, is opened up for the conscious individual – often a vulnerable figure armed only with perception, an artist or a woman.

Women are still very much signs, but their status as such in a world given meaning by shifting and confusing signification has somewhat changed. Women both signify and interpret – signification being their realm, they understand and proffer it. The figure of the powerful, older woman using her control of worldly representation to maintain the *status quo* and ensure her own status as wife, mother or hostess that was evident in Madame Merle, re-emerges here as Mrs Beale and Mrs Brookenham and, in another guise, Mrs Wix. Fixed culturally, these women assume power culturally to restrict others, representing a world of rigid meaning and convention. In *The Faces of Eve*, Judith Fryer comments on the inequality James perceived in American life as lying in:

> the growing divorce between the American woman (with her comparative leisure, culture, grace, social instincts, artistic ambitions) and the male American immersed in the ferocity of business, with no time for any but the most sordid interests, purely commercial, professional, democratic and political.[2]

This inequality, Fryer suggests, results in admiration of women, a sense of their importance and fear of their power.[3] Yet in James's work the resistance offered to this cultural rigidity does not come from a young man. Only the male artist isolates himself in order to see and interpret freely, other men, however restricted by the social world represented by these women, benefit from it. It exists for them, they own it, and are the inheritors of it. It is the young girl, destined through marriage to take her place in the scheme, who offers resistance.

This resistance forms its own tensions between the choice of escape and rejection of social structures and a developing attempt to change them and control them personally. Asserting a personal vision, the young girl attempts to signify *herself* to the world, and not a range of cultural meanings. The privacy and relativity of the worlds of *What Maisie Knew* and *The Awkward Age* lend weight to the attempt of one vulnerable and powerless, but conscious, individual to assume some ability to re-name and re-interpret, rejecting the stasis of her imposed sign function. This privacy, a sense of an enclosed world in which anything might mean something and then change in meaning again, is carried over into the last novels, and in *The Wings of the Dove* and *The Golden Bowl* it is also a young woman who attempts to control and transform the structures of the society surrounding her.

The desire for love, a desire for a continued relation with the social world rather than a rejection of it, enforces the need to communicate the woman as self through the very structures of signification she is attempting to reject. There is a swing between an assertion of self, which is unacceptable, and a mysifying control of meaning, which directs the attention of the male subject towards herself, but as sign.

Maisie and Nanda both function as signs of innocence and ignorance in corrupt societies. Their innocence, and the need to protect it, mystifies and expands the 'knowledge' they are excluded from. As both in fact learn and discover the secrets of their worlds, they become inadequate signs of girlhood – or the signifying function becomes an inadequate expression of them. Nanda rejects the mystification outright and attempts to present herself in direct opposition to the significations of girlhood – defined by being in opposition to them she becomes a problem, and in so doing exposes the specific sordidnesses of her mother's world which the mystification of excessively signified forbidden knowledge had exalted. Maisie, however, adopts the mystification of knowledge, in order to play 'with' the adults rather than against them. She re-designates herself in order to play for higher stakes, and the incongruity once again dislocates her social existence. Maisie no longer signifies childhood innocence nor yet adult femininity; her intelligent consciousness obtrudes the fact that she is not the little girl society would have her be. No longer knowing how to take her, her society does not know what to do with her. When women are no longer immediately recognisable as signs, they have to fight for social existence. Maisie attempts to do this through an excess of signification, suggesting that if you only look hard enough, you will find something; Nanda gives up, and recedes.

Both girls also make the attempt at direct communication of their complex selves, the selves which overspill their existence as sign, to a man. Woman assure themselves of an integrated existence in social life if they have established a relationship to a man, if they have been recognised and interpreted by a male subject. In a strange inversion, the men of the late period novels become the spoils, the prey, because it is they who can validate the existence of the various women struggling for social identity and the communication of love. Women become competitors with each other for the beloved man, who is often morally weak in comparison. He is led and explained to by the women who exist in the world of representation and interpretation, who obscure from him the knowledge of himself which he is afraid of. *The alienation of mystery and fear into a woman safeguards the man from facing his own self* – the women all face their own fear of themselves, the knowledge of isolation, and work to fulfil their feminine function by protecting the man from that same fear.

Maisie, Nanda, Milly and Maggie all face that internal fear and in turn recognise the same fear in Sir Claude, Vanderbank, Densher and Amerigo, and in varying degrees try to shield the men from it. This fear relates to the process of signification because it is that process which gives form to and objectifies the desire for meaning without which they are left alone with themselves as they are. James seems to be suggesting in these late novels that it is those most intelligent women, who most complexly and subtly hold out the promise of meaning to men, who most totally face the lack of meaning themselves, and in doing so achieve a particular female subjecthood. Maggie is the only heroine who manages to sustain the promise of signification in the face of her own awareness – Maisie and Nanda, in different degrees and ways, both fatally go for 'honesty', a direct presentation of self as subject, and are rewarded with affectionate, even anguished rejection. Milly's honesty is forced out of her by an unexpected blow, an unlooked for degree of manipulation just as she sustains control of her self as sign for Densher.

For all four of these heroines, development of a feminine subjectivity involves an explicit awareness of themselves as signs within their social worlds, as occupying – however awkwardly or inappropriately – a specific place in a structure. Unlike Isabel Archer, who attains this awareness by the end of *The Portrait of a Lady*, these figures are given the chance to go forward from this point, in worlds which can be threatened, even destroyed, by their creativity, the creativity of the artist brought into personal form.

In the two novels of the 1890s that I wish to discuss, *What Maisie Knew* and *The Awkward Age*, power and freedom are seen to reside in the acquisition of knowledge, and ability to communicate that knowledge. The relativity of any perception or knowledge is both a threat to social communication and a chance to assert an individual consciousness. It provides a fluid alternative to the failure of any public, rigid system of knowledge – the anarchism, feminism or aestheticism that were exposed as inadequate in the novels of the previous decade.

The theme of knowledge emerges naturally from a rejection of conventional ideas and systems. If what we know is individually acquired and understood and is continually changing, then it is both harder to use that perception in relation with the world and yet more possible to see it as true in conflict with the world's truths. The perception of the artist can be purer or more real than that of conventionally understood reality but this mode of experience also threatens both madness and isolation – a theme most fully explored in the *Sacred Fount* (1901). The fear of madness or of having been wrong and of having wasted artistic endeavour is repeated in the many 'artist stories' of the 1890s, together with the sense of isolation for the artist, the lack of communication with the world and the world's impositions of its expectations of art. Such stories as *The Middle Years* (1893), *The Death of the Lion* (1894), *The Next Time* (1895), and *The Figure in the Carpet* (1896) all hinge on the artistic attempt at knowledge. This theme of the relativity of perception is echoed in the use of the supernatural in stories like *Owen Wingrave* (1892) and *The Real Right Thing* (1899), and is most openly expressed in the culminating fear of the governess in *The Turn of the Screw* (1898): If he *were* innocent, what then on earth was *I*? (vol. 10, p. 136).

Intelligence and sensibility can remain an excuse for isolation and a retreat from love and involvement, a theme James explored in *The Altar of the Dead* (1895), and later in *The Beast in the Jungle* (1903). Though experience is frightening and continually changes perspective, it is exactly what modifies perception and ensures against a new creation of stasis. Rejection of it is easier for the middle aged man who figures in these stories, in that he is not seen, does not have demands made upon him by the world. The love offered him is passive and patient, it needs his active acceptance. The burden of perception being on the individual, the greatest fear and threat to harmony and fulfilment becomes fear of oneself and one's own inadequacies.

On a lighter note, James also continued his stories of behaviour and relations in society, and probed less painfully at the same theme of perception in his continuing treatment of the importance of appearances and their relation to the individual who so appears. As it is women who are most dependent on how they appear in order to succeed and survive socially, they are the centres to the tales *The Wheel of Time* (1892), and *Glasses* (1896). In fact, the dependence of women on succeeding socially, marrying and manipulating the marriages of other women, is also prominent in stories such as *The Chaperon* (1891), *Lord Beaupré* (1892), *The Visits* (1892), and *The Patagonia* (1888). Powerless in political and financial terms, and defined for the world by their appearance and marital status, women can assert themselves only by choosing the manner of their disposal, by fighting among themselves for the opportunities of marriage and social success. In *Lord Beaupré*, for instance, the weak young man is nonetheless desirable because he possesses social power and status; he becomes a tangible aim for the women who parade themselves for him. The social order which fixed women through marriage and representation is most vehemently maintained by those who are rendered most powerless if they fail to succeed in it. Paradoxically, men become more desirable and more passive than women, and their passivity perpetuates in turn the acceptance of the paramount nature of marriage in women's lives.

I have indicated the range of James's interests in this period – one permeated by a sense of disillusionment and fear of failure which can be at least partially ascribed to James's catastrophic attempts at writing for the stage. These interests come together in the two novels I wish to explore, novels in which James begins a return to an affirmative sense of possibilities, though mingled with the taste of renunciation and isolation and the corruption of society. In *What Maisie Knew* and *The Awkward Age*, the individual confronts society again, but from a very different position than that of Daisy Miller.

The kind of girls that James chose as heroines for these English stories possess qualities very different from those of the American girl, or the beauty and talent of the Princess Casamassima and Miriam Rooth. The expectations of the society surrounding them are of a passive and useful innocence or goodness. As individual, they are socially unimportant and dependent on the use to which they can be put by others – either men or women who have accepted conventional values and determined to survive according to them. James touches directly on the unimportance of such figures in the Preface to the *Spoils of Poynton*, when he acknowledges the eccentricity of making a 'free spirit' out of a 'mere little flurried bundle of petticoats'.[4] Referring to the *Spoils* and to *A London Life* (1888), and *The Chaperon*, he pinpoints the combination of the conventionally unimportant with the personally important: 'very young women' who possess 'a certain high lucidity'.[5] The assertion of self, of unconventional values and of a rejection of social patterns was to be more incongruous and difficult in the very young girl than in any other figure. Her youth, her lack of a secure and permanent home, her complete poverty, her social insignificance – all these render Maisie and Nanda vulnerable to manipulation and appropriation in the way no male character could be, however poor and artistic. Even the little boy in *The Pupil* (1891) had to be given a weak heart to even the score. At the same time, this social helplessness is juxtaposed with the female potential that James is so interested in developing against such odds, the qualities so often appropriated and crudely objectified by conventional demands. This potential takes the form here not so much of freedom or spontaneity or beauty but of *intelligence*. In the Preface to *The Spoils of Poynton*, James says of Mrs Gereth that she 'was not intelligent only clever'.[6] Intelligence means understanding from the point of view of others as well as from your own, it means intellectual sympathy as well as perception. This was very much a feminine quality to James, as were the related ones of awareness and sensitivity – ones he felt a little boy simply wouldn't have had enough of to figure as the child centre to *What Maisie Knew*. These qualities of intelligence and sympathy are shared by Mary Gosselin in *Lord Beaupré*, Mrs Ryves in *Sir Dominic Ferrand* (1892), Fleda Vetch in *The Spoils of Poynton*, and even the anonymous heroine of *In the Cage* (1898) (though in this case in a rather distorted degree). They are possessed in abundance by Maisie and Nanda. The perception of this repressed potential in women involves the risk of reducing it to a principle, and rendering the individual possessor unimportant or static because of it. But in these heroines their actual, physical vulnerability, and the need to fight for a place to live and exist, ensures that their intelligence is linked to their own needs as well.

The heroines also share unconventional looks in which only the perceptive observer finds charm or beauty. And they possess the sense of self and of the way the self may be appropriated and manipulated by the world (Maisie acquires it very early in the novel) and thus *begin* from Isabel's climax of 'motionlessly seeing'. The 1890s' heroines also differ from Isabel in that they accept their inescapable involvement in the world and in experience – they long even for that which they recognise to be corrupt, they love passionately. For each of them, it is the attempt and success of identifying with the passion and understanding of another person that shapes and gives meaning to their behaviour.

The acquisition of knowledge, learning and understanding forms the linguistic pivot of *What Maisie Knew* and *The Awkward Age*. The deepening perception of the heroine develops away from the received knowledge and common sense of the world, and yet takes its importance from its relationship *to* the world.

The novels share the fundamental structure of a weak man being struggled for by the conventional woman desiring social status, marriage and justification for her existence, and by the young girl wanting to establish a relationship of 'free' love, one based on a union of perception. The sterility and materialism of the social settings for these works are emphasised by the specific expediency of the social function of feminine innocence or virtue. The attempts to appropriate the young girl as a symbol of life, freedom and individualism have been replaced by the appropriation of the young girl as an emblem of a hate filled divorce, or an empty notion of socially awkward girlhood. Having a lover or a husband is the only justification for female existence, identifying with and representing a man is the only assurance of a place in society and of a relationship to property, income and home. Being appropriated and submerged in marriage or an affair is a greater security than being socially obsolete. But whereas the women up to this point faced the alternatives of losing selfhood in marriage or remaining singly isolated the young girls of these books insist on their right to a more idiosyncratic love. What emerges is that the refusal to be appropriated, the insistence on a relationship with the world on one's own terms and in full knowledge and criticism of the world is so unacceptable to society as to be dangerous and implicitly powerful. Maisie and Nanda seek to know the world as well as themselves, and to remain true to that knowledge in their relation to the world.

In *What Maisie Knew*, three structures of knowledge are established as alternative ways of interpreting the world – the conventional materialism of Mrs Beale, the rigid moralism of Mrs Wix, and the intelligent love of Maisie. All centre on an attempt to establish a relationship with the world and what it offers women in the figure of the (weak) Sir Claude. The emergence of these alternatives is presented through the vision of Maisie, who develops her knowledge during the book. With Maisie, James explores the gradual processes (rather than the moments of adult illumination) by which she acquires her personal consciousness in resistance to the many forms of appropriation and knowledge imposed upon her by the adult world.

In the Preface to *What Maisie Knew*, James describes how: 'the small expanding consciousness would have to be saved',[7] and those contemporary critics who deplored the exposure of such a consciousness as Maisie's to the world of adultery and hatred ignored the extent to which Maisie also has to be saved from the world of morality expounded by Mrs Wix. Both worlds attempt to fix and define Maisie for their own purposes – possessing her, as sign of innocence and purity, would validate the possessor.

As a little girl, Maisie is the epitome of helplessness and self-effacement. She has no importance as self, only as reflection to the adult world. She does not even have the potential importance of a little boy.

Miles, in *The Turn of the Screw*, impressed the governess by his: 'whole title to independence, the rights of his sex and situation' (vol. 10, p. 90); even in young children degree of social importance and power is implicit. But James recognised that:

> the very principle of Maisie's appeal . . . that vivacity of intelligence by which she indeed does vibrate in the infected air . . . may pass for a barren and senseless thing, or at best a negligible one.[8]

In the opening chapters of *What Maisie Knew*, two important events take place in Maisie's mind, linked by the explicit statement of her conscious awareness: 'from the first Maisie not only felt it, but knew she felt it' (vol. 11, p. 11).

She realises that she is being used by her parents, and she attempts to oppose this use by reserving and controlling part of her*self* from the outside world. The one follows from the other, sense of self arises directly as a result of realising how the world manipulates her as representative and object:

> The theory of her stupidity, eventually embraced by her parents, corresponded with a great date in her small, still life: the complete vision, private but final, of the strange office she filled (vol. 11, p. 15).

In her essay on *What Maisie Knew*, Juliet Mitchell points out how literally Maisie functions as an *object* of communication in adult games as billiard ball.[9] From the first, Maisie sees her relation to the world – she doesn't understand much of the purpose of it, or how other people relate to each other, but she has a 'complete vision' of her inextricable existence within the world of other people and also of a corresponding responsibility for this social existence: 'everything was bad because she had been employed to make it so' (vol. 11, p. 15).

Maisie both rejects the use made of her, and embraces the necessity to use herself in the world, to maintain the responsibility of human, social existence. She even struggles to exert her personal responsibility, reiterating how she has brought Sir Claude and Mrs Beale together, and searching to arrange love for her mother. Yet for any of this to take place the act of self-assertion in resistance to imposed reflections of herself must be performed:

She had a new feeling, the feeling of danger; on which a new remedy rose to meet it, the idea of an inner self or, in other words, of concealment (vol. 11, p. 15).

Maisie's perception of the strange office she fills includes an understanding of the way in which she is a 'thing' for her parents, an emblem of their feelings about each other, and of no intrinsic value in herself. Thus the rules of the game change according to Ida or Beale's circumstances, and when Ida and Sir Claude become engaged Maisie realises that the object of the struggle: 'would now be *not* to receive her' (vol. 11, p. 48).

The knowledge given to Maisie by the adult world is insufficient, and accords little with her personal sense of experience. The illusion of reward for the kind of 'goodness' that is socially useful and non-disruptive is experienced early:

Waiting patiently . . . seemed to Maisie a long way round – it reminded her of all the things she had been told, first and last, that she should have if she'd be good, and that in spite of her goodness she had never had at all (vol. 11, p. 20).

Mrs Wix is the constant agent of such goodness, seeking to fortify Maisie with the acceptable morality of the world – a morality which Maisie can already recognise as inadequate in explanation:

Her [Mrs Wix's] conversation was practically an endless narrative, a great garden of romance, with sudden vistas into her own life and gushing fountains of homeliness (vol. 11, p. 27).

Although Mrs Wix also uses Maisie as a substitute for a lack in her own life, she does care for the child as a child rather than primarily as a weapon (though Maisie does become an approach to Sir Claude for Mrs Wix) and the intensity of her concentration on her is a wholly new experience for Maisie. Mrs Wix is 'safe' in her concern; however oblique and inadequate the knowledge she offers, it is impelled by love for Maisie and a desire that she shall survive in the world:

Somewhere in the depths of it the dim straighteners were fixed upon her; somewhere out of the troubled little current Mrs Wix intensely waited (vol. 11, p. 42).

Many critics have commented on James's play with the ideas of vision, and the reference of the straighteners to the crooked vision of Mrs Wix. Maisie herself appears to realise Mrs Wix's lack of any real knowledge, and also her lack of any power or status in the world. Near the end of the novel, when Maisie is deciding who she 'wants' in the world, she recognises that Mrs Wix is nobody, is as anonymous and expendable as Maisie herself. Compassion allows her to satisfy Mrs Wix's demand for a display of conventional response, but it doesn't prevent Maisie from being willing to sacrifice her if necessary.

From early on, Maisie realises that in order to meet the dangers of the world she must not only have an inner self, she must understand how things actually are, undistorted by the superficial morality and absolutism offered by Mrs Wix. Maisie is surrounded by 'ambiguity' and forbidden knowledge, she discovers that:

> Everything had something behind it: life was like a long long corridor with rows of closed doors. She had learned that at these doors it was wise not to knock (vol. 11, p. 34).

Her attempts to learn are usually met with laughter, whether derisory or sympathetic, and this response itself Maisie attempts to 'learn' playing adult to her doll's child, practising the power relationships prevalent in the adult world. Maisie's hunger for knowledge of any kind is denied her by the meaness of the grown ups who won't pay for her to go to school, by the ignorance of governesses, especially Mrs Wix, and by their laughter at her questions. When she gets even some muddled lessons from Mrs Wix Maisie is ecstatic:

> The year therefore rounded itself as a receptacle of retarded knowledge – a cup brimming over with the sense that now at least she was learning (vol. 11, p. 66).

But the knowledge dispensed by the world *as* knowledge, the formal tuition, both here and in the incomprehensible lectures that Maisie and Mrs Beale attend, is useless. Maisie is 'allowed' only such knowledge as will keep her innocent. Her real education comes from personal experience taken in a personal way. This is symbolised by her walks through London (and later through France) with Susan and, more importantly, with Sir Claude. As far as Mrs Wix is concerned, Maisie's chief education is to talk to her about Sir Claude. Generally Maisie learns and understands more and more about the people around her and her understanding is tinged with compassion and love. She joins Mrs Wix in gently deceiving Sir Claude about his puzzling gifts to them: 'it was a part of their tenderness for him not to let him think they had trouble' (vol. 11, p. 72).

Maisie's emotions are honest in a way that cuts right through the conventional labels and expectations. In her world, husbands and wives don't necessarily love each other, neither do parents and children. The formally assigned relationships of society have little to do with real knowledge of feeling. Maisie loves Sir Claude and recognises how little her mother loves her: 'Mamma doesn't care for me . . . Not really' (vol. 11, p. 83).

In struggling to formulate her own desires and perceptions, Maisie recognises the need to free herself from being appropriated and submerged in the desires of other people. As opposing 'sides' become clearer: 'Maisie of course in such a delicate position, was on nobody's' (vol. 11, p. 95); and the tension of the struggle intensifies her hold on her only salvation: 'her sense of freedom to make things out for herself' (vol. 11, p. 99).

It isn't long before Maisie's clearness of perception outstrips everyone, she insists on, even cannot help, seeing things as they are. Walking in the park with Sir Claude, he weaves a romantic fantasy about the couple in front of them:

> Maisie's fancy responded for an instant to her friend's idea that the sight was idyllic; then, stopping short, she brought out with all her clearness, 'Why mercy, – if it isn't mamma!' (vol. 11, p. 140).

Maisie's love for Sir Claude comes from two sources. One is his value as part of the beauty of the world, he is: 'by far the most shining presence that had ever made her gape' (vol. 11, p. 57).

But as well as this, he responds to her and to her need for knowledge, he is: 'with the exception of Mrs Wix the only person she had met in her life who ever explained' (vol. 11, p. 36).

On this basis, the developing relationship between Maisie and Sir Claude is more complex than that between Fleda and Owen in *The Spoils of Poynton*. It involves not only her love for the world in all its weakness, but the potential for a reciprocal relationship, which is never entirely convincing in *The Spoils of Poynton*. Sir Claude, who is desired by all women, wants to escape these patterns in dealing with Maisie. Interestingly, he attempts to divest their relationship of potential polarisation not only by responding to Maisie as child, but as a de-sexed equal. He entrances her by his: 'pleasant fraternising, equalising, not a bit patronising way' (vol. 11, p. 80) and calls her 'Maisie boy', and 'old chap'. Sir Claude also helps Maisie to understand how all experience and all knowledge has to be 'paid for'. Maisie's lack of power in the world means that she does a great deal of 'paying', and gets very little in return, she is cheated by those more knowing than herself:

> It all came back – all the plans that always failed, all the rewards and bribes that she was perpetually paying for in advance and perpetually out of pocket by afterwards – the whole great stress to be dealt with introduced her on each occasion afresh to the question of money (vol. 11, p. 137).

A great many practical alternatives and lifestyles for Maisie, Sir Claude, Mrs Beale and Mrs Wix have to be rejected on the grounds of expense. Money is power, and part of Sir Claude's weakness comes from his lack of it – even so, he has to pay Mrs Beale and Mrs Wix, just as Maisie's father, in an inversion of convention, is paid for by his American countess. Knowledge is the other source of power, less respected by the world and yet more valuable. But it is hard to get at one without the other. Penniless, Maisie finds it difficult to assert her demands for explanation – she has no bargaining power: 'She was to feel henceforth as if she were flattening her nose upon the hard windowpane of the sweet-shop of knowledge' (vol. 11, p. 137).

Maisie's first attempts to act in the world, rather than be used by it, are acts of love for other people, and involve rejecting conventional morality for the personal wisdom of lying and deceiving. In her compassion for her mother, she forces a confession of love from the Captain and exposes her emotion to him by weeping. She then resists Sir Claude's attempt to use her against Ida, by lying to him. Confronted by her father, Maisie transcends his devious perception in a dogged effort at understanding:

> an extraordinary mute passage between her vision of this vision of his, his vision of her vision, and her vision of his vision of her vision (vol. 11, p. 182)

yet Maisie finds it impossible to lie consistently to such a degree simply to please him; used by others to reflect what they want to see of themselves, she suddenly breaks down and asserts herself: 'I can't give you up'. Her father rejects her not simply for himself but in her very existence as a daughter: 'You know your mother loathes you' (vol. 11, p. 187).

In her final scene with her mother, Maisie again fails to be what her parents want, despite her utmost efforts for them, and her mother completes the destruction of Maisie as child: 'Your father wishes you were dead' (vol. 11, p. 220). As Ida searches for her own existence as a good mother in Maisie's eyes, we are told she:

> postured to her utmost before the last little triangle of cracked glass to which so many fractures had reduced the polished plate of filial superstition (vol. 11, p. 218).

Maisie's knowledge and development has rendered her unfit to be simply an object of representation or reflection, and there is no solution in attempting to represent good in any passive way. The child as medium of reconciliation is a popular sentimentality of the Mrs Wix variety, and a false justification for her kind of protection. As Maisie attempts this kind of action, she comes her nearest to despair at her failure to be what the world wants; her mother's fury at Maisie's mention of the Captain makes clear to her how truly corrupt the world is: 'There was literally an instant in which Maisie fully saw – saw madness and desolation, saw ruin and darkness and death' (vol. 11, p. 225). Her understanding of love and compassion is alien to the world around her, she still needs to understand reciprocally, to reach the feelings of other people.

As Maisie travels to France with Sir Claude she is at first happy to act as we have seen her acting on and off throughout the novel. She plays the part of 'a glad young lady taken into her first dinner'. Maisie postures not simply as a child longing to be grown up, but as an isolated consciousness attempting to camouflage her difference from the world by meeting its expectations. She has now become aware of how strange she appears, of:

> her tendency to produce socially that impression of an excess of the queer something which had seemed to waver so widely between innocence and guilt (vol. 11, p. 232).

But the journey to France is also a joy to Maisie, it represents a new opportunity to learn and to see life. She demonstrates her superior adaptability and familiarity with strange experience in her easy understanding of a foreign country: 'Her vocation was to see the world and to thrill with enjoyment of the picture' (vol. 11, p. 231). The pain of failure and manipulation is superseded by the potency of seeing and understanding:

> It came to her in fact, as they sat on the sands, that she was distinctly on the road to know Everything. She had not had governesses for nothing: what in the world had she ever done but learn and learn and learn? She looked at the pink sky with a placid foreboding that she soon should have learnt All (vol. 11, p. 281).

But as Maisie ponders on 'her personal relation to her knowledge' she appears to be soaring out of the reach of Mrs Wix and the demands of conventional morality. Maisie is not destined to be a spectator, partly because of her love of Sir Claude, partly because of the choices she has forced upon her. Mrs Wix is obsessed by the literal extent of Maisie's knowledge about sex, and confronts her with her lack of a 'moral sense'. This is perhaps the sublime irony of Maisie's situation; not only is she far beyond Mrs Wix's 'morality' in her accepting love of the people close to her, but she is ready to acquiesce to Mrs Wix's demands by another honourable lie – the pretence of a jealousy of Mrs Beale in order to show she is not simple. Mrs Wix can only confuse and obscure Maisie's understanding by seeking to impose the idea of innocence upon her, but the two communicate nonetheless through their love for Sir Claude. They: 'Exchange with each other as through a thickening veil confused and ineffectual signs' (vol. 11, p. 294).

The innocence and morality that Maisie is supposed to represent cracks under her development of personal intelligence. In preparing to sacrifice the intensity of her union with Mrs Wix, and the claims upon her of secure authority, she demands an equal sacrifice of Sir Claude – that he frees himself of the patterns of corruption that have led him to be responsible for Mrs Beale. Maisie's final step is to discover what she wants, and that is to be no longer an accessory, to be disposed of, to play: 'the passive part in a case of violent substitution' (vol. 11, p. 301).

She doesn't care about the morality of Mrs Beale's relation to Sir

Claude, but she rejects Mrs Beale all the same. This rejection seems to come from two sorts of emotional loyalty; one is to Mrs Wix and her anguish at the idea of losing Maisie to the sinful couple, Maisie can't forget: 'the picture . . . [of] an old woman and a little girl seated in deep silence on a battered old bench' (vol. 11, p. 336).

But also the symmetry of all Maisie's experiences up to now demands that if she is to be a protagonist, and no longer a little girl, then her love for Sir Claude must involve him relinquishing Mrs Beale. His taking her seriously is implied by his acceptance of this. So Maisie makes her choice: 'Him alone or nobody' (vol. 11, p. 309), for she knows now what she wants: 'All her learning and learning had made her at last learn that' (vol. 11, p. 357).

Sir Claude wants Maisie, but he cannot do what she asks. They both meet in mutual fear of themselves, fear of their inability to do what they want and what they feel to be right. Maisie understands Sir Claude's fear, and his weakness only makes her feel the more tender towards him. That he wants her at all makes her feel 'high', 'high', 'high' (vol. 11, p. 329). As they walk round the town, hand in hand, they communicate both their fear and their love to each other: 'If they were afraid of themselves it was themselves they would find at the inn' (vol. 11, p. 342).

By the time Maisie has confronted Sir Claude's inability to meet her in her challenge to him, her attempt to go with him to Paris, she has also conquered her fear of herself. All that remains now is to let him down gently: 'his fear of his weakness, leaned upon her heavily' (vol. 11, p. 347).

But even if he cannot rise to Maisie's level, Sir Claude gives her what Owen can never give Fleda – a recognition of her moral freedom, of her right to resist appropriation and make her own demands. Freeing her from the clutches of both Mrs Beale and Mrs Wix, he echoes the statement that has had such a contorted and distorted meaning when applied to all the other characters: 'She's free' (vol. 11, p. 359), and for the first time it rings true. As Maisie and Sir Claude part: 'their eyes met as the eyes of those who have done for each other what they can' (vol. 11, p. 363).

Maisie's knowledge has culminated in a union of understanding and in an act of love both precipitated on her own terms and in rejection of the terms acceptable to the world. Criticism which debates whether or not she is offering herself sexually to Sir Claude appears to be operating on the same level as Mrs Wix. Maisie's freedom is precisely freedom from the moral categories which underpin the possessive and competitive modes of experience around her. She is willing to try and act in the world, and risk the pain and assault on her sensibility that this involves. By acting, Maisie asserts that inner self, the accumulated knowledge that she has hitherto used as a protection against the world by concealment and apparent stupidity. But the manipulation of her by Mrs Beale, the imposition of morality on her by Mrs Wix, the offer of a redemptive place in the relationship between Sir Claude and Mrs Beale – all these places within the social world can no longer simply be resisted in silent perception. Refusing to play act as mirror or shuttlecock any longer, Maisie asserts her own vision of the world and her own sense of her worth in a relationship by demanding sacrifice and commitment. By risking so much, she conquers her fear of herself. By making her own demands, she also transcends (however briefly) the fixed status and meaning assigned her by her world.

Although Sir Claude cannot go with Maisie, he appears to love her freedom from the world he so completely inhabits, and to accept her vision of his fear and inadequacy. Maisie's joy in life and in learning, her culminating power to demand that finishes the novel, all serve to create a tone not simply of loss but of gain as well. The love and clarity that results from Maisie's vision of 'ruin and darkness and death' is an affirmation of feminine 'intelligence' and ability to survive as self in a dehumanising and predatory world. Although Maisie is sad to be different and not to have a Mrs Wix style moral sense, she appears to have accepted her strangeness to the world. Nanda, in *The Awkward Age* is a potentially more tragic figure than Maisie, torn as she is between Maisie's kind of informed criticism of the world, and a desire to function conventionally within it in order to fulfil her love for it.

The society of *The Awkward Age* is the most rigid and sterile of the societies presented in the novels of this period in that it not only excludes but condemns the intelligent love of the young girl. The extent to which the representative function of the young girl as innocent and pure actually maintains and justifies a predatory society conditions the rejection of Nanda, even by those who appreciate her. The structure of knowledge is somewhat less clear than that of the other novels, corrupt materialism and rigid morality being shared by figures like Mrs Brookenham and Vanderbank, and cleverness being allied with the material rather than the worldly morality of the conventional scheme. Nanda's function is complex in that her love for the world means a more fully realised sharing of its values, even to the extent of condemning her own knowledge and compassion. The damage and isolation caused by individual perception is of a totally different order to that suggested by *The Sacred Fount*, becuase here the 'truth' of Nanda's knowledge is never doubted, it is what the world demands her to see and to be that is so destructive, the appropriation practised on the feminine threatens to divest Nanda of her own most valuable qualities. The extra element that James adds is in the figure of Mr Longdon, a man also with intelligence and one who has had to give up a full emotional life in the world, but who can live freely in his own country retreat and whose 'difference' in no way threatens the social structure because it is related back to the past.

Both James's own discussion of *The Awkward Age* in his Preface to it, and a great deal of critical discussion of the book, concern the technical experiments it embodies. In writing *The Awkward Age* as a drama, James did so in full confidence of the extent to which form and content are indivisible.[10] It is thus worth asking how our sense of the content is affected by the form. By unfolding his story in conversation, James ensures that people are seen only in relation to other people, that all the characters are not only rendered meaningful but actual, in as much as they exist in the lives of other people. This is an important mark of change from such a novel as *The Portrait of a Lady*. Any attempt to develop a personal consciousness in the world of *The Awkward Age* has continually to take into account what one is for others, what one is made by others, and the degree of loss involved in isolation or retreat from society.

The opening chapters of *The Awkward Age* introduce us to society through Mr Longdon's bewilderment in the face of it. Mr Longdon is 'a man of intelligence', 'so fresh . . . so fine' (vol. 9, p. 6), to whom Vanderbank displays great cleverness and even appreciation of unorthodox values, but at the same time initiating him into the values of society, appearing to consider them immutable. In talking of Nanda he admits: 'She has in her expression all that's charming in her nature' (vol. 9, p. 25), but continues that she is not conventionally beautiful, and beauty:

> fetches such a price in the market that the absence of it . . . constitutes . . . a sort of social bankruptcy . . . she's at the age when the whole thing – speaking of her attractions, her possible share of 'good looks' – is still to a degree in a fog. But everything depends on it (vol. 9, pp. 25–6).

'Everything' is of course marriage, and marriage is 'everything' because it is the way a girl survives financially and socially. Vanderbank initiates here the two main pivots of his society, appearance and money. The two are inter-connected and vital. Appearance must be preserved at the cost of greater honesty, because it both determines price and justifies the buying and selling that takes place.

Mr Longdon, who feels as though he has been 'dug up from a long sleep', is attracted to Vanderbank and disturbed by the world he lives in. Jokingly, the question is raised 'is Van past saving?' At this point, it seems an irony. Van is attractive and perceptive, he speaks with understanding about Nanda and about Mr Longdon's own past history. His conversance with the ways of the world does not yet appear as an irrevocable commitment to them.

In Book Two, we are introduced to society in action and taken immediately backstage. The sordid relationship between Mrs Brook and her son Harold is reminiscent of the corruption of the mother/child relation in *What Maisie Knew*, when Mrs Brook says to him simply: 'You're odious' (vol. 9, p. 46). Yet her appearance for the world deals in different terms to this distaste and cynicism:

> She had about her the pure light of youth – would always have it; her head, her figure, her flexibility, her flickering colour, her lovely silly eyes, her natural quavering tone all played together toward this effect by some trick that had never yet been exposed.
>
> This was her special sign – an innocence dimly tragic (vol. 9, p. 42).

We are frequently told about her 'hanging head of a broken lily' (vol. 9, p. 46). Mrs Brook deliberately appears for the world in a manner that is acceptable, her life is spent hustling: for a job for her husband, for money, for a place for Harold, for marriage for Nanda, for social success for herself. To get these things, she must be for the world what it expects. As the Duchess arrives, we are shown the same conscious process of presentation:

> Her head, her chin, her shoulders were well aloft, but she had not abandoned the cultivation of a 'figure' or any of the distinctively finer reasons for passing as a handsome woman. She was secretly at war . . . with a lurking no less than with a public foe . . . the

colourless hair, the passionless forehead, the mild cheek and long lip of the British matron . . . were elements difficult to deal with (vol. 9, pp. 51–2).

This conflict between appearances is a primary demand of social existence for women, what they represent determines how they are taken. They must be not only feminine, but successfully feminine, and at moments of crisis the effort may be too great:

Mrs Donner's face presented, as she now crossed the room, something that resembled the ravage of a death-struggle between its artificial and its natural elegance (vol. 9, p. 112).

Even putting on make-up correctly is a mark of social initiation. For some women, the conflict is less because they are acceptable in themselves. Thus Lady Fanny (one of the more corrupt social figures) is: 'magnificent, simple, stupid . . . But the great thing in her was that she was, with unconscious heroism, thoroughly herself' (vol. 9, pp. 107–8).

Mitchy, on the other hand, although common, is rich. He can afford to look 'comic' because he is not dependent on how he appears. In fact his appearance is another kind of protection, from his real perceptive difference from society:

It was only on long acquaintance that his so many ingenious ways of showing he appreciated his commonness could present him as secretly rare (vol. 9, p. 78).

It is not that Mrs Brook or the Duchess are not what they appear, or that they are fundamentally alienated from their social selves. Their careful monitoring of how they are seen is itself intrinsic to their mode of life and survival.

In the first meeting between these two women, the marriages of Nanda and little Aggie are discussed. The need for marriage, its financial basis, the dependence of girls on whether or not men will find them acceptable, all this is quite explicit. Once again, knowledge is to be acquired only in a set social form, and at a set moment in life. Men don't like 'initiated girls', and Aggie's concern must be with what 'she was *not* to learn' (vol. 9, p. 55). 'Knowledge' means the rules and sins of society, and a prescribed attitude to both. The modernity that the Duchess frowns upon in Nanda is not so much a new knowledge as the learning of it too early, and in independence of marriage. As an 'initiated' young girl, Nanda would be socially immoral in the same way that Mrs Wix fears Maisie to be immoral, and as such failing to function correctly in society. The Duchess hints that the maintenance of social forms is as important to Van as to herself. Mrs Brook's attitude is less clear. She refuses to let concern for Nanda interfere with her life, yet later in the book accepts as a matter of course Nanda's social rejection and simply works to palm her off on Mr Longdon.

Little Aggie's appearance exemplifies the form of social morality and how it is used. She is shy and submissive:

> As slight and white, as delicately lovely, as a gathered garden lily, her admirable training appeared to hold her out to them all as with precautionary fingertips (vol. 9, p. 93).

Of course what Aggie represents *is* beautiful. It is the ignorance on which it rests, and the use made of it, which is so sterile and finally dishonest. This is something Nanda recognises in her admiration of Aggie and her attempt to save her from becoming like the Duchess by marrying her to the sweet and delicate Mitchy. As with the innocence of Verena or the freedom of Isabel, it is not the absolutes themselves that are corrupt or false so much as the use made of them and the inadequacy of static values themselves to harmonise, simply by unconscious existence, the complexities of experience.

The obscuring of communication in front of little Aggie is complemented by the bewilderment of Mr Longdon in his first exposures to Mrs Brook's drawing room. The language and names of this society are foreign to him, but unlike Aggie he has a language, a knowledge of his own. Once more, we see that learning is relative, and forms of knowledge both personal and social. Mitchy is confident that Mr Longdon will 'know' what a lady is in a quite different way from the same knowledge in Mrs Brook's drawing room.

Finally Nanda makes her entrance. Her overwhelming characteristic is her direct and honest perception. We are given her as: 'extraordinarily simple', 'downright' and 'of so fresh and sweet a tenderness of youth' (vol. 9, p. 137), possessing 'crude young clearness' (vol. 9, p. 148) and 'the directness that made her honesty almost violent' (vol. 9, p. 149).

Honesty of vision *is* violent as it threatens accepted vision. Van tries to humour Nanda, to treat her as a little girl, but the attempt is a failure:

> He had spoken as with the intention of a large vague optimism; but there was plainly something in the girl that would always make for lucidity (vol. 9, p. 136).

Nanda does not appear as a young girl in many ways. As well as her lucidity and her lack of conventional prettiness, she is very self-possessed: 'decidedly she was not shy' (vol. 9, p. 148). But Van and Mitchy both agree that Nanda is already 'sad' even 'tragic'. This is mentioned together with her lack of humour. Maisie, too, was subjected *to* a lot of laughter in her direct search for knowledge and does very little laughing herself. Laughter appears not as the benevolent good humour of some of James's work, but as the expression of being 'in' socially, of knowing the form and the jokes, of sharing a set of assumptions.

Mr Longdon finds Nanda even harder to take than he found Van. He, too, expects something from Nanda's appearance, though for different reasons, and is confused by the contradictions of her conversation and manner. Understanding this, she is gentle with him and her first movement towards him is a combination of understanding and emotion:

> What they [his eyes] were beginning more and more to make out was an emotion of her own trembling there beneath her tension . . . 'You are good,' she continued; 'I see already how I shall feel it.' She stared at him with tears, the sight of which brought his own straight back; so that thus for a moment they sat there together.
>
> 'My dear child,' he at last simply murmured. But he laid his hand on her now, and her own immediately met it (vol. 9, pp. 154-5).

'Seeing' comes before, and with, 'feeling', which is the quality that unites and communicates. In these novels, it is shared tears that signal real communication, expressing both its sadness and its explicit, dangerous nature. To cry in front of someone is to be willing to open yourself to them – the gift that Maisie gives both the Captain and Mrs Wix.

Mrs Brook exposes her lack of emotional understanding further by the wrong 'tone' she takes with Mr Longdon; she also makes her indifference to Nanda clearer by her willingness to sacrifice her to the Carrie/Fanny/Cashmore intrigue. The world to which Nanda has now fully 'come down', is displayed as basically lacking in compassion or regard for feeling.

Unlike Maisie, Nanda comes down fully formed as a conscious subject. We see her as alert, critical and above all self-aware. Knowing what she should be in her society – a blank sign like Aggie waiting to be allotted to a specific signified (or man) – she also knows that she is not what she should be. She is, in the terms of Mrs Brookenham's drawing room, socially unacceptable from the start. Knowing this, she yet loves the society that would limit and deny her complexity. Unable to indulge in self-denial, she attempts to reach out *as* herself.

In Nanda and Van's conversation in the garden at Myrtle, the first direct manifestation of her love for him is enacted. She tells Van she is afraid of him, then declares simply: 'Oh Mr Van, I'm true' (vol. 9, p. 211). Her fear is the same 'sacred terror' that Mitchy talks about Van inspiring in women, and says that he himself will never inspire. This terror is at least in part the intensity of sexual force which makes the love Nanda feels for Van into passion, and passion of a completely different order to her love of Mitchy or Mr Longdon. Sexual love, in James's novels, often represents the kind of passionate involvement in the world that is so treacherous and so difficult to align with other forms of knowledge and perception. Nanda's fear of Van is reminiscent of Fleda's fear of Owen in *The Spoils of Poynton*, and both allow for an understanding of the man's weakness in other respects. Van can cope with Nanda's feeling only by transferring it on to another plane, and declaring his interest and concern for her: 'Don't talk, my dear child, as if you didn't really know me for the best friend you have in the world' (vol. 9, p. 210).

Nanda can tell Van only that she is what she is, she can never be transformed into the appearance of anything else: 'What I am I must remain . . . I'm about as good as I can be – and about as bad' (vol. 9, p. 214).

Van can never accept this, but Mr Longdon, in contrast, is already beginning to.

In Nanda's ensuing conversation with Mr Longdon, she talks with a frankness that still astonishes him. Yet her discussion of the affairs of her mother's circle are always full of concern and humanity, in direct contrast with her mother's conversation. Nanda worries about shocking Mr Longdon, yet she knows that to pretend would be to threaten the very basis of their communication:

> unable to pretend, to play any part, and with something in her really that she couldn't take back now, something involved in her original assumption that there was to be a kind of intelligence in their relation (vol. 9, p. 229).

The use of the word 'intelligence' here sounds almost like secret knowledge, and so it is, in that they are forming a relationship on the basis of a perception that alienates them from the common knowledge of the world. Unlike Fleda's fear of Owen's destruction of her carefully constructed wall of defence, Nanda (like Maisie) finds great relief in the sharing of her inner self.

The sadness that is already implicit in Nanda is now expressed by her. As Mr Longdon expresses his wish for her to marry she replies: 'I shall be one of the people who don't. I shall be at the end . . . one of those who haven't' (vol. 9, p. 232).

Loving Van as she does, and yet being what she is, Nanda accepts that not only will Van never be able to perform the same act of personal perception and isolation that she has managed, but neither can she pretend to go back on what she has become. She would like to be a part of the world, to be an innocent young girl and loved by Van. She feels that knowledge does involve a degree of corruption and change that one can never return from, as she expresses later to Mitchy in her description of herself as a drainpipe with 'everything flowing through' (vol. 9, p. 358). The loss for Nanda seems greater than the gain of understanding. Her attempts to act in the world are frustrated by the limitations of it; she can arrange Aggie's marriage, and make sure that Van provides company for her mother, but the complex relationship of her rejection of the manner of her society to her love of its values and prizes make her too exacting a presence to be tolerated. Van is ultimately not so much disapproving of Nanda's premature initiation as frightened, almost repelled, by her transcendence of worldly knowledge and the criticism of the society that he moves in that that implies: 'I'm only afraid, I think, of your conscience . . . The thing is, you see, that *I* haven't a conscience. I only want my fun' (vol. 9, p. 504).

When Nanda tells Mr Longdon in the garden that she will never marry, her part in the novel is done until the final acts of help and freedom at the end. She is right and she sees as clearly now as is possible. The rest of the novel is a matter of letting the reader and Mr Longdon catch up with her, and her realisation that Van will never propose. And in so doing, of establishing the relative largeness of response of Mr Longdon, Van, Mitchy and Mrs Brookenham in facing the intractable presence that Nanda now constitutes.

Mr Longdon comes to see how the great difference between Nanda and little Aggie is not simply a matter of degree as to how much they know, but consists of Nanda's existing as an autonomous individual being who will interact with experience, and of Aggie's having no being or selfhood at all, of being merely a passive receptor of social conditioning:

> The elements of that young lady's nature [Nanda] were already, were publicly, were almost indecorously active. They were practically there for good or for ill; experience was still to come and what they might work out to still a mystery; but the sum would get itself done with the figures now on the slate. On little Aggie's slate the figures were yet to be written; which sufficiently accounted for the difference of the two surfaces. Both the girls struck him as lambs with the great shambles of life in their future; but while one, with its neck in a pink ribbon, had no consciousness but that of being fed from the hand with the small sweet biscuit of unobjectionable knowledge, the other struggled with instincts and forebodings, with the suspicion of its doom and the far-borne scent, in the flowery fields, of blood (vol. 9, pp. 238-9).

And of course for him communication with Aggie is impossible: 'She understood too little – he gave it up' (vol. 9, p. 239).

The juxtaposition of social intrigue with the blank innocence of Aggie that gives it its significance is a form of knowledge that Mr Longdon finds particularly oppressive:

> The child herself . . . understood nothing; but the understandings that surrounded her, filling all the air, made it a heavier compound to breathe than any Mr Longdon had yet tasted (vol. 9, p. 245).

Mr Longdon's attempt to bribe Van to marry Nanda is both a misunderstanding of Van and a misvaluation of Nanda. Ultimately, to support her, he must do so directly and not through the agency of a social convention. His development is in his willingness to learn and to change and to accept Nanda for what she is. He comes to offer her emotional commitment as well as money, compassion as well as understanding, and they are united finally in a second show of emotion and acknowledgement of Nanda's passion and shame.

Van, on the other hand, cannot begin to cope with what Mr Longdon offers. When Mrs Brooks tells him three times: 'You won't do it', he finds her unemotional confidence a relief: 'She offers me the truth, as she sees it, about myself, and with no nasty elation if it does chance to be the truth that suits her best' (vol. 9, p. 302).

It is the fact that society does consist of 'mere words', however brilliant, that suits Van best. He enjoys handling ideas, playing with perceptions, but he doesn't want the commitment and demands of the 'intelligence' that Nanda and Mr Longdon possess. When he sees Nanda at Mr Longdon's house in Suffolk he is intensely nervous – again we see the fear of self that was so justified in Sir Claude and is so again in Van. Yet like Sir Claude and Maisie, he does Nanda the justice of recognising her fineness and clarity:

> so she appeared to put it to him, with something in her lucidity that would have been infinitely touching; a strange grave calm consciousness of their common doom and of what in especial in it would be worst for herself (vol. 9, p. 344).

But he misses his chance, and the moment for proposal goes past.

Talking to Mitchy, Van says of Nanda: 'She always knows everything, everything' (vol. 9, p. 377), but it is Nanda's mode of knowing, the distinctions she is capable of making, that really disturb him. Nanda explains to Van that it is the 'unutterable' that is corrupting. Knowledge retains power only in being kept secret; Tishy Grendon cannot corrupt Nanda because she is frank with her. Nanda can protect Tishy from a bad French novel, on the other hand, because she knows enough to recognise the danger of false partial knowledge.

The final exposure of Nanda at Tishy Grendon's dinner party, and Nanda's three interviews with Van, Mitchy and Mr Longdon, rescue *The Awkward Age* from the same note of muted resignation as *The Spoils of Poynton*. However sad Nanda is, however poignant her loss, she does end in a very different position to that of motionlessly seeing. Nanda's knowledge, her awareness of self and her relation within society, has taken various forms. Not only does she understand what as a 'girl' she should be, but she has rejected the opportunities to compromise on her losses – to marry another social outsider in Mitchy or to pretend to an innocence she hasn't got. In resisting manipulation and remaining faithful to her own vision in contrast to the world's, she not only achieves autonomy, she projects outwards on to the world, and effects change in it.

Nanda's attempts at conventional manipulation in getting Mitchy to marry Aggie is a failure. But her refusal to compromise herself at the dinner party shatters the society that condemns her. Van conceives of this destruction as having been engineered by Mrs Brook, but the cause is unquestionably Nanda and what she *is* rather than what she appears. The effect is also unquestioned, Mrs Brook now sits alone in her drawing room and Mitchy speaks to her with an 'approach to coldness' (vol. 9, p. 473). The world of *The Awkward Age* will 'never grow together again' (vol. 9, p. 439); surely this looks forward to the devastating effect of Milly on the lives of Merton and Kate in *The Wings of the Dove*.

In her final encounter with Van and Mitchy, Nanda takes full responsibility for her relations with them. She acts *for* them in a way they can barely understand. Van, regarding her now as infinitely more knowing than himself, sees her as being socially powerful in her isolation, as: 'a perfect fountain of curious knowledge . . . You always seem to me to hold the strings of such a lot of queer little dramas' (vol. 9, p. 503).

Though he means to be kind 'he was embarrassed enough really to need help' and Nanda lets him off easily by requesting his help for her mother. Van can acknowledge only how Nanda acts for him and let her control the situation, and they too have their moment of shared perception: 'the longest look on any occasion exchanged between these friends' (vol. 9, p. 503).

Nanda is concerned now to protect and defend her friends to each other: Van to Mr Longdon, and Aggie to Mitchy. Mitchy grasps at the possibility of shared communion with Nanda:

> What does stretch before me is the happy prospect of my feeling that I've found in you a friend with whom, so utterly and unreservedly, I can always go to the bottom of things (vol. 9, p. 520).

but even Mitchy cannot know as much as Nanda, and has to agree to leave everything to her.

In relation to her mother, in relation to Mr Longdon, Nanda is now 'old'. This implies both sadness and strength. She is no longer a vulnerable young girl, and this is acknowledged by all those around her who defer to her ordering of their relations with her. As Mr Longdon realises, Nanda's feminine potential, whether exploited by others or generously employed for them, appears to give her very little for herself. She says: 'But being a woman . . . has then . . . its advantages' and he replies: 'It strikes me that even at that, the advantages are mainly for others' (vol. 9, pp. 536–7).

But she does retain the right now to be herself, and insists: 'I'll come if you'll take me as I am' (vol. 9, p. 538), and 'her anxiety that he should understand gave her a rare strained smile'. Mr Longdon can no longer play the artist and control and order people's lives with the personal detachment that Van and Nanda's marriage would have given him. Forced by Nanda to admit exactly how 'impossible' she is, they commit themselves on that basis, that Nanda: '*is*, you know, for a girl – extraordinary' (vol. 9, p. 543).

The very values which are exalted in the young girl as sign – freedom of the American girl, the purity ·of the girl-child – are limited and trivialised without a subjective awareness of their position within the structures of alternative values. The subjective awareness which could make Isabel Archer's freedom more real by at least giving her some awareness of what she is choosing, is explored here as forbidden knowledge. Knowledge is safely given to women only when married, when socially placed and defined. In a young girl, it is unacceptable and threatening. The only way it can be incorporated socially is when it is mystified – thus Nanda is rejected as herself by Van; yet he can respond to a new idea of her as 'knowing', as holding out some mystified version of events, some clue to the meaning of the 'little dramas' which make up social life.

The young girl is reassimilated as a possessor of meaning and knowledge (both in herself as sign and as a keeper of signs) which she undertakes to use on behalf of the beloved man – the 'he', the individual. Yet 'he' cannot completely escape knowing that even as she parades the possibility of meaning *in* herself she controls the process, and thus reminds him of the existence *of* herself as separate subject. We return to the paradox posed by de Beauvoir, where woman is:

the wished for intermediary between nature, the stranger to man, and the fellow being who is too closely identical. She opposes him

with neither the hostile silence of nature, nor the hard require-
ment of a reciprocal relation.[11]

and yet:

Man wants woman to be object; she makes herself object; at the
very moment when she does that, she is exercising a free activity.
Therein is her original treason.[12]

7 The Wings of the Dove

In Chapter 2 *The Scarlet Letter*, I discussed how Hester, alienated from and marked by her society, develops her own resisting subjecthood in response to the awareness this alienation provokes. This subjecthood leads not to her rejecting the A she wears, but ultimately to her insisting on it to the extent that its significance is transformed:

> She had returned, therefore, and resumed, – of her own free will, for not the sternest magistrate of that iron period would have imposed it, – resumed the symbol of which we have related so dark a tale . . . the scarlet letter ceased to be a stigma which attracted the world's scorn and bitterness, and became a type of something to be sorrowed over, and looked upon with awe, yet with reverence too.[1]

Not only has Hester retained a place within her society, there is a suggestion that she has attained some control over the way she is seen: that as signifier she is no longer bound to socially pre-determined signifieds provoking shame or scorn. But this control, her resisting subjecthood, is still communicated to the world through the A – there does not appear any possibility that Hester can live without the A, simply communicating herself as herself.

Thus Nanda, in *The Awkward Age*, who attempts to dispense with the A, retires from society, and from its prize in the form of a loved man. In *The Wings of the Dove* (1902), Milly wears the A before she even realises it herself. The 'dove' of the title, she is also called a Byzantine princess, an angel, a Bronzino portrait, a religious martyr, a Christ figure, a priestess and an American girl. Milly moves from feeling that her subject existence is so obscured by her visibility as sign that 'I think I could die without its being noticed' (vol. 19, p. 228), to forcing Merton Densher to be intensely aware of her and her desires: 'The drop, almost with violence, of everything but a sense of her own reality – apparently showed in his face' (vol. 20, p. 247). And until the very end Milly sustains Merton's focus upon herself not through rejecting her function as sign, but by reworking and augmenting it, and by letting him see that this is what she is doing. She presents herself as manipulating meaning for his benefit. Having accepted the determining factor of social naming, that what she is called she must in some sense be (to even respond to the name), Milly becomes even *more* of a dove, of an American girl, so that her spectators are pulled further in than they intended to go.

In *Decoding Advertisements*, Judith Williamson describes the process of 'hermeneutics':

> By this I simply mean interpreting, but interpreting in the sense of deciphering a code, or translating from one language to another: it is an interpretation along given channels.[2]

By drawing the readers into a pre-determined interpreting game, the makers of the advertisement force them to look at it in their (the makers') terms. Deciphering the deliberate puzzle (perhaps a missing word or missing person) we dón't look at what the puzzle is doing there in the first place, at the process of the advertisement. In discussing *The Wings of the Dove*, I want to suggest that in her relation to a reader, or male subject, if woman cannot discard the reading process altogether she can at least set up her own puzzle, make the man look at her on her own terms, even withhold or mystify the answer. Milly attempts to do this on a complex and powerful level. By making the puzzle personal, and suggesting that the clue to decipherment is personal, the attention is focussed back on to the woman as signifier, rather than to easily determined meanings.

The dependence of personal activity of this kind of social and conventional structures is reinforced not simply by Milly's starting point being the names given her, but by the emphasis on the factors shaping a personal or transforming activity. Milly's wealth facilitates both social responses in terms of 'innocence' or 'purity', and also her own ability to control the way events appear.

If we put Chad Newsome, Merton Densher and Prince Amerigo to one side and consider the rest of the characters in the last three novels, we find that each of them (with the exception of certain minor figures) has two aspects. Each appears as an individual in the world of the novel; yet each functions as one of the impulses determining human behaviour, or as one of the ideal limits of moral motion. Newsome, Densher and Amerigo are the figures on whom or within whom these impulses operate – who approach or recede from the ideal limits.[3]

Quentin Anderson is certainly not unusual among critics of *The Wings of the Dove* in assuming that Merton is the 'subject' of the text. Both in the *Notebooks* and the Preface to the novel James, however, suggests that, in conception at least, the story was very much to be about Milly, and her register of suffering and experience:

> The idea, reduced to its essence, is that of a young person conscious of a great capacity for life, but early stricken and doomed, condemned to die under short respite, while also enamoured of the world; aware moreover of the condemnation and passionately desiring to 'put in' before extinction as many of the finer vibrations as possible, and so achieve, however briefly and brokenly, the sense of having lived.[4]

James goes on to state that it is the behaviour (manipulation) of other people in relation to her that will precisely represent Milly's sum of experience. Having envisaged the situation from Milly's angle he then goes on to view it from the other side: 'her stricken state was but half her case, the correlative half being the state of others as affected by her'.[5]

James sensed, however, an ultimate lack of correlation in his two halves of the 'case', a failure in the end to have dealt directly enough with the initial idea of Milly's subjectivity and suffering, resulting in what he called the 'false and deformed half', the second half of the book.[6]

But there is no doubt that Milly's consciousness, however fully or inadequately presented, *is* presented differently from Merton Densher's, and to this extent I would agree with Anderson. Densher very consciously moves in a 'circle of petticoats' (vol. 20, p. 289); his subjecthood is an established state which gropes and guesses in the world of changing and opposing meanings sustained by women – meanings which serve, finally, to protect him from any real knowledge of himself. The women that we see as conscious subjects at all *do* exist under 'two aspects', in that they achieve their own subjectivity precisely through their awareness of themselves as other, as sign for their world. The novel does not have one subject, or even two, but three – and of those three only Densher can fully *be* Densher, where Milly must always take into consideration the extent to which she is also a dove, and Kate Croy the extent to which she is also a handsome girl.

Although different, indeed vitally opposed, to each other, in their struggle to achieve their goals, Milly and Kate are displayed as far more akin to each other than to Densher. We see the constitution of their awareness of the world and their place in it, as we do not see his, and out of the constitution of this specifically feminine subjectivity we see the assumption of a kind of social intelligence which bears the burden of both interpretation and mystification for the male subject. The different levels at which Kate and Milly operate are determined by money. Not for Kate the luxury of transforming the power of the material into a form of spiritual or artistic power; her poverty forces her into a particularly vulnerable position as woman, and her efforts are to manipulate convention, to 'work' the world that so relentlessly works her.

'What the dove brings is an awareness of the limitations of human language and the perpetual need for interpretation in a world of time.'[7] In his essay on *The Wings of the Dove*, J. C. Rowe, while not exploring the issue of Milly as subject, does make the point that the novel displays signification as a process. The elaboration and subtlety of that process, the tempting layers of imagery and symbolism, have often had the effect of drawing the reader into the interpreting game, however, of coming up with 'solutions' of Milly as Christ, as art or, once again, as American individualism. The kinds of controls that Milly (and, in her way, Kate) exerts over these displays are somehow submerged; the violent realisation that Merton gets of 'a sense of her [Milly's] own reality' is all too often avoided by the critic.

There are in the novel three main levels of reference, three main 'symbolic systems', perhaps, which in their inter-dependence demonstrate both the relationships between aspects of physical and social reality and the extent to which these *are* systems, constructed to facilitate social relationships. These three levels are the commercial, the aesthetic and the moral or spiritual, and the extent to which they invade each other can be shown through a look at one of the novel's central signs: wealth.

When we are introduced to Aunt Maud, at home in Lancaster Gate, we see through Densher's eyes the extent to which possessions speak for their owner, and to which meaning resides in the human 'shell' that Madame Merle champions in *The Portrait of a Lady*. So we see Aunt Maud's 'massive florid furniture, the immense expression of her signs and symbols' (vol. 19, p. 76). Yet possessions signify not only the physical or financial standing of their owner, for money itself has inextricable links with morality: 'the general attestation of morality and money, a good conscience and a big balance' (vol. 19, p. 79). Much later in the novel, Kate bluntly describes Milly as 'an angel with a thumping bank account' (vol. 20, p. 51).

Milly's angelic qualities are inseparable from her wealth, for Kate and for everyone else. The pearls she wears around her neck are heavy and pure but they are also a symbol of wealth and power. At Milly's death, Mrs Lowder is moved to exclaim 'The mere money of her, the darling' (vol. 20, p. 341), as a natural expression of sorrow and pity. Attraction, innocence, moral responsibility and power, all are highlighted and even made possible by wealth. Materialism is another name for spiritual potential, as John Goode demonstrates in his essay on *The Wings of the Dove*[8] or, to put it slightly differently, it makes morality/spirituality possible. Kate's potential for integrity is eroded by the sheer economic squalor of her circumstances – she and Milly might be an exposition of Emerson's statement in his essay on wealth that:

> Wall Street thinks it easy for a *millionaire* to be a man of his word, a man of honour, but that, in failing circumstances, no man can be relied on to keep his integrity.[9]

In Emerson's essay, the equation is not an inevitable one, however, money does not prescribe integrity so much as render it more possible, it imposes some kind of responsibility on its possessor but its realisation may be various: 'Money is representative, and follows the nature and fortunes of the owner'[10] and 'each man's expense must proceed from his character'.[11]

Wealth can be the motive power behind an essentially conventional materialism, a social conformism, or it can be expressive of a jumping off point, a means to quite other ends. Aunt Maud uses her money to enhance her social morality whereas Milly has at first no use for her money because she has not yet taken her active place in the world. In as much as wealth is potential, one can be spiritually wealthy, and accumulate such wealth:

> The true thrift is always to spend on the higher plane; to invest and invest, with keener avarice, that he may spend in spiritual creation, and not in augmenting animal existence.[12]

Yet in reverse one can be spiritual, or religious, about money and worship it, dedicate oneself to the pursuit of it, becoming a priestess in the temple of wealth. As Santayana points out in *The Genteel Tradition*, this fusion of wealth and morality so integral to the nineteenth century American social fabric is a product of a much older tradition: 'Was not "increase", in the Bible, a synonym for benefit? Was not "abundance" the same, or almost the same, as happiness?'[13] Notions of richness, power and spiritual dedication take meanings from each other – the available symbolism is still symbolism, whether it glorifies Milly as priestess, or reduces her to rich girl, and this is demonstrable in the interchangeable vocabulary of the levels of appropriation.

On the other hand, there are clues to the exposure of this process both in the deliberately familiar use of certain images and in the irony and ambiguity with which James puts his symbolism to work. This can be observed, for instance, in the central images of Milly as dove and as American girl.

Hawthorne's *The Marble Faun* is often put forward as an obvious source for the dove imagery in James's novel. James himself wrote about *The Marble Faun* in *Hawthorne*, describing Hilda as 'this pure and somewhat rigid New England girl', and goes on to enforce the sense of purity in describing Hilda's 'Catholic' confession, how she 'comes away with her conscience lightened, not a whit the less a Puritan than before'.[14]

Rigidity is of course very useful in a symbol, and Hilda's simplicity as a pure dove-like New England girl is interesting to compare with the complexity of Milly Theale in the same role. Hawthorne's vision of Hilda herself (whatever problems he has with the purity she symbolises) is entirely straightforward: 'What a pretty scene this is,' thought Miriam, with a kindly smile, 'and how like a dove she is herself, the fair, pure creature.'[15]

Miriam of course has no designs on Hilda, she merely observes her with admiration. Kate Croy, on the other hand, has, we know, a motive for everything she says and does, which makes questioning of her observation inevitable: 'Because you're a dove' (vol. 19, p. 283). Spoken to Milly, this therefore involves her, and Milly's response is far from straightforward: '*That* was what was the matter with her. She was a dove' (vol. 19, p. 283).

Milly's involvement in others' perception of her is a key articulation of the whole great difference between the treatment of Hilda and that of Milly. Milly is reacting and changing within the novel. The evil perpetrated is perpetrated on her. Hilda, in James's words, is simply: 'accidentally the witness . . . of the dark deed'.[16] Hilda is not an artist but a copyist, she interprets, and as a symbol she interprets values in the action of the novel. When Milly Theale visits the National Gallery in London, exhausted and anxious, she reflects:

> She should have been a lady-copyist – it met so the case. The case was the case of escape, of living under water, of being at once impersonal and firm (vol. 19, p. 288).

As fast as Milly represents á value for one character in the novel, she becomes aware of it, involves herself in the representation and thus changes it. The interaction of what she 'is' (for instance, a dove) with her head-on experience of it, results in continual irony and ambiguity in the use of such symbolism. Thus we see Milly 'practising' being dovelike to Aunt Maud and realising 'She should have to be clear as to how a dove *would* act' (vol. 19, p. 284).

Qualities in Milly suggest the dovelike. Kate perceives her as dove. Milly responds to Kate's perception. The process is continuous, and continually reopens the question of what the qualities themselves are, and where they come from – the world's perception, the female self, or a process of reaction between the two.

Yet Milly does share with Hilda the quality of being 'seen' as something, however much more various and ambiguous that something may be – and the problem of personal resolution, of moving beyond the representative, is fraught with pain and misunderstanding, solved only at the moment of defeat. Milly Theale dies, just as Daisy Miller does – the conventional alternative is of course to exchange one symbolic function for another, which is precisely what happens to Hilda. Domesticised by Kenyon, she exchanges her wider significance for a private one, inspiring not many but one:

> So Kenyon won the gentle Hilda's shy affection, and her consent to be his bride. Another hand must henceforth trim the lamp before the Virgin's shrine; for Hilda was coming down from her old tower, to be herself enshrined and worshipped as a household saint, in the light of her husband's fireside.[17]

In contrast to this decorous and stable movement from one

representation to another, Milly Theale shifts her appearance with dazzling rapidity according to the viewer. For Merton Densher she is most simply an American girl, and Milly herself recognises and enjoys presenting this reflection of her qualities. Her American girlness is simply a part of herself, but one which she knows is understood, is cultural common property:

> She had long been conscious with shame for her thin blood . . . of her unused margin as an American girl . . . She became as spontaneous as possible and as American as it might conveniently appeal to Mr Densher . . . to find her (vol. 19, pp. 295–6).

> what he especially recognised was the character that had already several times broken out in her and that she so oddly appeared able, by choice or by instinctive affinity, to keep down or to display. She was the American girl as he had originally found her (vol. 20, pp. 214–5).

> It was settled thus for instance that they were indissoluble good friends, and settled as well that her being the American girl was, just in time and for the relation they found themselves concerned in, a boon inappreciable (vol. 20, p. 254).

Exhibiting this image consciously and at specific times, Milly exposes its inadequacy as a total manifestation of herself.

However opposed in value or in terms of structure, Kate and Milly both undergo the same processes as women, their difference lying in their response. As I remarked earlier Densher, throughout the novel, is aware of being surrounded by a 'circle of petticoats' and reflects, despite his mounting claustrophobia, that 'women are wonderful'; including in this Milly, Susan Stringham, Kate and Aunt Maud. The feminine world is one of perception, imagination – it demands an ability to read the signs correctly, to understand what is being represented. Merton Densher moves through this world, trying to make sense of it. Kate herself not only understands how social existence is represented, she early on recognises her function as representer, and the paradox implicit in being a value both for others and for oneself.

Just as Milly, at the hands of critics, all too often becomes the articulation of some world view, or religion, so Kate is forced into the same kind of scheme (Merton, of course, remaining a 'person'). Simplistically Milly is a dove, a pure maiden, a dying heiress – no more. So Kate is a dark counterpart, sexual passion and tainted vitality. James's own stress on social forces, and individuals' contradictory and conflicting responses are, apparently, to be examined only in the bewildered male. James himself found such moral absolutism, as the kind that labels Kate 'villainess' or 'evil', ridiculous:

> It is almost impossible to pronounce an individual . . . positively good or positively bad without bodily detaching him from his entourage in a way that is fatal to the truth of history . . . We are compelled to look at them [individuals] in connection with their antecedents, their ancestors, their contemporaries, their circumstances.[18]

But the habit of regarding female characters as structural and moral signposts goes too deep for writers such as Leslie Fiedler, Maxwell Geismar, J. A. Ward and others for whom Kate is the 'dark lady'.[19] The irony lies in James's recognition of this way of taking experience (and, by inference, this way of taking characters in a novel), as a starting point for his own exploration of the conflicts implicit for the dark lady and the pure maiden themselves.

Kate's initial encounter with her father is reminiscent of Maisie's last meeting with her father in *What Maisie Knew*. There is the same demand for lying and rejection in order to free the parent as an act of love by the child. But Kate is making her last effort to escape the conventional world for herself, and, frustrated in this by her father, she is not 'moved by charity' (vol. 19, p. 11). Forced back to Lancaster Gate, she assumes her place in the world as a visible, a 'sensible' value. Just as Milly will later, Kate allows people to see her as they like:

> It wouldn't be the first time she had seen herself obliged to accept with smothered irony other people's interpretation of her con-duct. She often ended by giving up to them—it seemed really the way to live – the version that met their convenience (vol. 19, pp. 25–6).

At Aunt Maud's, after her mother's funeral, Kate is at a stage of crisis, of conscious entry into the material world. She is made anxious by new discoveries, one being: 'how material things spoke to her', and she realises that: 'The world was different—whether for worse or for better – from her rudimentary readings' (vol. 19, p. 28).

The process of Kate's seeing and understanding the way of the world, the price of 'material things', and her own status as an object of value rather than purchaser or appropriator, is traced in a scene very similar to the one in *The Portrait of a Lady* where Isabel sits in front of the fire and realises how she has been exploited. So Kate:

> knew more than she could have told you, by the upstairs fire, in a whole dark December afternoon. She knew so much that her knowledge was what fairly kept her there, making her at times circulate more endlessly between the small silk-covered sofa that stood for her in the firelight and the great grey map of Middlesex spread beneath her look-out. To go down, to forsake her refuge, was to meet some of her discoveries halfway, to have to face them or fly before them; whereas they were at such a height only like the rumble of a far-off seige heard in the provisioned citadel (vol. 19, p. 29).

She further reflects:

> The more you gave yourself, the less of you was left. There were always people to snatch at you, and it would never occur to *them* that they were eating you up (vol. 19, p. 33).

Powerless, like Maisie and Nanda, in that she has no money, Kate faces different problems from those of Isabel and Milly. Desiring the social values, her ability to take her place in the world is complicated by her understanding of the denial of her self that this involves: 'There was no such misfortune . . . she further reasoned, as to be formed at once for being and for seeing' (vol. 19, p. 33).

Consciousness is a complication for Kate – her pragmatism leads her to accept conventional values, forces her to play predator in order to gain the best results as prey. Yet knowledge leads her to want to retain herself and her control over herself, epitomised in her decision to make her own marriage choice (a disastrous one in social terms) rather than accept her aunt's. As she says to Densher: 'I shall sacrifice nobody and nothing, and that's just my situation, that I want and that I shall try for everything' (vol. 19, p. 73).

John Goode calls Kate the real subversive in the novel,[20] and both the extent and failure of her subversion lie in her determination to 'sacrifice nobody and nothing', to 'try for everything'. In effect, Kate forces upon herself a kind of schizophrenia.

She hides her identity as subject, and allows the world to see her in their terms. This means that what she signifies for it is comparatively simple; compared to the symbolism surrounding Milly we know that Kate's 'value' is her beauty. Her father responds to this: 'It gave him pleasure that she was handsome, that she was in her way a tangible value' (vol. 19, p. 9), and at the opposite end of the scale, so does Milly, for whom Kate is always 'the handsome girl'. And as a handsome girl, Kate's significance in the world's eyes will depend on the sort of marriage she can obtain in exchange for her beauty – the social level she can aspire to represent. She is watched to see whom she will marry, not just by Aunt Maud, or even her own sister, but by such bystanders as the Misses Condrip, so that early on Kate feels resignedly that she already has 'five spectators' and that: 'What was expected of her by others . . . could . . . present itself as beyond a joke' (vol. 19, p. 43).

A successful marriage would mean both money and status – things that Kate, by virtue of her intelligence and beauty would wear particularly well. To the point that wealth means power, and power to act, it confers upon women a certain wider range – still 'other' as Britannia of the Market Place, Aunt Maud is nonetheless a public force, capable of exerting her will, of being seen in action as well as framed in repose. Densher is struck by how Aunt Maud, who is a 'private lady' can look like 'big cold public men' (vol. 19, p. 83). She cannot be masculine, but she can at least function in the world of public power rather than simply that of private virtue. And this realm appeals to Kate, she feels her ability to be 'magnificent' in conventional terms.

Her relationship with Densher appears to be the one area in which she can communicate herself. Seeing him as male, as somehow apart from the structures of signification that so intimately concern her, she responds to him as 'different'. She is willing to take care of social existence for him, to function as feminine in that way, yet she makes it clear that she does it consciously and deliberately as herself. This is the core of her attraction for him, that her conversation: 'banished the talk of other women . . . to the dull desert of the conventional' (vol. 19, p. 70), and that

> when, in talk with him she was violent and almost unfeminine, it was quite as if they had settled, for intercourse, on the short cut of the fantastic and the happy language of exaggeration (vol. 19, p. 65).

Yet Merton can never really understand the double life that Kate is immersed in to the extent of her whole identity. Nor, finally, does he want to. By her assertion of herself to him Kate implicates him in the manipulation and objectification of Milly that takes place. The process whereby Milly's exploitation is justified and obscured by her existence as sign is the process that Merton does not want to face. Ultimately he cannot share this knowledge with Kate, her function as woman to hide it from him takes precedence over any communion of subjecthood. Like Vanderbank in *The Awkward Age* Merton shies away from the clear, appraising assessment of society that Kate can offer, albeit more calculatingly than Nanda.

Women are placed in a world where they are both subject and object, only they can totally understand the power of representation, form and language: 'Men don't know. They know in such matters almost nothing but what women show them' (vol. 19, p. 99). Although Kate refers specifically here to 'refinements . . . of consciousness' she is explaining to Densher the nature of her need, or her freedom, to deceive. Her attempt to have 'everything' – both success in, and in opposition to, the world, is to be achieved through deception. By hiding her emotional centre, she hopes to maintain outer and inner selves in opposition. In this sense, she is the other side of the coin to Milly – the alternative attempt. Internal and external existence are not to be fused, but maintained by further division and concealment.

Merton's maleness in opposition not only to Milly but to Kate, Aunt Maud and Susan as well, is stressed at several points. Not only does his subject status free him from the need to understand the process of representation and its manipulative potential, it prevents him from possessing a full understanding of what it is to be 'other' and therefore of projection into the suffering of another consciousness. His intellectual faculties take him only so far with Milly, in the end he hides from her pain and acquiesces to Aunt Maud's judgement: 'Besides – oh, I know – men haven't, in many relations, the courage of women' (vol. 20, p. 338).

Kate's re-reading of the world, her understanding of her place in it, and sense of herself through her spectators, takes place at the beginning of the novel. When we first encounter Milly at the beginning of Book Two, she is as yet outside the world, in a state of social innocence. Presented obliquely through Susan Stringham's romantic vision, Milly's 'value' is immediately transposed away from the straightforward material level of Kate and on to a level of metaphor and suggestion, of emotion and spirit. The irony is, of course, that this transposition depends on the one solid fact about Milly, her enormous wealth. The fact that she is outside of speculation about 'good' marriages, that she is free of the need to sell herself and can instead please herself, makes the romantic legitimate. Yet Aunt Maud and Milly both have money but nothing else in common: wealth *is* capable of transformation and ambiguity in this framework. For instance, though Milly's wealth expresses so much about her freedom and potential it simultaneously expresses nothing at all. Any attempt to define Milly simply as 'heiress' collapses in the face of such as Aunt Maud who does define all relations with the world simply through her bank balance. Aunt Maud 'sat . . . in the midst of her money', but Milly 'is far away on the edge of it, and you hadn't . . . in order to get at her nature, to traverse . . . any piece of her property' (vol. 19, p. 196).

Ambiguity and paradox are the notes sounded in the first glimpses we get of Milly, as Susan Stringham finds herself dedicated to personal subtlety and observes the far from traditionally blonde and beautiful princess:

> the striking apparition, then unheralded and unexplained: the slim, constantly pale, delicately haggard, anomalously, agreeably angular young person, of not more than two-and-twenty summers, in spite of her marks, whose hair was somehow exceptionally red, even for the real thing, which it innocently confessed to being (vol. 19, p. 105).

Milly is 'rich, romantic', has 'thousands and thousands a year . . . youth and intelligence . . . a high dim charming ambiguous oddity' and enjoys 'boundless freedom, the freedom of the wind in the desert'. (vol. 19, p. 110). Yet she is totally without practical experience, particularly experience of, and with, other people. She is: 'reduced by fortune to little, humble minded mistakes' (vol. 19, p. 110), and Susan reflects:

> That the potential heiress of all the ages should never have seen anyone like a mere typical subscriber, after all, to the 'Transcript' was a truth that – in especial as announced with modesty, with humility, with regret – described a situation (vol. 19, p. 109).

And this situation is seen by Susan, a writer, as more real than literature, a vision of the romantic life. The temptation to 'interpret' Milly, to search for a meaning in her wealth and freedom, is epitomised by Susan, with her literary and aesthetic approach to life, her tendency to label, to generalise and to see the likeness/ portrait more clearly than the person. At one point, she specifically likens Milly to one of the heroines in her own books (vol. 19, p. 171).

Already the conflicts of Milly's situation are implicit – the object existence imposed upon her by the world which sees her as 'heiress' and more romantically as 'princess' – both will confine her:

> Milly Theale was a princess . . . It was a perfectly definite doom for the wearer – it was for everyone else an office nobly filled. It might have represented possibly, with its involved loneliness and other mysteries, the weight under which she fancied her companion's admirable head occasionally, and ever so submissively, bowed (vol. 19, p. 120).

> the girl couldn't get away from her wealth . . . She couldn't have lost it if she had tried – that was what it was to be really rich. It had to be *the* thing you were (vol. 19, p. 121).

Yet at the same time, Milly already has a sensitivity towards appearance and an ability to transform and control the way she appears. She has:

> the art of being almost tragically impatient and yet making it as light as air; of being inexplicably sad and yet making it as clear as noon; of being unmistakeably gay and yet making it as soft as dusk (vol. 19, p. 115).

In order to be for the world what it expects Kate Croy has to conceal her feelings and responses. Here it is suggested that Milly can be both impatient, sad and gay and yet render it acceptable and encompassable to the world.

Susan's view of Milly on the mountain-top in Switzerland is the climax of this section, and is an image that reverberates throughout the novel. As the religious language that surrounds Milly builds up toward and after her death, I think it is important to remember the contradiction contained in this first image of Milly as Christ:

> If the girl was deeply and recklessly meditating there she was not meditating a jump; she was on the contrary, as she sat, much more

> in a state of unlimited and uplifted possession that had nothing to gain from violence. She was looking down on the kingdoms of the earth, and . . . it wouldn't be with a view of renouncing them (vol. 19, p. 124),

and Susan gains:

> a conviction that the future was not to exist for her princess in the form of any sharp or simple release from the human predicament . . . It would be a question of taking full in the face the whole assault of life (vol. 19, p. 125).

Christ did renounce the kingdoms of the earth; presumably Milly's embrace of them points to her functioning on a more human and social level. But the distinction less often made is that the association with Christ is not only with the spiritual, but with the whole principle of acting/dying *for* others – and this notion is easily and glibly applied to Milly, especially as a way of justifying the eager acceptance by others of what she *can* do for them. Thus Kate at the end: 'She died for you then that you might understand her . . . She did it *for* us' (vol. 20, p. 403).

But Milly's desire to take 'full in the face the whole assault of life' is a personal desire to live, and to experience – and this experience comes to mean the desire for a personal passion, the experience of mattering as herself to one beloved. Her action towards Densher is in the light of her passionate love for him, not in the light of an abstract moral or religious system. The one thing she doesn't want to do is to relinquish all personal claim in order to act *for* other people.

The nature of Milly's course having been decided, she and Susan prepare to go to London – sign of her entry into social existence in her search for emotional experience.

Society is an 'element'. Milly observes within both herself and others as though for the first time. She knows she has been 'jumped at' by London society, but does not really understand why – she has no real understanding of herself as reflected to her by others, and thus her involvement is only partial. She is still very much an observer, capable of removing herself at will:

> while this process went forward [dinner] our young lady alighted, came back, taking up her destiny again as if she had been able by a wave or two of her wings to place herself briefly in sight of an alternative to it (vol. 19, p. 160).

Athough Milly's first glimpse of London society is guided by conversation with Lord Mark, it is Kate who fascinates her from the start. Kate reflects Milly's sense of difference – and gradually the reverse is also true. It is as though each sees in the other what they are not (and therefore, more strongly and clearly, what they are) as social beings. Sense of female identity is shaped and reinforced by awareness of one's existence as other, for other people. Milly's progression into social relations, which she shapes as an overwhelming desire for a personal relationship, is made possible by her developing sense of what she is for other people – and this sense is centred in the developing awareness that she and Kate have of each other. Milly first turns to Lord Mark for an explanation of this – a direct comparison of herself and Kate: 'She might learn from *him* why she was so different from the handsome girl' (vol. 19, p. 153). Yet all she learns is that Kate is 'difficult' whereas she herself is 'easy', and this is challenged immediately by Milly's questioning of the extent of Lord Mark's wisdom:

> You're blasé, but you're not enlightened. You're familiar with everything, but conscious really of nothing. What I mean is that you've no imagination (vol. 19, p. 162).

Imagination, that quality of transforming and personal perception, Milly has in abundance – but as yet no knowledge of the material her imagination is to work on. Like Isabel Archer, her very separateness from the social world, her independence of it, means that she cannot comprehend its manipulation of herself, its treatment of her as legitimate prey. Unlike Isabel, Milly wishes to understand through reflection the ways in which she is treated as object.

> Lebowitz speaks of the struggle in this novel of the object to become subject, but . . . Milly's struggle is to become the subject of those to whom she is object, and to control what they see.[21]

As Kate and Milly develop in their intimacy, Milly learns to see herself for the first time from the outside:

> it was a fact – it became one at the end of three days – that Milly actually began to borrow from the handsome girl a sort of view of her [Milly's] state (vol. 19, pp. 174–5).

Kate, on the other hand, is intensely aware of the limitations of her own social status, and her dependence on the generosity of others, in contrast to Milly's freedom. Seeing Milly in terms of the power and freedom that wealth confers, Kate is all the more conscious of the helpless and passive fate imposed on those who possess only feminine status:

> It wasn't obscure to her that, without some very particular reason to help, it might have proved a test of one's philosophy not to be irritated by a mistress of millions, or whatever they were, who, as a girl, so easily might have been, like herself, only vague and cruelly female (vol. 20, p. 176).

The different degree of their comprehension of their social existence is measured by Kate using her own perception of Milly to view her own state, whereas Milly uses Kate's perception of herself to view herself. Milly is thus undergoing a direct experience of what she 'is' to someone else. Kate is socially initiated to the extent that she acts both as subject – viewing Milly – and as object, in thus comparing her own value and potential.

Milly develops from this intimate exchange of self-knowledge to a realisation of Kate's existence for other people. This is of great significance for Milly – it seems to mark a comprehension of the whole process of making a person other, of alienation. Her relation with Kate is intimate, then she realises that Kate knows Merton Densher. From then on, Milly is fascinated by the fact that Kate is out of her reach in her existence for Merton. The Kate who has reflected to Milly what she (Milly) is, is now distanced and estranged from Milly through her separate knowledge of Merton – and Milly seems to be distanced and estranged from her own self-reflection which has been given to her by Kate. So we are told that Kate's 'other self' is revealed through her closeness to Merton. Milly realises that she will never wholly 'know' Kate – as one can never share the subjectivity of another – and thus feels herself becoming 'other' (James's word here) through this alienation, 'on the edge of a great darkness' (vol. 19, p. 190).

As Milly learns the essential nature of social relations, her vulnerability within them is stressed. The contrast between her wealth and Aunt Maud's is discussed in terms of motive. Not having any motive in regard to her wealth (unlike Aunt Maud), Milly is wide open to the appropriation of her potential by others. Still learning what she is, she cannot yet extend that knowledge into an active relation with the world, cannot yet use her growing understanding of herself as object to guide her assertion of her subject status. Still learning through seeing Kate function socially, Milly observes how Kate can be whatever the occasion demands, can sink her identity for the purpose of others. Milly's observation is couched in language which suggests that, as we know, this is a process controlled by Kate, whose subject self is engaged in self-denial as a process of social survival:

> Kate had for her new friend's eyes the extraordinary and attaching property of appearing at a given moment to show as a beautiful stranger, to cut her connexions and lose her identity, letting the imagination . . . make what it would of them (vol. 19, pp. 211–12).

Milly's usefulness as object is already coming to be defined not only by her wealth, but by her lack of motive for its use, by her separation from social convention. Her absence of conventional deployment of her money marks her off as 'different from the world' (Lord Mark) and therefore as all the more useful to it as an elevated and impersonal sign of potential. As she is shown the Bronzino portrait which so resembles her, Milly recognises the extent to which she is being denied subjectivity, as expressed by passion, and fluid changing life:

> The lady in question, at all events, with her slightly Michaelangelesque squareness, her eyes of other days, her full lips, her long neck, her recorded jewels, her brocaded and wasted reds, was a very great personage – only unaccompanied by a joy. And she was dead, dead, dead. Milly recognised her exactly in words that had nothing to do with her. 'I shall never be better than this' (vol. 19, p. 221).

Watching the picture in tears, Milly is isolated by her recognition of herself as an impersonal object for others and by Lord Marks's inability to share her emotion. Kate's closer perception, her insistent placing of Milly as 'superb', reinforces for Milly the extent to which she has no personal existence. Under the eyes of 'her painted sister', the Bronzino, she says: 'I think I could die without its being noticed' (vol. 19, p. 228).

At this stage, Milly has lost her social blankness. Comprehension of possible manipulation and denial are parallelled by a new physical collapse. Yet immediately Milly begins to respond by 'being' what she is for others as forcefully as possible. Newly distrustful of Kate, she reinforces her trusting friendship by asking Kate's help. From here on, Milly attempts to exist as subject by so completely fulfilling her object role as even to ask for help from those around her in sustaining it, and thus gradually takes control of the whole process into her own hands. Her monitoring of the treatment, by others, of her illness, is the immediate, continuous example of this.

In the interview with Sir Luke Strett, Milly experiences with intensity the perception of her 'condition' by another. His knowledge comforts her, that he knows she is alone, that he pities her. Pity and isolation are not things that she wants to acknowledge, but that acknowledgement to another marks itself her first real communication, unobscured by the search for reflection that conditions the relationship between Kate and herself. So with Sir Luke: 'there actually passed between them for some seconds a sign, a sign of the eyes only, that they knew together where they were' (vol. 19, p. 241).

The extremity of Milly's situation is itself productive of the great irony for her, it both isolates her to the extent that she cannot share with one person, on an intimate basis, her predicament, and yet the only solution, the only way of coping, is to search for that kind of personal passion. Thus, leaving Sir Luke, Milly 'went forward into space', knowing that: 'No one in the world could have sufficiently entered into her state' (vol. 19, p. 247).

She can 'be' only in relation to the total desire for life, the human race and its grey immensity. She leaves the protected glimpses of life and plunges into the reality, the pain of it for herself and others:

> she had come out, she presently saw, at the Regent's Park, round which on two or three occasions with Kate Croy her public chariot had solemnly rolled. But she went into it further now; this was the real thing; the real thing was to be quite away from the pompous roads, well within the centre and on the stretches of shabby grass . . . here were wanderers anxious and tired like herself; here doubtless were hundreds of others just in the same box. Their box, their great common anxiety, what was it, in this grim breathing-space, but the practical question of life? (vol. 19, p. 250).

This kind of impersonal compassion and empathy is paralleled by the impersonal symbolic status as Bronzino or Byzantine princess, that is gradually being imposed on Milly by those around her. Yet Milly still wishes to 'live', and she does not underestimate the pressure and the urgency of the search for some kind of experience for her*self*:

> It was perhaps superficially more striking that one could live if one would; but it was more appealing, insinuating, irresistible in short, that one would live if one could (vol. 19, p. 254).

Her perceptions sharpened by the new momentum given to her situation by her interviews with Sir Luke, Milly sees Kate more and more clearly as 'other' as the 'handsome girl' known to Merton Densher. At the same time, she determines not to be herself impersonalised further into, literally, an 'object' of pity. She will control the response to her illness by 'allowing' others to pretend it doesn't exist. Thus James describes a 'current' in Milly that others control because she lets them. Confronting Kate clearly and directly for the last time, Milly allows Kate to teach her about the predatory nature of society, to warn her that she will be appropriated even more for her difference; her use lies in her being: 'an outsider, independent and standing by yourself; you're not hideously relative to tiers and tiers of others' (vol. 19, p. 281).

Milly's response is more and more intensely to be what she is seen to be. She is conscious of 'the American mind as sitting there thrilled and dazzled' (vol. 19, p. 277), and she learns not just from what Kate says but from their relation as they talk. Kate appears to want, at the last moment, to release Milly from the appropriation she herself has had to accept, to tell her to run from the whole world of Lancaster Gate. In doing so, she helps Milly to see how she will be taken by the world, the terms in which she functions for it, and therefore the terms through which she can attempt to communicate and assert herself: 'Because you're a dove' (vol. 19, p. 283). '*That* was what was the matter with her. She was a dove' (vol. 19, p. 283), and so she begins to practise being dovelike.

At this point, Kate more or less ceases to communicate directly with Milly. Having attempted to free her momentarily for her own sake, she now reinstates Milly as object, and as somehow deserving of exploitation in her very generosity and magnificence. Although perceptive of Milly's needs, Kate sees them now only in order to use them and thus to fulfill her own attempt at self-assertion via secrecy and denial.

With the meeting between Merton, Kate and Milly in the National Gallery, Milly's experience moves beyond the initial curious searching for herself in another that she engaged in with Kate, and operates within the framework of the third person. Her communication takes into account now her own existence for others, and others' existence for her, within a social framework that pre-determines impressions and responses. She sees Merton through the eyes of fellow tourists in the Gallery, commenting on his English style. In the embarrassment of the triangular meeting she copes – as she is beginning to learn to do – by being what is most apposite. But because Milly's motivation is not social success, but experience, she pushes beyond what would suit the occasion in order to assert herself:

> She became as spontaneous as possible and as American as it might conveniently appeal . . . *What Milly thus gave she therefore made them take – even if . . . it was rather more than they wanted* (vol. 19, p. 296). (my emphasis).

Merton being the one with whom Milly wants personally to connect, the extent to which she presents herself to him and he accepts the presentation is at first simply disheartening, because he has not yet come to see *how* she is controlling and ordering that process in order to make things easy. With him, more than anyone, she consciously plays the American girl. The very conscious use of this part of her persona is again a means to subjectivity – not by rejecting one's significations, but by consciously employing them. Not only the representation of Hilda as dove, but James's own Daisy Miller, point up the difference in treatment. Yet the danger lies in failing to penetrate beyond the general acceptance of the symbolic or representative, and Merton Densher initially takes Milly simply as she appears: 'her heart could none the less sink a little on feeling how much his view of her was destined to have in common with . . . *the* view', which makes 'relations rather prosaically a matter of course' (vol. 19, pp. 300–1).

Like Merton, most critics of *The Wings of the Dove* see Milly as dove or American girl, without accepting as an intrinsic part of her presentation her own conscious manipulation of these qualities. Kate pinpoints the problem both within and without the structure of the novel: 'You're right about her not being easy to know. One *sees* her with intensity' (vol. 20, p. 42).

Milly's representative richness and complexity make it all too easy to explore no further. By contrast, in invisible secrecy from the world, Kate and Merton share the kind of committed personal desire that Milly precisely doesn't have and so desperately wants:

> It was all they had together, but they had it at least without a flaw – each had the beauty, the physical felicity, the personal virtue, love and desire of the other (vol. 20, pp. 54–5).

As Kate and Merton develop Kate's plan in the urgency of their love, designating Milly as victim, as Aunt Maud unconsciously abets them through wanting to use Milly to get Merton out of Kate's way; the basic act of manipulation is achieved, and Milly's new acquisition of perception is not proof against such conscious scheming. We are told: 'So Milly was successfully deceived' (vol. 20, p. 69).

Meanwhile, Milly moves towards her realisation of a life as subject, a life of experience in relation to others. She first exerts herself towards others in relation to her own illness – refusing pity and attempting in turn to pity or support others, she controls the response to her own predicament, emphasising in turn her wealth, her gentleness, her pathos or her Americanness. Merton's understanding that Milly is consciously presenting herself to him as not-ill is his first move towards communicating with her:

> she was never, never – did he understand? – to be one of the afflicted for him; and the manner in which he understood it . . . constituted . . . something like a start for intimacy (vol. 20, pp. 73–4)

and this is reinforced by Milly's ability to pity Merton, through her false understanding of Kate's having rejected him.

Similarly, Milly controls her relationship with Susan by rejecting pity and instead giving support to Susan in the difficult task or 'seeing her through', 'the pledge of protection and support was all the younger woman's own' (vol. 20, p. 102).

On what is essentially an impersonal plane, Milly can retain her own self and exist as subject – she can control how she is taken by the world, and by extending compassion and making the taking easier she lends meaning and importance to what she signifies. But personal and involved experience eludes her on this plane. It reinforces a certain distance. By making things easier for everyone round her, even Sir Luke – 'Him too she would help to help' (vol. 20, p. 124)*– Milly allows them to see her as all the complex of significations that have clustered around her. It is only with shared acknowledgement of her deliberate control over this that they will begin to appear as inadequate as a representation of Milly herself. This acknowledgement is denied by Kate, and gradually, painfully arrived at by Merton, whose importance is in this role of accepting what Milly is doing. Subjectivity is meaningful only when recognised, when deferred to, by the world, which tends to a recognition of you as other. For Milly simply to be a princess out of love and sympathy for the world would be simply for her to be object, if that process were not understood from without as well. Venice, and the return to London, thus belong to Densher's vision, his struggle to retain his loyalty to Kate, and the patterns of manipulation she embodies, and his final acknowledgement of how Milly's action is both of love and exposure.

By removing herself to Venice Milly chooses to live on a plane of appearance – prosaic and symbolic. Choosing her palace as a great gilded shell, she allows herself to be 'understood' by all the world, by Eugenio or by Susan Stringham. Milly enjoys Eugenio's understanding of her value in simple financial terms, yet she allows herself to be valued on a variety of planes. For the first time, she has her own territory instead of staying on other peoples', and it is an expressive, symbolic one where even the weather corresponds to her moods and she can appear, or disappear upstairs, entirely at will. Controlling appearance, Milly can choose to deny exposure or intimacy, and returning in the evening to remove the social mask with Kate becomes the most masklike activity of all.

Merton, pressed by Kate into behaviour which he feels forces him to deny his own convictions, resists the available reverberative associations that surround Milly. She responds to this, allowing him to see her in simple, undemanding terms:

> Mrs Lowder, Susan Shepherd, his own Kate, might . . . see her as a princess, as an angel, as a star, but for himself, luckily, she hadn't as yet complications to any point of discomfort: the princess, the angel, the star, were muffled over, ever so lightly and brightly, with the little American girl who had been kind to him in New York (vol. 20, pp. 173–4).

Yet against his will Merton begins to respond to the nature of what Milly is doing:

> This spectacle had for him an eloquence, an authority, a felicity . . . for which he said to himself that he had not consciously bargained (vol. 20, p. 184).

The inadequacy of mere intellectual perception as a response to Milly's plight is signalled in her first Venetian interview with Lord Mark. He can see her as the dead Bronzino, he can feel sympathy and even know what it is she is searching for as an antidote to her death, yet he, like Kate, perceives without intimacy. He is willing to prey on her and to expect in turn to be preyed on. The straightforward exposition of social relations that Milly achieves with Lord Mark enables her to 'let go'; she has nothing to lose by allowing him to pity her: 'she would be kind once for all; that would be the end: "I'm very badly ill"' (vol. 20, p. 155).

Her refusal to expose her illness to the others is a product of *her* need as much as an act of charity for them. Lord Mark understands what it is Milly lacks: 'You want to be adored' (vol. 20, p. 156); 'You want somebody of your own' (vol. 20, p. 161).

As Merton (on the other hand) is touched more strangely by the vision Milly creates, he can afford less and less to look at what she wants, and his own manipulation of it. He turns more and more to the reality of his desire for Kate as a way of retaining integrity: 'Good God, if you'd only *take* me' (vol. 20, p. 198).

The full extent of the manipulation that Kate intends him to practise upon Milly is articulated at the moment of Milly's greatest presentation, the Veronese dinner party. Usually dressed in black, Milly chooses to appear that evening as the pure dove, dressed in white like Hawthorne's Hilda. Unlike Hilda, she is also a princess and an heiress, and she wears a heavy string of pearls around her neck. Assuming a beatific mildness (product of her practising at the dove-like?) she creates an element that they all 'swim in'. Merton becomes acutely aware of Milly's appearance as a social act, and one which she controls. For him, as always, she is thus primarily the American girl:

> It affected him as a large though queer social resource in her—such as a man, for instance, to his diminution, would never in the world be able to command (vol. 20, p. 215).

When most fully object and subject in the world, the woman reverberates beyond herself in a way the anonymous male onlooker can comprehend but not experience or share.

Merton's seeing what Milly *is* for Kate, what Kate wants him precisely to do, and his exertion of pressure on Kate for the first time, are all inter-connected. His perception of Milly subtly alters his relation to Kate – their love becomes an act of demand rather than of recognition. As Merton sees more and more towards a communion of perception with Milly, his relation with Kate tends more and more *away* from the shared knowledge of their early days toward a passionate escape from knowledge.

Kate gazes at Milly at the party and repeats 'She's a dove', but Merton knows that she is really moved by the sight of Milly's pearls, the great 'symbol of differences' that has displaced any community between the two women, and which Kate now seeks to blur in language by stressing Milly's moral 'magnificence':

> Yet he knew in a moment that Kate was just now . . . exceptionally under the impression of that element of wealth in her which was a power, which was a great power, and which was dove-like only so far as one remembered that doves have wings and wondrous flights (vol. 20, p. 218).

J. C. Rowe, discussing James's three late novels, comments that: 'the symbolism in the later novels constantly frustrates the characters' demands for meaningful definition'[22] showing, for instance, how in *The Wings of the Dove* the ironic use of religious imagery and the Christ imagery surrounding Milly points up the extent to which there is no external source of order outside the consciousness. Therefore, as a 'symbol of differences' in her many aspects:

> Milly Theale ultimately brings the characters of the novel to a consciousness of one another, forcing them to recognise the distance that separates their respective desires.[23]

This reading prevents any simplistic symbolic interpretation, and focusses on the irony and multiplicity of the symbolism instead, thus exposing the symbolic *process* as being the central issue. By demonstrating the inadequacy of any one set of images to make ordered or meaningful either Milly or the other characters' experience, we are forced to look at the symbolic process as a mode of exploitation and justification for the working out of personal desires and comprehension.

But once again, Rowe views the story from one side – deals with half of the structure. Not only are we finally concerned with the effect that Milly has on others' lives but on the extent to which their (or Merton's) response *to* her changes, and to which his and Kate's actions affect her attempts at involved experience, her desire to 'live'. The change that takes place when Milly starts to live in Venice is most fully expressed in the party scene: she orchestrates and controls the effects that she studied so carefully in London. She places herself in a setting (or set), selects the supporting cast, dramatically changes her costume and appears as . . . the princess, the heiress, the dove, and for Merton, the little American girl. And Milly begins again to 'make them take . . . rather more than they wanted'.

Forcing Kate to come to his rooms for a night is Densher's final attempt to give reality and passion to that relationship, and thus to diminish Milly's control over the experience encapsulated in Venice. Obsessively he fears Milly coming to his rooms which are now a sanctuary of his self, the self which he can still acknowledge, which has retained its commitment to Kate. But, in her element, Milly knows now how to control her relation to the world, how to be sign and yet so order the understanding of that signification that it becomes personal and leads straight back to her. If the only order exists in the consciousness, then Milly's consciousness here takes the imaginings of Kate, Aunt Maud and Densher, and transforms them into something else:

> He then fairly perceived that – even putting their purity of motive at its highest – it was neither Kate nor he who made his strange relation to Milly, who made her own, so far as it might be, innocent; it was neither of them who practically purged it . . . Milly herself did everything . . . Milly herself, and Milly's house, and Milly's hospitality, and Milly's manner, and Milly's character and, perhaps still more than anything else, Milly's imagination (vol. 20, p. 239).

In the final days of their relationship in Venice, Milly and Merton reach some communion of understanding of Milly as subject controlling her appearance for him as sign and thus sustaining and consoling, making their relations to each other safe and ordered.

Milly's passion *as* subject is made quite clear to Merton; she repeats:

> 'I want so to live.'
> 'Well, that I know I *can*.'
> 'If I want to live I *can*' (vol. 20, p. 246)

and this assertion of self breaks down *his* concealment of self and he says that she can come to his rooms, aware that: 'the drop, almost with violence, of everything but a sense of her own reality – apparently showed in his face' (vol. 20, p. 247).

Yet sharing this knowledge of Milly's needs and demands as conscious subject, not simply existing for others, remote and detached in her palace, is potentially dangerous for Merton. Knowing this, Milly facilitates their communication, preserving the structures of signification that Merton can recognise. They 'rely' on her being the American girl:

> They really, as it went on, *saw* each other at the game; she knowing he tried to keep her in tune with his conception, and he knowing she thus knew it. Add that he again knew she knew, and yet that nothing was spoiled by it, and we get a fair impression of the line they found most completely workable (vol. 20, p. 255).

Structures of meaning have almost become the rules of a game, yet a game which Merton completely depends on and which must be sustained as 'real', even while he and Milly share the knowledge of its conscious construction.

Lord Mark's arrival and destruction of the fragile Venetian world in effect smashes Milly's ability to sustain her performance. The strength of London, the social world, the weight of past decisions and impositions, appear to submerge the personal creativity of Milly's display. Bereft of her sustaining powers, her ordering of experience as sign, Merton is left in fear of himself. He attempts to dissociate himself from the past, first by blaming Lord Mark: 'The weather had changed, the rain was ugly, the wind wicked, the sea impossible, *because* of Lord Mark' (vol. 20, p. 263). Then he blames himself, but *as* another; he sees his actions with detached disbelief through the eyes of Eugenio, as those of another man who is an abject fortune hunter. Like Sir Claude and Vanderbank, the one thing that Merton cannot cope with is the knowledge of himself and his own responsibility for the manipulation of the woman as sign, as a social convenience to sustain his subjectivity. Exposed by the stark presentation of the girl as herself, they are all afraid of themselves. Merton 'knew soon enough that it was of himself that he was afraid' (vol. 20, p. 282).

Milly dies, and she dies because the weight of manipulation and objectification she has to face as being perpetrated on her shatters her ability to control her existence in the world. Yet her death shadows the book from the beginning. She left New York specifically because she was ill. Unlike the pattern of *Daisy Miller*, which suggests that Winterbourne might have saved Daisy and which minimises the ripples caused by Daisy's death, *The Wings of the Dove* weights the destructiveness of social structures more heavily, and also increases the importance and implications of Milly's resistance to them.

Both Susan and Sir Luke are prepared, in their different ways, to let Merton off. From now until the end of the novel life in the social world is suddenly made easy for him. Aunt Maud accepts him. Kate welcomes him. Milly makes him rich. Destroyed herself, the impact of Milly's relationship with Merton nonetheless underlines its reality. Milly's attempt to live is, ironically, most vital in its destruction.

In Venice, Merton clings to his identity by at least refusing to lie further. His final interview with Milly is known only by impact. Back in London, everything is altered – Merton's relationship with the world at large and with Kate in particular. The process of signification – of ordering and interpreting individual response into some kind of 'meaning' – is carried on by Kate and Aunt Maud. Merton's response now is to resist their interpretations.

Their alienation is now continually present. Kate *would* have denied their engagement had she been in Merton's place, would have continued the manipulative process to the bitter end. Kate understands that Milly acted from personal love for Densher, yet uses even this to justify their actions – that after all Milly: 'realised her passion' – 'We've succeeded' (vol. 20, pp. 332–3). Kate is playing with language, playing with the idea of Milly as other, getting what she wanted as a static quantity, experiencing passion.

Merton, on the other hand, cannot directly face the extent of how he and Kate have destroyed Milly, her: 'consciousness, tortured, for all he knew, crucified by its pain' (vol. 20, p. 339), and he sees himself still as other, as a reflection of Milly's passion:

He saw a young man far off and in a relation inconceivable, saw him hushed, passive, staying his breath, but half understanding, yet dimly conscious of something immense and holding himself painfully together . . . The essence was that something had happened to him too beautiful and too sacred to describe. He had been, to his recovered sense, forgiven, dedicated, blessed (vol. 20, p. 342–3).

The irony is still present. Religious language still mingles with echoes of the financial. After all, Merton has been left a great deal of money. His attempt to reject the money and marry Kate without it heralds a final inability to confront squarely what he and Kate have done, he never really faces his new knowledge of himself in the way that Kate can: 'She understood everything, – and things he refused to; and she had reasons, deep down, the sense of which nearly sickened him' (vol. 20, p. 349). Released by her death from confronting Milly further as subject, Merton can transcend his manipulation of her as something taken out of his hands and sanctified by her. The responsibility for the meaning of his earlier actions can be returned to Kate.

In these final scenes, James reminds us of the need which drives Kate, her vulnerability which, so different from Milly's, nonetheless renders her object in the world. Back with her family, with the spectre of her father once more present, she is made desperate by her setting in a way Merton would never be because as a woman she is so largely defined by her environment, her appearance. Merton, in the end, can afford not to face the pain that both Milly and Kate can understand, and Milly and Kate even understand that: 'Your attitude, my dear, is that you're afraid of yourself . . . You've had to do yourself violence' (vol. 20, p. 386).

Kate attempts to retrieve her relationship with Merton by explaining and ordering what has happened:

But your change came . . . the day you last saw her; she died for you then that you might understand her. From that hour you *did* . . . She did it *for* us . . . I used to call her, in my stupidity, a dove. Well she stretched out her wings and it was to *that* they reached. They cover us (vol. 20, pp. 403–4).

But Merton cannot accept this version of events, any more than he can accept Aunt Maud's – he distances himself from Kate as subject, seeing her appearance more and more clearly, and sharing only sexual passion:

> their final impulse or their final remedy, the need to bury in the dark blindness of each others' arms the knowledge of each other that they couldn't undo (vol. 20, p. 392).

Sexual passion is an escape from perception and shared knowledge, as it is for Isabel Archer in Caspar Goodwood's arms, and as it is for Maggie Verver in Amerigo's.

It is Kate who can most clearly acknowledge the power of Milly's display and the shattering effect of its breakdown, the disruptive assertion into the social world of Milly as subject, manipulated, and destroyed by this manipulation: 'We shall never be again as we were' (vol. 20, p. 405).

Both Kate and Milly, recognising themselves as other in the world, attempt to establish a relationship in that world, through Merton; a relationship in which in different ways they can be both subject as well as object by controlling appearance and meaning. In the end, neither Milly's love nor Kate's determined exploitation is quite enough to maintain both existence as subject and retain validation (through love) as sign, for the bewildered male subject. They achieve a feminine subjectivity at quite a cost in a world which sees them as merely beautiful and magnificent. The penalty for failing to maintain the social function, for stepping beyond designated structures, is displayed in *The Wings of the Dove* in Milly's death and Kate's final impotence, still poor, still dependent. In James's final completed novel, *The Golden Bowl*, we see the bleak implications for success for the woman as conscious and self-directed signifier, retaining the prize of social existence.

8 *The Golden Bowl*: Signification as Power

In primitive thought there is clearly something else in what we call a 'commodity' that makes it profitable to its owner or trader. Goods are not only economic commodities, but vehicles and instruments for realities of another order, such as power, influence, sympathy, status and emotion.[1]

For . . . James the expression of man's *desire* for unity is what ultimately describes both his art and his history . . . Words present their own significances in a world otherwise devoid of meaning. For . . . James language affirms the separation of man from the world. A sign is not a transcendent third term through which man may approach the reality of his condition. The need to speak or write is a constant reminder of an external world which man can neither know nor have.[2]

Naomi Lebowitz, in *The Imagination of Loving*, describes how *The Golden Bowl* (1904) is made up of fairy tale elements – the prince, the princess, the wicked stepmother, the advice giving fairy godmother, the magic bowl, and so on.[3] Certainly in this novel, significantly less than in *The Wings of the Dove*, for instance, James makes little attempt to render a recognisable, particular social world outside of the tight coterie of the four main characters plus the Assinghams and, barely, Lady Castledean. The use of place and time is far more like that of *The Sacred Fount*; houses mark off arenas for certain kinds of action, characters oscillate between 'company' and privacy, human behaviour is pondered in language of extremity and violence after observed confrontations in ballrooms and on country house terraces. The lack of reference to the details of the material or temporal (in so far as they exist beyond the immediate action of the novel) opens the way to the accumulations of symbolism in the book. By the time Maggie's half begins everyone is watching for, waiting for, reading and interpreting signs. Everything apparently means something beyond itself, whether it is Charlotte's voice as she displays Adam's art treasures, or a friendly after dinner game of bridge. As in *The Wings of the Dove*, I shall suggest that James is concerned in *The Golden Bowl* partly with the *process* of signification itself, rather than simply with meanings or events thus signified.

From the first, *The Golden Bowl* is laden with notions of exchange, of buying and selling. The central exchanges are marital, in both cases it is both explicitly an economic transaction and one laden with complex ideas of what is being transacted. The values assigned are both contradictory and interchangeable – cultural, historical, sexual, financial and aesthetic – and control of one, any, or all of these values means a degree of control over the processes of exchange and re-exchange that continue throughout the novel. Conversely, representation of values renders one object, and therefore to be controlled and subsequently exchanged.

The Golden Bowl displays a world of total 'civilisation' in which power (or control) in some degree affects every human relationship. This power rests in varying abilities to control the means of signification, in possessing the goods which generate the values of the social world. Degrees of power vie against each other – the fundamental patriarchal power which both Adam and Amerigo can wield toward Charlotte and Maggie is temperd by the challenge of economic power which Adam in turn can assert against Amerigo. Words associated with Adam are 'bland', 'anonymous', 'modest', 'impenetrable', 'inscrutable'; he is least clearly to be 'seen' of all the characters, and is the one with greatest ownership and control.

The social structure is created by the transformation of goods into 'instruments for realities of another order' – the goods which are bought or exchanged are representative beyond themselves. Whereas Maggie recognises and creates her sense of self out of her representative functions as wife and daughter, Amerigo's function for the Ververs apparently obscures his private identity without threatening it – but his existence as subject, free of signification, is implicit in his relationship to Adam and Maggie, and finally conflicts with his representative status.

To expose the disharmony between the social construct of meaning and value and the particular people and relationships and behaviour that supposedly figure these meanings forth, Maggie both creates the way to overt disharmony by *not* fulfilling her representative status (breaking the code in its own terms by remaining of Adam rather than becoming of Amerigo) and, in comprehending that disharmony, holds the power to expose it. The enormous effort of *The Golden Bowl*, that which gives it its overriding effect of strain and tension, of being an agonisingly sustained balancing act, is that Maggie chooses not to expose the signifying process and the contradictions it creates and obscures. Instead, she closes the gap as far as she can in order to gain the prize of social existence denied to James's other heroines: 'for love'. In doing so, she experiences power and control herself and has to accept the wielding of it; the price of social success (in the broadest terms) is the adoption of social methods.

In the harmonious scheme of reality represented by the marriages, Maggie is willing to take her place, to fulfill her function – alienating as that might be – if the others will maintain the representation as well. The apparent marriage of the disparate elements that provide the axes of the novel: America/Europe, timelessness/history, individual/world, aesthetic/economic, is maintained in a series of power exercises manifested in the most fundamental marriage of disparate elements, the marriage of man and woman. Marriage bonds groups through the exchange of women, who represent the world they come from (the father) and the world they go to (the husband). This fusion involves the control of women, so that they function as signs over and above their existence as individuals. You could say that it is Adam and Amerigo who *marry* – the marriage of America and Europe takes place through the exchange of Charlotte and Maggie. The conflict arises through the imbalance of this marriage whereby Adam seeks to absorb Amerigo and his world, rather than achieve a balance with it (and uses his over-riding power of money to do this), and through the added unwillingness of either man or woman to abandon the relationships they already have.

Adam in fact attempts to render the Prince feminine, the woman in their marriage, by controlling the Prince as sign (of history, Europe, etc.). The Prince's revolt against this constitutes the first half of the novel – the domination of the old world by the new is resisted in subterfuge and in resort to the fundamental control of Charlotte as sign. Maggie then facilitates the adjustment of this unequal 'marriage' to a balanced exchange, a social harmony and fusion of old and new elements by threatening the whole signifying process on which the marriage rests – yet only threatening. Adam finally has to accept Charlotte as his representation of the old world, and has to relinquish Maggie (as representation of the new) to the

Prince. By making sure that she and Charlotte still function as married women, Maggie ensures this reciprocity.

Maggie, like Milly Theale, is tortured and dehumanised by her representative function, by her acceptance of the function of signifier. Like all women, she learns the rules of language and of representation because they are the rationale of her existence – they define her. But social existence (and on another level, love) also depend on them; and thus women can threaten to deprive the patriarchal world of its civilised and consoling framework by exposing the 'reality' that supposedly corresponds to the signified – and therefore the arbitrary nature of the sign.

> To allow this fact, that woman is not above us and below, is to leave her just beside us, shorn of the magical power we know we as men very well lack . . . To accept woman as one of us, to give up her mystificaton, alternately suppression and exaltation, is to recognise and accept that we are, in our own world, alone.[4]

Maggie does not attempt to demystify herself in the way, for instance, that Nanda does – to do so would be to lose Amerigo's love. Rather, by sustaining the fictions by which they, and we, all live, she attains some control over them and knows the power of the artist while·assenting to the oppression of the woman as sign. In it for better or worse, it is women in the end who manage the ramifications of society, their resistance is to exalt the process of signification beyond the control of those who possess the signifiers. The ambiguity of such an achievement, the sacrifice in terms of direct communication and acceptance of selfhood that it demands, is central to the ambiguous resolution of *The Golden Bowl*.

Maggie's control over language (exemplified in lies) and over social order by the end of *The Golden Bowl* allies her inextricably with the signifying activity, the 'constant reminder of an external world which man can neither know nor have'. *The Golden Bowl* is a novel in which the power, manipulation and objectification potential in all social relations is confronted in terms of intelligence, compassion and suffering, and yet apparently accepted as an integral material of such relations, to be used, if not for the 'worst', then for the 'best'. However triumphal, Maggie remains image in her relation to her world – her achieved selfhood expresses most fully her alienation from her social appearance.

Although *The Golden Bowl* is divided into two halves, 'The Prince' and 'The Princess', and although it is possible to see the novel as being fundamentally 'about' Amerigo,[5] the difference in effect of the two halves is considerable. Maggie's half, which takes up the story at the moment of action and change, is relayed almost entirely through her consciousness, *her* sense of what is happening. The Prince's half spends a considerable amount of time away from the Prince, with Adam Verver, Adam and Charlotte, Fanny and the Colonel, and even Maggie herself. It establishes the situation from without (as much as the book ever does) as well as from within, preparing the way for the internal tension of the second half, 'The Princess'.

THE PRINCE

The nature of Amerigo's achievement in marrying (or becoming engaged to) Maggie Verver, and the bond that this constitutes, is outlined in the early chapters. Maggie and Adam constitute a – still undivided – unit, yet there is a distinct difference in Amerigo's sense of Maggie and of Adam. Maggie he has captured, Adam has captured him. In Maggie, Amerigo·has acquired a wife, and her qualities as a wife will reflect on him: 'He expected her, desired her, to have character; his wife *should* have it, and he wasn't afraid of her having too much' (vol. 23, p. 19). From the first, we get a sense of Amerigo's sexual power, something developed in later chapters, and the fact that it is in the exericse·of this power that he deals with all and any women: by making, or not making, love.

But Amerigo's engagement to Maggie is perceived by him as having little to do with the personal, with himself. He knows what he signifies *for* the Ververs and renders up these qualities in exchange for emerging signifieds of the new world – wealth. Amerigo has history, family, culture – he is the 'creme de volaille' to Adam's 'natural fowl' – both need to 'eat' each other, to complement and exchange. But the balance is unequal. In marrying Maggie, the Prince is not so much taking to himself the qualities of American good faith, romance and innocence (and money) as being taken *to* America through Adam's undissolved bond with Maggie, his retention of the purse strings. Thus Amerigo becomes a representative object, 'a part of his collection . . . You're a rarity, an object of beauty, an object of price' (vol. 23, p. 12). It is Adam's collection he is acquiescing to enter, not Maggie's. She has money only in identification with her father – alone she is vulnerable to possession herself, and when she says: 'Yes, if you mean that I'd pay rather than lose you' (vol. 23, p. 13), she is referring to a different kind of currency, the material is not within her control.

At this stage, Amerigo appears to feel that the arrangement is satisfactory. The marriage is necessary in terms of what he signifies; his family needs a new history and 'He perfectly recognised . . . that the material for the making had to be Mr Verver's millions' (vol. 23, p. 16).

He senses that Adam will take him as he is, accept him as representative and yet not chameleon-like. Unlike the woman in marriage, he will not have to respond and reform: 'He was to constitute a possession, yet was to escape being reduced to his component parts' (vol. 23, p. 23).

Amerigo carries his aesthetic beauty and his history with him:

> His look itself . . . suggested an image – that of some very noble personage who, expected, acclaimed by the crowd in the street and with old precious stuffs falling over the sill for his support, had gaily and gallantly come to show himself: always moreover less in his own interest than in that of spectators and subjects whose need to admire, even to gape, was periodically to be considered (vol. 23, p. 42).

The arrogance implied here is perhaps part of Amerigo's dissoci-ation of his self from his appearance. Recognising the importance of what he represents he will place himself in the relation of object to Adam, yet disdains to consider the world of object and representa-tion further – that is to be done by others, particularly by women. We are told that Amerigo has no interest in interpreting signs, he simply acknowledges their presence. The whiteness of America is unnerving because it appears to give no signal at all. The Prince is, in many relations, a reader and user of signs, not a constitutor or creator, nor an interpreter. His relation to Adam – as an object of historical and aesthetic value – is constituted by Adam's superior wealth, his power over Amerigo. Yet as a man Amerigo can exert other forms of power, he can expect not only to offer himself to the 'white curtain' but to also do something for himself – the masculine self which can look to women for representation, aid and submis-sion. As Quentin Anderson says: 'Amerigo's sense of himself depends on his ability to subordinate women to himself'.[6]

Initially, Amerigo's relation with Maggie hardly exists, she is simply the means to Adam's millions. She too sees his history and not his self, very like *Miss Gunton of Poughkeepsie* (1900). In union with her father, Amerigo is to her an object of value. With Fanny Assingham, however, and of course with Charlotte, the Prince already exerts his form of power, and demands the activity of interpretation and, indirectly, of signification, to be carried on for him. Thus Fanny will 'see him through' the world of difference that America represents. Fanny will represent for him what the white curtain conceals – the white world into which he is voyaging.

This act of interpretation is the same as that which Fanny performs for her husband – and the word is 'performs'. Representation extends beyond simply being 'other' into the realm of discussing, interpreting and extending the implications of such an activity. Women signify and explain signification, their world is that of seeming. To the Prince, Charlotte is fundamentally a woman; she is inevitably the loser, inevitably other, and also inevitably the bearer of the burden of investing experience with order and meaning:

> She always dressed her act up, of course, she muffled and disguised and arranged it, showing in fact in these dissimulations a cleverness equal to but one thing in the world, equal to her abjection: she would let it be known for anything, for everything, but the truth of which it was made . . . She was the twentieth woman, she was possessed by her doom, *but her doom was also to arrange appearances*, and what now concerned him was to learn how she proposed (vol. 23, p. 50). (my emphasis).

Charlotte performs *for* the Prince, arranges appearances to tide over not only herself but him as well. As man he has a subject power, is a watcher, acquirer and waiter in the way that Adam is in relation to him. This is parodied in the even less concerned spectatorship of Colonel Assingham:

> He watched her [Fanny] accordingly in her favourite element very much as he had sometimes watched at the Aquarium the celebrated lady who, in a slight, though tight, bathing suit, turned somersaults and did tricks in the tank of water which looked so cold and uncomfortable to the non-amphibious. He listened to his companion tonight, while he smoked his last pipe,

he watched her through her demonstration, quite as if he had paid a shilling. But it was true that, this being the case, he desired the value of his money. What was it, in the name of wonder, that she was so bent on being responsible *for*? (vol. 23, p. 65).

Not only does Fanny Assingham function in an element quite alien to that of her husband – that of the interpretation of signs – but she is watched as she does so; it is in itself a performance which renders her on display, which in itself signifies a kind of feminine mode (being responsible for) that is accessible voyeuristically to the (money-controlling) male.

As Amerigo senses with regard to Charlotte, this condition of being seen renders women vulnerable, doubly so as they, defined through observed behaviour, have no existence beyond it. Amerigo's observable value is finite – beyond it he can look out for the chance to do something for himself, bu Charlotte's whole existence is social, involves representation and performance. As such, it necessitates attitude and display and thus a form of transparency – ultimately she will display some sign if she is only watched long enough:

> Once more, as a man conscious of having known many women, he could assist, as he would have called it, at the recurrent, the predestined phenomenon, the thing always as certain as sunrise or the coming round of saints' days, the doing by the woman of the thing that gave her away. She did it, ever, inevitably, infallibly – she couldn't possibly not do it. It was her nature, it was her life, and the man could always expect it without lifting a finger. This was *his*, the man's, any man's, position and strength – that he had necessarily the advantage, that he only had to wait (vol. 23, p. 49).

Amerigo's power lies in his necessity as a man to women, and in their rendering up to him in recognition of that power the reading, the significations of the representative world they form and reform. He has only to wait. Maggie outwaits him – she does not discard the representative so much as obscure it and keep the key to the code to herself. She thus transforms herself from helpless other to a controlling other through the (concealed) acquirement of consciousness. This obscuring process is prepared for by the Prince's sense of the Americans as impenetrable, and his experience of them as being analogous to Poe's *The Narrative of Arthur Gordon Pym of Nantucket*. Amerigo is aware of being potentially out of his depth in the plane of meaning signified by Adam, through Maggie, in a way that he will never be with Charlotte. Once more, the commercial, aesthetic and moral coincide, fuse, and remain distinct. Not only do the Americans possess money power they hint at moral power, and it is in this realm that Maggie can outwit and outwait – referring to an alien code until Amerigo gives up the attempt to recognise it. Throughout the first half, throughout his book, we are reminded that he still doesn't understand the Ververs. Of course at this stage it doesn't matter, the basic import of the representational world surrounding him tells him not to worry: 'He [Amerigo] liked all signs that things were well, but he cared rather less *why* they were (vol. 23, pp. 138–9). When the situation changes, Amerigo's inability to interpret will be forced into prominence by the effort that constitutes Maggie's growth into selfhood – her refusal to explain.

At this stage, however, Amerigo's relation to Charlotte and Maggie is defined in terms of imbalance: in his favour. He is an art-object to Adam, Charlotte and Maggie are art-objects to him. But he possesses them not through money but through male sexuality. The note of this sexuality is ownership: 'But it was, strangely, as a cluster of possessions of his own that these things in Charlotte Stant now affected him' (vol. 23, p. 46).

She is a Florentine sculpture, an intricate working model, she has:

a likeness also to some long loose silk purse, well filled with gold-pieces, but having been passed empty through a finger-ring that held it together. It was as if, before she turned to him, he had weighed the whole thing in his open palm and even heard a little the chink of the metal (vol. 23, p. 47).

The ensuing chapters in which Charlotte and Amerigo hunt for Maggie's wedding present, and the Golden Bowl is introduced, continue the note of possession and imbalance. Charlotte wants some kind of relationship *to* Amerigo – he is anxious for the social harmony to be maintained at least cost and trouble at all:

He might get on with things as they were, but he must do anything rather than magnify. Besides which it was pitiful to make her beg of him. He *was* making her – she had begged; and this, for a special sensibility in him, didn't at all do (vol. 23, p. 93).

what she asked was little compared to what she gave (vol. 23, p. 95).

Charlotte stresses that what she does ask is not simply to have her hour with Amerigo, but for him to understand, to hear – to be aware and see what she is doing and sacrificing. Amerigo watches her 'demonstration' politely and breathes a sigh of relief to be 'let off' any further performance. This sense that it is she who creates and represents their relationship is reinforced when they arrive at the shop in Bloomsbury and he tries to buy her a present. She says:

'A ricordo from you – from you to me – is a ricordo of nothing. It has no reference'.

'You don't refer, she went on to her companion. '*I* refer' (vol. 23, pp. 108–9).

In the discussion that follows about the bowl – its purity, its beauty and its possible flaw – Charlotte ponders and considers, whereas Amerigo simply sees the bowl and responds instinctively. The signs are there, and he senses danger, withdrawing, unconcerned to follow them further: 'one does know. *I* do at least – and by instinct. I don't fail. That will always protect me' (vol. 23, p. 120).

Amerigo, in fact, doesn't operate on a general or symbolic level at all; he lives according to event and action and responds to the signs surrounding him at any one time without pursuing it further. Adam Verver reflects:

It came back . . . to his own previous perception – that of the Prince's inability, in any matter in which he was concerned, to *conclude*. The idiosyncracy, for him, at each stage, had to be demonstrated – on which, however, he admirably accepted it (vol. 23, pp, 157–8).

At first glance, this is almost a reversal of a story like *Dasiy Miller*, where Daisy represented and Winterbourne attempted to interpret. But in fact here the women represent as well as interpret – and depend utterly on their relation to those for whom they interpret. Their function is to mediate experience for those in control; to order either by representation, or by arranging existing appearances and making sense of them.

Amerigo's controlled, civilised, quasi-brutality in his relations to women is in explicit contrast to the way he is being controlled, treated as other by Adam Verver. He is 'a pure and perfect crystal'. It pleases Adam that there is apparently an absence of 'friction upon Amerigo's character as a representative precious object' (vol. 23, p. 140). Transposed as object within the Verver's world, Amerigo is become 'a domesticated lamb tied up with pink ribbon' (vol. 23, p. 161).

At the same time, Amerigo is already bored, restless for his own world and his home. Several times it is stressed how the Prince has absolutely nothing to do. As man, he cannot transpose himself in marriage, to represent to another culture the precious object of European history. The danger looming in this incomplete transaction, whereby Maggie is still representative of the Ververs, and Amerigo an addition, is figured in the nature of the relation that Maggie *does* have personally to her husband: that of her identification and subjection as a woman to him as a man (the signification of national and aesthetic values disappearing):

> She never admired him so much, or so found him heart-breakingly handsome, clever, irresistible, in the very degree in which he had originally and fatally dawned upon her, as when she saw other women reduced to the same passive pulp that had then begun, once for all, to constitute *her* substance (vol. 23, p. 165).

In contrast, Adam Verver is a source of power – a forge, a cloud. He owns everything, he can observe and look. Impressions exist for him, whether they are of beautiful museum pieces or of his daughter's capacity for love and tenderness:

> His freedom to see – what could it do but steadily grow and grow? It came perhaps even too much to stand to him for *all* freedom (vol. 23, p. 150).

What he sees however is his business, we never know and neither do the other characters in the novel. He is no interpreter, he exists of and for himself, and his fears and responsibilities are those of one who controls others: 'he . . . feared, hauntedly, himself . . . to say No – he lived in terror of having to' (vol. 23, p. 133).

Adam's relation to Maggie is undoubtedly one of intimacy – they protect each other instinctively and unquestioningly. She is mother, wife and daughter to him (continually stressing how 'young' he is). The change that they have both resisted is their separation out into distinct people:

> They had had fears together, just as they had had joys, but all of hers at least had been for what equally concerned them. Here of a sudden was a question that concerned him alone, and the soundless explosion of it somehow marked a date (vol. 23, p. 154).

No longer represented in exclusiveness by Maggie, there is now a gap in Adam's existence, his personal private precinct which others will try to fill. Maggie and Adam try to convert their social relations into variants of their relationship with each other, to augment rather than to exchange – so with Amerigo, and so with the baby:

> It was of course an old story and a familiar idea that a beautiful baby could take its place as a new link between a wife and husband, but Maggie and her father had, with every ingenuity converted the precious creature into a link between a mamma and a grandpapa (vol. 23, p. 156).

Their love and intimacy is not that of two separate selves, it is the indissolvable and unspoken bond of mother and child before absence has been accepted or undergone. The Ververs' helplessness in their felicity is threatened by the demands of social existence which necessitate exchange and re-bonding with others. They attempt to let this process take place by proxy, through possessing Amerigo and then Charlotte and being represented by them to the external world. Maggie can arrange this for her father, but it is not she who controls it. Charlotte and Amerigo perform for him, he pays them. The social world flourishes on exchange, here the old world with its concomitant values of history, art and tradition exchanges with the new and its values of timelessness, wealth and individualism. On each side, a woman is exchanged – yet the man is unwilling really to part with her, she is unwilling to go. In result the excess power signified by Adam Verver's wealth absorbs the whole set of incomplete transactions, controlling all and rendering the old world self, in Amerigo, sign and therefore alienated. In leaving her father to go completely to her husband Maggie finally restores Amerigo's masculinity and re-establishes the basis for social order. The shattering of social harmony that precipitates this move also shatters her innocence, her one-ness with her father and the enclosed world she inhabits. In taking upon herself the function of restoration, of pretence, fiction and representation she denies her authentic self, yet asserts enormous power through the image she projects. The process of assertion constitutes her development of an authentic self, however concealed and mystified it must ultimately be.

Once Adam has collected Charlotte, simultaneously collecting some antique tiles in Brighton, then Amerigo, together with Charlotte, assumes a more obviously passive and dependent position, one which the two stress to the extent of irony and concealed impatience. As Charlotte explains to Fanny, it is largely a question of accepting decorum, of representing a 'situation' and of losing the liberty to act as oneself:

'Your situation's perfect,' Mrs Assingham presently declared.
'I don't say it isn't. Taken in fact all round I think it is. And I don't, as I tell you, complain of it. The only thing is that I have to act as it demands of me . . . Isn't it acting, my dear, to accept it?' (vol. 23, p. 261).

She has just explained how she and the Prince know their place, how Maggie 'likes to arrange', and how she, Charlotte, follows suit: 'Certainly I have to arrange' (vol. 23, p. 259). But because Maggie arranges still for Adam, Charlotte, the implication runs, must arrange for Amerigo.

The dissatisfaction which Charlotte can express to Fanny – that she is not really a wife to Adam, that her loss of liberty is not compensated for by a satisfactory function – is echoed by Amerigo. His obligation, in terms of his heritage, to Adam's wealth, is forcing him more and more to the passive feminine status of Charlotte. He is 'paying' his debt with object (abject) behaviour:

it had been up to now her [Fanny's] conviction that his idea was to behave beautifully enough to make the beauty well nigh an equivalent. And that he had carried out his idea, carried it out by continuing *to lead the life, to breathe the air, very nearly to think the thoughts*, that best suited his wife and her father . . . His acknowledgement of obligation was far from unimportant, but she could find in his grasp of the real itself a kind of ominous intimation. The intimation appeared to peep at her even out of his next word, lightly as he produced it. 'Isn't it rather as if we had, Charlotte and I, for bringing us together, a benefactor in common?' (vol. 23, pp. 268–9). (my emphasis).

The ominous intimation is clear enough: the Prince and Charlotte can justify their being thrown together to the extent of using it as a form of assertion against the distorted balance of their situation. For Amerigo, it is the way to exert subject existence against Adam's control – to escape periodically and to take Charlotte with him. He has explained to Fanny that while Charlotte is 'naturally in Mr Verver's boat':

am *I* not in Mr Verver's boat too? . . . The 'boat', you see . . . is a good deal tied up at the dock, or anchored, if you like, out in the stream. I have to jump out from time to time to stretch my legs, and you'll probably perceive, if you give it your attention, that Charlotte really can't help doing occasionally the same. It isn't even a question, sometimes, of one's getting to the dock – one has to take a header and splash about in the water (vol. 23, p. 270).

Apart from the sexual innuendo, furthered in Fanny's guessing at a 'suggested wink' from Amerigo, the notion of Adam's 'boat' is linked with other appearances of the same idea of boats, coaches and trains. The conveyance – whatever it is – is owned and controlled by someone, it represents territory. Maggie still occupies Adam's territory, she sits in his coach while Amerigo and Charlotte push it. Sexually, she already occupies Amerigo's territory, and one of her great acts of resistance takes place as they go home in a coach. Maggie, like Charlotte and Amerigo, acts by jumping out of her father's coach – eventually to jump in again, but to Amerigo's and not Adam's conveyance. The use of transport rather than houses to signify this idea of territory emphasises the notion of time inherent in each situation. Situations develop and change, and control over active changing life rests largely in the hands of those driving. Amerigo has his own boat in the early description of his drifting towards the terrifying whiteness of the Pole, like Arthur Gordon Pym, but his little craft – his firm ground of selfhood over which he has control – has been taken over and subsumed into the larger craft of Adam Verver. Maggie and Charlotte, as women, must look to be taken aboard somebody else's boat or coach, and the images of flight suggest an escape from control or a search for a new relation. Right at the end of the novel, Maggie reflects on the extent to which she has had to travel over to Amerigo's territory – and that he *has* territory. The recognition that she hasn't goes far beyond her signifying America, for she realises that *her* only territory is that of the fundamental passions.

Amerigo begins to rebel through the re-valuation of functions. Charlotte, who controls the foursome's social relations and takes on the act of representation at large achieves a wider and more reverberative signification. Maggie, in contrast, diminishes almost to a cliché of the feminine – not expressing through any signifying function anything particular to herself, so that Amerigo sees in her an:

> approximation, finally . . . to the transmitted images of rather neutral and negative propriety that made up, in his long line, the average of wifehood and motherhood (vol. 23, p. 322).

Reverting to his world, through Charlotte, who 'does the worldly' for Maggie and Adam (rather than acquiring the new world through Maggie) Amerigo can now regard the Ververs as 'good children'. The innocence of the Ververs is a quality necessary to the anchoring of social relations, yet also to be resented. Maggie (as vicarious good conscience to Amerigo) is totally inadequate at this stage, because she does not really represent him – her innocence has no relation to his social existence. His going about with Charlotte in a state of childlike innocence, 'the state of our primitive parents before the fall', is the climax of his being made to represent the Ververs and all they signify. Amerigo resents and destroys this signification, asserting, through his acquisition of Charlotte on his terms, his male subjecthood, his right to be represented.

At Matcham, Amerigo begins to feel his power again, most directly through his effect on women – not just Charlotte:

> he had after all gained more from women than he had ever lost by them . . . What were they doing at this very moment, wonderful creatures, but trying to outdo each other in his interest – from Maggie herself, most wonderful, in her way of all, to his hostess of the present hour . . . All of which besides, in

Lady Castledean as in Maggie, in Fanny Assingham as in
Charlotte herself, was working for him without provocation or
pressure (vol. 23, pp. 350–1).

Strolling on the terrace, waiting for Charlotte, Amerigo reflects that
what makes the day so lovely: 'was his extraordinarily unchallenged, his absolutely appointed and enhanced possession of it'
(vol. 23, p. 350). His good humour can survive even a reminder of:

> how . . . as an outsider, a foreigner, and even as a mere
> representative husband and son-in-law, he was so irrelevant to
> the working of affairs that he could be bent on occasion to uses
> comparatively trivial (vol. 23, p. 352).

Amerigo can detach himself now, in the moment of regaining
himself, can ponder the vagaries of the British and the blankness of
their social world in which the signs convey little or nothing to him
(without some explanation), the lack of a 'discerned relation
between a given appearance and a taken meaning' (vol. 23, p. 354).
For today: 'nothing mattered, in the relation of the enclosing scene
to his own consciousness, but its very most direct bearings' (vol. 23,
p. 355).
Charlotte is the 'same' as the Prince, she can most fully represent
his impulses. At the moment of their intimacy, it is she who puts a
form round his impulse, who arranges and articulates. And it is his
reward for having:

> given up so much, and bored himself so much; he knew why he
> had at any rate gone in, on the basis of all forms, on the basis of his
> having, in a manner sold himself . . . It had all been just in order
> that his – well, what on earth should he call it but his freedom? –
> should at present be as perfect and rounded and lustrous as some
> huge pearl. He hadn't struggled nor snatched; he was taking but
> what had been given him, the pearl dropped itself, with its
> exquisite quality and rarity, straight into his hand (vol. 23, p.
> 358).

Defined against the experience of existing as sign, as transfixed
object of value, Amerigo's freedom, his pearl, his self, is signified
now by his taking Charlotte.
Charlotte knows on every level what they're doing. Referring

back to the Golden Bowl (which Amerigo has to struggle to remember) she declares herself ready to risk the 'cracks'. On a more prosaic note, she has worked out the appearance of the day, their story and the train times home.

> He had taken it in, but there was always more and more of her.
> 'You mean you've arranged – ?'
> 'It's easy to arrange' (vol. 23, p. 360).

She has taken over, for Amerigo, the signification of their experience – even to the extent of promising in the future to be 'stupid' and not to understand, Amerigo tells Charlotte he wants to avoid 'rifts within the lute' and, at this moment, the rifts have finally been made. The basis of his relation to Adam and Maggie – his existence as a pure and perfect crystal, like the bowl, is now flawed, in the establishment of Charlotte's relation to and for him.

The immediacy of this crack reverberates to London – Maggie knows. Preparing the effect of the change, the stirring into action, Fanny tells us: 'Maggie's awake', and the long process of pretence, of arranging still further, begins. Fanny already prepares for a long siege of lying and pretending and waits for Maggie to learn to do the same, to save the social order out of her knowledge of its artificiality:

> I like the idea of Maggie audacious and impudent – learning to be so to gloss things over. She could – she even will, yet, I believe – learn it for that sacred purpose, consummately, diabolically (vol. 23, pp. 396–7).

Fanny explains, like the Greek chorus commenting now on the whole first half of the novel; she is the arranger, the interpreter for the reader. She explains how Maggie has never had Amerigo, how Charlotte has never had Adam, how, in fact, the exchange and bonding of marriage has not yet taken place. There is no question of Adam concerning himself with arranging or re-arranging to accommodate the development until he is given the 'sign' by Maggie. Maggie, as woman, bears responsibility for not seeing, understanding and representing. She must understand unhappiness, and 'Evil', in other words the polarities of experience, in order really to transfer herself to Amerigo and, now, in order really to come alive herself. She will live and be awake only by controlling the process – of artifice, of painting, of signifying. Women can exert power socially only by retaining the clues to meaning, by continually going beyond the signified to new obscurities of the signifier. Condemned to paint, to seem, their selfhood lies in their ability to do it 'consummately, diabolically'. Maggie has only just awoken to the one, let alone the other; in her determination to retain the conventional order, the appearance, she must look like a fool. By not being one she will enter the tension of female subjectivity in a male world. Nanda, Maisie, ultimately even Milly, refuse (or are unable) to play the game, to look like 'fools', however innocent or angelic. Maggie chooses to keep on playing – and her reasons for doing so are James's great concession to the power of non-intellectual passion and love.

THE PRINCESS

Naturalism characteristically deals in heroines: perhaps specifically heroines rather than female heroes. There is a long line stretching from Emma Bovary to Esther Waters and Crane's Maggie which would include examples as diverse as the Goncourts 'Woman of Paris' and Hardy's Tess. In this perspective, heroines are not so much saving consciousnesses as consecrated victims, passive sufferers of brutal process.[7]

Freed from the constraints of naturalism, Maggie Verver explores the resistance to 'brutal process' through the operations of consciousness. The opening paragraphs of 'The Princess' describe a process of alienation, actively achieved. Maggie is suddenly outside 'the situation', its bright 'beautiful but outlandish' artificiality rears up before her as a completed structure which has suddenly excluded her. Her response is a result of a new action, she had 'done . . . something she was not always doing', it is 'the fruit, positively, of recognitions and perceptions already active'. She herself has reached out her hand and made a 'difference' (vol. 24, p. 3).

In fact, Maggie realises that the pagoda has not suddenly excluded her but that she has not tried to enter before – she has suddenly discovered its exclusion. Tentative, modest, qualifying the importance of her actions Maggie now knocks for admission. Everything about the pagoda is artificial, the porcelain, the silver bells, the way in which it is 'coloured and figured and adorned' (vol. 24, p. 3). It is not only 'the' situation, it is in a sense any situation. It's a construction, an artefact in a natural world. It is: 'The pagoda in her . . . garden' – social and cultural existence in all its complexity and strangeness rising out of 'rich', fertile and innocent soil. Maggie now sees the impenetrability of the pagoda in a reversal of the way that Charlotte feared for cracks in the Golden Bowl. The bowl contains; and contains the indefinable: constituted by consciousness of, and in, relations. The pagoda excludes and hardens in shape – Maggie needs to enter it, to fill the emptiness of the particular set of social relationships that have been established at this point in the narrative. Whereas the danger to the bowl is in its form – potentially flawed – the insidious nature of the pagoda lies in its sealed emptiness. Form must be made to contain, and the contents of the bowl must be given a truer, less deceptively gilded form. Fusion will take place on a social level, however, not for Maggie the shattering of form as a challenge for a new order.

Maggie wants to enter the pagoda, to enter the social (artificial) world from the garden she and Adam have occupied for so long. The fact that the pagoda and the garden are so distinct, and that there is no door from one to the other, she understands as resulting from the false nature of the marriages. By acquiring Amerigo and, subsequently, Charlotte, the Ververs have remained in their garden and left their spouses to 'do the worldly' for them inside the pagoda. Maggie, it is worth noticing, takes the responsibility for this arrangement, and also: 'found . . . a measure of relief from the idea of having perhaps to answer for what she had done' (vol. 24, p. 5).

Woman as artist, representing in a deliberate and constructive way, interpreting and ordering – these parallels are strong throughout *The Golden Bowl*, and seem to offer a new, more alienating (yet also potentially corrupting) power or consolation for the designation as feminine that in other works threatens with exposure. Maggie grasps immediately at the consolations of creation: however strange and outlandish a child, the pagoda is hers:

> we progress from the solid block of inherited and assumed masculinity represented by the Prince to the subjective domain and dominance created for herself by The Princess.[8]

Pearson describes the novel in terms of Maggie's 'epic of a selfhood achieved', but sees that selfhood as being wrested out of its relations to the other characters, out of its definition *by* relationship at the expense *of* those relationships:

> in *The Golden Bowl*, Maggie ceases to be in any traditional sense a
> heroine, and becomes the hero of her book: her roles of daughter,
> wife, mother becomes issues and aspects of an entirely individual
> and non-generic struggle for identity.[9]

J. C. Rowe, on the other hand, sees Maggie's activity being carried
on for the other characters rather than for herself – as an assertion of
artificial social forms against real knowledge or intimacy: 'Milly's
sacrifice brings the world of Lancaster Gate to a consciousness of
itself, Maggie's power is used to restrict the imagination of others.'[10]
Maggie protects the others against intimacy, against a shared
acknowledgement of the corruption and manipulation integral to
the process of signification via which social existence is created and
maintained.

I think both these judgements are true as partial readings of the
text. Maggie's development into active consciousness does focus the
second half of the novel around her struggle as self, as assertive
subject. Yet the very form that struggle takes involves a protection
and conservation of social forms. Her 'non-generic' struggle for
social identity takes place as she searches for an entry into the
pagoda – the disharmony recognised by Maggie in the incomplete
marriages is not seized on as the flaw which can shatter them.
Instead, she seeks to repair the breach, to complete the transaction
whereby she will no longer be the blood relative, all-in-one
daughter, wife and mother to Adam, but will cross over to Amerigo
as his wife and force Charlotte to do the same and assume her
representative function solely as wife to Adam. If Maggie is to
preserve social form and take her place within it – rather than suffer
the permanent degree of privileged isolation accorded Maisie,
Nanda and, more tragically, Milly – she has to function in recognisable forms, speak understandable language. The fact that this
involves lying and deceit reminds us of the self-assertion that is
simultaneous within this process of repair and conservation. Maggie
pretends to be a fool, she pretends to be an unchallenged and
unchallenging wife. But because Amerigo and Charlotte can
suspect that she is not these things without ever being confronted
with their suspicions, they have to wonder what she *is*. Her selfhood
is asserted through concealment, her signification is that of opacity
and mystery and she gains, if not the intimacy of being, for another,

her self, at least the attention of the Prince. He is left watching for signs, she attains centrality but as more entrenchedly feminine than ever. To put it crudely: faced with the choice of being the embodiment of uninteresting, domestic womanhood or being the mysterious feminine of the pedestal, Maggie chooses the pedestal – the transfer involves tremendous evolution of a conscious identity as self, but that is kept hidden.

But this is not described as the intellectual process it sounds. The pivot of Maggie's book, her decision to bend her new capacity for action to the maintenance of those very forms which render her object and passive, is her reason for living, her passion for Amerigo. Vanderbank, Sir Claude, Merton Densher, the civilised, intelligent and sexually attractive young men of James's later work, are all committed, one way and another, to the 'world'. They exist within a world of representation and signification which constitutes the illusion of the other, which will express them and console them. Within the world they are active and individual – the owners. For a woman to participate, she takes her place in this delicately balanced relationship, representing and arranging in return for a relation to life and experience. Nanda, Maisie and Milly all try for this relation to experienced, passionate life, but are defeated by the disparity between their function as signifiers and their selves. They can maintain the lie for other people, but finally, in relation to the loved man, insist on an intimacy that involves an acknowledgement of failure/illusion. Maggie foregoes such intimacy, maintains her illusion to the end. Even in her one confrontation with Amerigo she neither displays, nor allows display of, acknowledged distress or guilt.

The strength of Maggie's passion for Amerigo is the reason she never becomes the monster she threatens to be; it is also the reason that she is not the angelic princess that any disinterested action would also tend to make her. Her desire for the world, in Amerigo, that she is a product of, is in a way the internal honesty of a book devoted to an exploration of artifice, miscorrespondence and obscuration. Not only Amerigo and Charlotte, but the readers, are to be confused.

The depth of Maggie's innocence, her unbroken child-status signified by her effortless intimacy with Adam, is exposed by the coincidence of her awareness of the 'situation', of something wrong, and her awareness of her passion for Amerigo, for the very world that her father has so blandly assumed control of. It is the recognition at the moment of loss (disappearance) of what is:

> She had never doubted of the force of the feeling that bound her
> to her husband; but to become aware almost suddenly that it had
> begun to vibrate with a violence that had some of the effect of a
> strain would, rightly looked at, after all but show that she was,
> like thousands of women, every day, acting up to the full privilege
> of passion (vol. 24, pp. 7–8).

The extent to which this new knowledge of self constitutes action is
expressed both overtly and in implication. Maggie is a 'timid tigress'
who is learning the potential of her power:

> she was no longer playing with blunt and idle tools, with weapons
> that didn't cut. There passed across her vision ten times a day the
> gleam of a bare blade. (vol. 24, p. 9).

She starts to watch, to look, to see – all active processes in contrast to
being watched, being seen. And by the smallest acts she in turn is
seen as sharply different, as suggesting change – she is 'within' and
has to work simultaneously with her own struggling consciousness
and with its reception. When Amerigo returns home to find her
unexpectedly waiting for him there, he is alerted to look for some
sign:

> she had felt overwhelmingly that she was significant, that so she
> must instantly strike him, and that this had a kind of violence
> beyond what she had intended (vol. 24, pp. 15–6).

The power Maggie has as seer resides in the possibilities of being
seen.

The direction of any action is uncertain at first. Maggie sees how
she has remained in her father's territory, and how Amerigo and
Charlotte have been coopted together to maintain their world:

> She might have been watching the family coach pass and noting
> that somehow Amerigo and Charlotte were pulling it while she
> and her father were not so much as pushing . . . Maggie found in
> this image a repeated challenge; again and yet again she paused
> before the fire: after which, each time, in the manner of one for
> whom a strong light has suddenly broken, she gave herself to

livelier movement. She had seen herself at last, in the picture she was studying, suddenly jump from the coach. (vol. 24, pp. 23–4).

In a characteristic fireside meditation, Maggie rejects the present situation; as she is looking for a new direction the door opens and Amerigo comes in. But the ensuing effort is not only towards regaining Amerigo without exposing too intimately what is happening (and thus managing to keep his love) but towards maintaining Adam Verver's privileged distance from the reality of the world he controls. Maggie's strongest source of power is the dependence of them all, as social and material beings in the existing world, on Adam's benevolence. To expose her knowledge to Amerigo would be destructive enough, to expose it to Adam would be to expose the basis of his power, his collecting, his taste, and the false relation of all these to their objects.

Maggie doesn't formulate it like this, of course, she simply accepts the maintenance of convention through the conventional function of 'arranging' for Adam. In return he will do as she wants and give her up. But her function as representative of Adam – until she hands it over fully to Charlotte – gives her the incredible manipulative ability that Fanny recoils from in such horror:

> Her tone might by this time have shown a strangeness to match her smile; which was still more marked as she wound up. 'And that's how I make them do what I like!'
> It had an effect on Mrs Assingham . . .
> 'My dear child, you're amazing.'
> 'Amazing?'
> 'You're terrible' (vol. 24, p. 115).

Maggie denies this with her threefold assertion 'For love', eluding Fanny's questions about the object of that love. Yet however motivated Maggie is by love, by her desire to keep Amerigo and protect the world of her father, there is excitement for her in learning to 'make them do what I like'.

Going to visit Charlotte after her first confrontation with the Prince, Maggie is intensely aware that she has sprung into: 'action quite positively for the first time in her life, or, counting in the previous afternoon, for the second' (vol. 24, p. 33).

She reflects that Charlotte and Amerigo 'treat' her 'beautifully', that they pander to her and protect her, immersing her in a 'bath of benevolence':

> Baths of benevolence were very well, but, at least, unless one were a patient of some sort, a nervous eccentric or a lost child, one was usually not so immersed save by one's request. It wasn't in the least what *she* had requested. She had flapped her little wings as a symbol of desired flight, not merely as a plea for a more gilded cage and an extra allowance of lumps of sugar (vol. 24, p. 44).

The protection Maggie is so smothered by is both a sign of something to be protected from and an indication of the repression of freedom necessary in a society founded on appearance and arrangement, the world that now gives Maggie: 'The sense of a life tremendously ordered and fixed' (vol. 24, p. 66).

Although Maggie is struggling free of her particular golden cage, Charlotte is being locked further into hers, and the final images of her are of a savage repression necessary to harness her power to social ends.

Maggie seems at times to exalt in her new power of action and of violence. However painful her discoveries, however strong her desire to submit to Amerigo, to remake the world in its old image, she discovers at the same time the pleasure of control and power. James uses words of violence and extremity again and again to describe Maggie's consciousness: the sheer importance of what is happening is stressed by the language. In a return to a familiar idea the haunted becomes the haunter, Maggie is gadfly and hunter. She discovers the power of mystification, of appearing different to one's apparent significations, of suggesting new departures and unexplained actions. Before now her signification, her worth, could be accurately and obviously assessed like that of an expensive doll:

> I cost originally a great deal of money: cost, that is, my father, for my outfit, and let in my husband for an amount of pains – toward my training – that money would scarce represent (vol. 24, p. 51).

Now she is trembling with the excitement of new knowledge and the superior advantage it gives her:

> She didn't yet wholly see . . . quite how she herself should handle them; but she was dancing up and down, beneath her propriety, with the thought that she had at least begun something – she so

> fairly liked to feel that *she was a point for convergance of wonder*. It
> wasn't after all that *their* wonder so much signified – that of the
> cornered six *whom it glimmered before her that she might still live to drive
> about like a flock of sheep*: the intensity of her consciousness . . . was
> in the theory of her having . . . captured, the attention of
> Amerigo and Charlotte (vol. 24, pp. 51–2). (my emphasis).

Maggie's gradual assertion of her self puts her into a different
position socially, whether it is her ability to manipulate her dinner
guests or her ability now to demand in turn a certain amount of
representation. The hierarchy places everyone according to their
various attributes, and Maggie's deference to the fundamental fixed
status of her father and her husband nonetheless forces her to be
powerful and ruthless with the more flexible and dependent women
in the game. Thus Maggie sees Fanny Assingham as someone who
can help her arrange appearances:

> Our young woman's idea . . . was that her safety . . . would
> proceed from this friend's power to cover, to protect . . . even
> showily to represent her . . . (vol. 24, p. 100).

> Maggie, who had no small self at all as against her husband or her
> father and only a weak and uncertain one as against her
> stepmother, would verily at this crisis have seen Mrs Assingham's
> personal life or liberty sacrificed without a pang (vol. 24, p. 101).

The more central each person is to her, the more difficult the act of
resistance and control. As Maggie learns to pit herself against others,
she experiences not only power and love, but also pity. She doesn't
want to pity either Amerigo or her father, the harmony of the social
order rests on their strength, in the end she strives to protect them
from the need for pity, and in doing so realises the extent to which
Charlotte, all women, must suffer for it.

Having given in so luxuriously to Amerigo's sexual power, the
night of his return from Gloucester, Maggie now begins a time of
resistance to it. Sexuality here is an expression of the relation of the
struggling female self to the pleasure of the appropriating world, the
sensuality of being dissolved and taken over, and relinquishing all
consciousness and responsibility for self:

> It was for hours and hours later on as if she had somehow been
> lifted aloft, were floated and carried on some warm high tide

beneath which stumbling blocks had sunk out of sight (vol. 24, p. 25).

He had been right . . . as to the felicity of his tenderness and the degree of her sensibility, but even while she felt these things sweep all others away she tasted of a sort of terror of the weakness they produced in her (vol. 24, p. 29).

Later Maggie refuses to give way, she makes the greatest effort of her life to refuse Amerigo what he wants in order, at this point, simply to *know*:

What her husband's grasp really meant, as her very bones registered, was that she *should* give it up [her advantage]: it was exactly for this that he had resorted to unfailing magic. He *knew how* to resort to it . . . She should have but to lay her head back on his shoulder with a certain movement to make it definite for him that she didn't resist. To this as they went every throb of her consciousness prompted her – every throb, that is, but one, the throb of her deeper need to know where she 'really' was (vol. 24, pp. 56–7).

Maggie longs for the freedom to submit again – right at the end she luxuriates in the nearness of her goal:

He was so near now that she could touch him, taste him, smell him, kiss him, hold him; he almost pressed upon her, and the warmth of his face . . . was bent upon her with the largeness with which objects loom in dreams . . . Then it was that from behind her closed eyes the right word came. 'Wait' (vol. 24, p. 352).

It is as though her great assumption of active consciousness is assumed in order to restore balance, and then to be relinquished again as far as it can be. Certainly in Maggie's final scenes with Amerigo she dreads any explanation, any discussion – any change in their relationship into an intimacy of knowledge rather than an intimacy of sensual possession.

Maggie retains the divisions so that she and Charlotte as women 'arrange' in their different ways; Amerigo's attempt to explain, to participate, to do anything but be, and watch Maggie, would destroy the masculine status that is the source of his powerful attraction for Maggie. Maggie even feels collusion with Charlotte by the end, that the two of them have striven to make appearances anew, to signify new balances and harmonies out of the fear and repression they both experience – and that any offort to confront will shatter those efforts:

> But what instantly rose for her between the act and her acceptance was the sense that she must strike him as waiting for a confession. This in turn charged her with a new horror: if *that* was her proper payment she would go without money. His acknowledgement hung there, too monstrously, at the expense of Charlotte, before whose mastery of the greater style she had just been standing dazzled. All she now knew accordingly was that she should be ashamed to listen to the uttered word (vol. 24, p. 368).

Maggie's fear that Amerigo will make a wrong move comes from her recognition that she achieved her new power as image for him by baffling him. She has taken up her function as representer for him, as signifier, in his world, of a series of values which leave him at sea, which go far beyond his own 'touchstone of taste':

> She mystified him . . . she recognised again in the light of it the number of the ideas of which he thought her capable. They were all apparently queer for him, but she had at least with the lapse of the months *created the perception* that there might be something in them; whereby he stared there, beautiful and sombre, at what she was at present providing him with (vol. 24, p. 344). (my emphasis).

Charlotte's 'mastery of the greater style', her power to represent and signify on a scale wider and more successful than Maggie, is what Maggie relies on to save Charlotte. Her fear of Charlotte as a rival comes from this greater expertise in the arts of representation (dress, 'socialising') but her final gamble rests on a dependence that Charlotte will stick to the creation through style that justifies, quite literally, her existence. The two meetings between Charlotte and Maggie have a deliberate formality of style all their own. On the terrace, Maggie waits while Charlotte comes out to her, in the garden Charlotte waits while Maggie comes to her. They carefully and deliberately allow the other to lie, and formally, publicly, declare allegiance to their social marriages, to the existence of social propriety, and seal it with a witnessed kiss:

'It's much more, my dear, than I dreamed of asking. I only
wanted your denial.'
'Well then you have it.'
'Upon your honour?'
'Upon my honour.'

She saw it in Charlotte's face and felt it make between them, in the
air, a chill that completed the coldness of their conscious perjury.
'Will you kiss me on it then?'

Her husband and her father were in front, and Charlotte's
embrace of her – which wasn't to be distinguished for them,
either, she felt, from her embrace of Charlotte – took on with their
arrival a high publicity (vol. 24, pp. 251–2).

The two women demand a high level of style successfully to uphold
the new structure they are building. As the process of signification is
central to social existence, at moments of tension it must be
performed with a ritualised perfection and artifice in order to stand
up to the threat of honesty and unadorned meaning:

She [Maggie] was ready to lie again if her companion would but
give her the opening. Then she should know she had done all.
Charlotte looked at her hard, as if to compare her face with her
note of resentment; and Maggie, feeling this, met it with the signs
of an impression that might pass for the impression of defeat (vol.
24, p. 316).

In between the two scenes that Charlotte and Maggie play out, is
Maggie's return to the garden with Adam to complete *their*
transaction in the allotted form.

Although Maggie has understood how she must relinquish her tie
with her father in order to go fully to Amerigo's world, she is 'of'
Adam, she represents him in the fullest sense, and it is this that she is
finally taking to Amerigo. But Adam remains (for her, and for the
world of the novel) the most powerful owner. The world is his by
right of wealth – he 'gives up' Maggie to Amerigo, consenting fully
to 'take' Charlotte in exchange. Right to the end Amerigo and
Charlotte remain, for him, possessions: his concession to the integrity
of Amerigo's world, his territory, is made by the substance he has
imparted to it by the gift of his daughter.

Maggie's fear with her father is rather like her fear with Amerigo – that he will be unequal to the signifying process that exists for his benefit. The real betrayal would be: 'The day you've ceased to believe in me' (vol. 24, p. 272), as Adam says.

By believing in his qualities as worth representing, worth trusting to, Maggie can see both of them through. She sees how:

> His very quietness was part of it now, as always part of everything, of his success, his originality, his modesty, his exquisite public perversity, his inscrutable, incalculable energy (vol. 24, p. 273).

Inscrutable and incalculable are what Adam remains. His bland surface, his quiet unemphasised ownership lurk in the background of the crisis. His sacrifice, his final giving up of Maggie, are what she has to depend on – that he will fulfill the act necessary to the appearance she – and Charlotte – have created. In this sense, Adam has the final power over Maggie, she gains her vindication through him, her creation is validated by him:

> The sense that he wasn't a failure, and could never be, purged their predicament of every meanness . . . It was like a new confidence, and after another instant she knew even still better why. Wasn't it because now also, on his side, he was thinking of her as his daughter, was *trying* her, during those mute seconds, as the child of his blood . . . It swelled in her fairly; it raised her higher, higher: she wasn't in that case a failure either – hadn't been, but the contrary; his strength was her strength, her pride was his, and they were decent and competent together. This was all in the answer she finally made him.

'I believe in you more than anyone' (vol. 24, pp. 274–5).

But Maggie's function as her father's child, as the signifier of the success and harmony of his appropriation of the world, still relies on the *unspoken*, on their pretending, even knowledgeably, to each other. The fear of himself that for Adam, as total subject, is the only fear he is prey to, can be kept at bay only by the signification of himself performed by Maggie, and now by Charlotte. Relinquishing Maggie, Adam possesses Charlotte in a new manner, the repression of an existence defined by acquiescence to 'convention', in its purest sense, is brilliantly manifested in Maggie's understanding of

Charlotte's defeat:

> Charlotte hung behind . . . she stopped when her husband
> stopped . . . and the likeness of their connexion would not have
> been wrongly figured if he had been thought of as holding in one
> of his pocketed hands the end of a long silken halter looped round
> her beautiful neck. He didn't twitch it, yet it was there; he didn't
> drag her, but she came (vol. 24, p. 287).

> The high voice went on; its quaver was doubtless for conscious
> ears only, but there were verily thirty seconds during which it
> sounded, for our young woman, like the shriek of a soul in pain.
> Kept up a minute longer it would break and collapse – so that
> Maggie felt herself, the next thing, turn with a start to her father.
> 'Can't she be stopped? Hasn't she done it *enough*?' (vol. 24, p. 292).

When Maggie speaks from the depth of her remembered experience:
'I see it's *always* terrible for women', the Prince's response could be
read as an agreemènt, for the terrible itself emerges from the endless
deployment of power and possession practised: 'Everything's terrible, cara – in the heart of man' (vol. 24, p. 349).

Amerigo abandons Charlotte totally, and fixes in all intensity on
the mystifying image of his American wife. She will now lead him
through the world of meaning in the way that he originally
depended for on Fanny and Charlotte. Adam can go back to the
American city in all his terrifying anonymity with Charlotte to
enhance and crown his collection – that which represents the fruit of
his sight.

In *What Maisie Knew* and *The Awkward Age*, James presents the
momentary loss of signification, itself an illusion residing in the
language of the novel. Maisie, by refusing simply to be disposed of
as an innocent child; Nanda, by insisting on her goodness and
badness, her individuality; even Milly, by failing to maintain her
dovelike illusion and turning her face to the wall; all three expose the
gap between signifier and signified, the illusion of the social world
and of the other beyond the self. The ensuing communication, face
to face, subject to subject, results in a fear of self – the fear that results
when:

> To accept woman as one of us, to give up her mystification,
> alternately exaltation and suppression, is to recognise and accept
> that we are, in our world, alone.[11]

Maisie and Sir Claude know that: 'If they were afraid of themselves it was themselves they would find at the inn' (vol. 22, p. 342).

Maisie conquers that fear and isolation, Sir Claude does not, and she loses him. Nanda has to accept Van's abject fear of himself in relation to her lucidity and honesty, and to accept that it is only with Mr Longdon, another inhabiter of the social fringes of loss and renunciation, that she will be able to communicate:

> unable to pretend, to play any part, and with something in her that she couldn't take back now, something involved in her original assumption that there was to be a kind of intelligence in their relation (vol. 9, p. 229).

Milly is destroyed in the process of trying to protect Merton from himself – and in failing, confronts him with knowledge he cannot accept without further, desperate mystification, so that it is left to Kate to say: 'Your attitude, my dear, is that you're afraid of yourself . . . You've had to do yourself violence' (vol. 20, p. 386).

Maggie finds herself alone, and conquers that fear. At the moment she could most possibly confront Amerigo with the ugliness, the lack of correspondence between their selves and their appearance, she determines to protect him. She doesn't want to see Amerigo's fear, to rob him of that superiority which makes him so much the centre of her life:

> she knew once more the strangeness of her desire to spare him . . . It was extraordinary, this quality in the taste of her wrong which made her completed sense of it seem rather to soften than to harden . . . she felt, within her the sudden split between conviction and action (vol. 24, pp. 285–6).

Maggie chooses not to follow through her knowledge, not to share the fruits of her own hardly-won consciousness. By continuing to function as obscurer, as signifier of order while standing in front of the smashed bowl, the evidence of her power to withdraw that function, she confronts the Prince not with her subjecthood, but with his dependence on her objecthood as his wife. She knows that now he will 'be *really* needing her for the first time in their whole connexion' (vol. 24, p. 186). In order to keep his love in the form in which it has potency, she chooses to maintain the structures of objectification and taste the power implicit for the manipulated when the structures themselves become indispensable. The full weight of that responsibility – for the helplessness of Charlotte, the compulsion for ever to lie, the distortion of herself into a sign that fills the Prince's sight – culminates in Amerigo's obsession with Maggie as vision:

'See? I see nothing but *you*.'
And the truth of it had with this force after a moment so strangely lighted his eyes that as for pity and dread of them she buried her own in his breast (vol. 24, p. 367).

There are no happy marriages for James's major heroines – until the 'pity and dread' of Maggie and Amerigo's union. Yet even here woman as conscious subject is left in a position of alienation and confinement, and yet also of responsibility and control. The heroines of James's later novels acquire subjectivity through a recognition of their function as sign and the burden of representation. We see them come to an awareness of what they are for others; Isabel Archer meditating by the fire is joined by Kate Croy, Maisie's bewildered interpretation of herself as a culpable object in a complex adult game is echoed by Milly's sudden awareness that '*That* was what was the matter with her. She was a dove' (vol. 19, p. 283). This feminine subjectivity takes into account a perpetual tension between self as other, between being defined as sign and yet attempting to assert subjectivity through multiplication and mystification of the signified, thus focussing attention back to the signifier. Woman as consciousness thus continually takes in both sides, perception of the world and also of her place in and for it. As James's heroines attempt to act for themselves within a world which consistently appropriates them as carriers of meaning, as legitimate objects of control, they are present as both object and subject of the text. The tension between the two perspectives is articulated in the exposure of the social construction of the woman as sign.

Within the range of his fiction, James does locate sources of oppression and restriction within the economic and social spheres; the factors of money, class, education, employment, the legal restrictions of marriage, are all at some point raised and affirmed *as* problems. But it is only in each individual's world of subjectivity, language and personal communication, that James can suggest the possibility of action and resistance. And yet that action and resistance through consciousness, by the women in these later novels, is written about as a process sustained with such passionate effort that it communicates a conviction of its importance. Seen in the light of the overall situation of women in the nineteenth (and twentieth) century it may not be enough, but it seems to me that a major constituent of women's control and oppression – denial of primary subjecthood; existing 'for' ourselves – has been recognised and confronted.

Notes and References

INTRODUCTION

1. J. Williamson, *Decoding Advertisements* (London, 1978) p. 17.
2. See C. Lévi-Strauss, 'Introduction a l'oeuvre de Marcel Mauss', in M. Mauss, *Sociologie et Anthropologie* (Paris, 1950) p. xix.
3. C. Lévi-Strauss, *The Elementary Structures of Kinship*, trans. J. Harle Bell, J. R. von Sturmer and R. Needham (London, 1969) p. 496.
4. R. W. Emerson, Nature, in *Nature, Addresses and Lectures* (London, 1903) p. 78.
5. S. de Beauvoir, *The Second Sex*, trans. H. M. Parshley (Harmondsworth, 1974) pp. 172-3.
6. Ibid, p. 626.
7. A contemporary example of this is the freedom from reproductive sexuality which modern birth control methods have begun to give to women and the subsequent conflict in the ideology of woman's role; I shall discuss it in Chapter 1 with regard to the ideal of the American girl.
8. S. de Beauvoir, *The Second Sex*, p. 218.
9. J. Mitchell, *Psychoanalysis and Feminism* (Harmondsworth, 1975) p. 405.
10. J. Fryer, *The Faces of Eve: Women in the Nineteenth-century American Novel* (New York, 1976).
11. M. Ellman, *Thinking About Women* (London, 1979).
12. J. Goode, 'Sue Bridehead and the New Woman', in M. Jacobus (ed.), *Women Writing and Writing about Women* (New York, 1979) p. 102.
13. J. Fetterley, *The Resisting Reader: A Feminist Approach to American Fiction* (Bloomington, 1978).
14. J. Piaget, *The Origin of Intelligence in the Child*, trans. M. Cook (London, 1953) p. 189 ff.
15. H. James, *The American Scene* (New York, 1907) p. 335.
16. Ibid, p. 415.
17. J. Berger, *Ways of Seeing* (Harmondsworth, 1972) p. 46.
18. H. James, 'Howells's "A Foregone Conclusion"', in *Literary Reviews and Essays*, A. Mordell (ed.), (New York, 1957) p. 211.

1: WOMAN IN THE NINETEENTH CENTURY

1. See B. Welter, *Dimity Convictions* (Athens, Ohio, 1976) ch. 2.
2. See J. Mitchell, *Psychoanalysis and Feminism* (Harmondsworth, 1975) pp. 410-16.
3. B. Welter, *Dimity Convictions*, p. 4.
4. L. Appignanesi, *Femininity and the Creative Imagination* (London, 1973) p. 2.

5. See S. Delamont and L. Duffin, *The Nineteenth-Century Woman* (New York, 1978), ch. 6.
6. K. Millett, *Sexual Politics* (New York, 1971) p. 89.
7. See B. Welter, *Dimity Convictions*, ch. 6.
8. M. Praz, *The Hero in Eclipse in Victorian Fiction*, trans. A. Davidson (London, 1956) p. 116.
9. C. Patmore, *The Angel in the House* (London, 1866) p. 28.
10. Ibid, p. 39.
11. Ibid, p. 85.
12. Ibid, p. 117.
13. J. S. Mill, *The Subjection of Women* (London, 1869) p. 27.
14. Ibid, p. 38.
15. N. Baym, *Woman's Fiction: A Guide to Novels By and About Women in America, 1820–1870* (Ithaca, 1978).
16. A. B. Fuller, Preface to M. Fuller, *Woman in the Nineteenth Century* (New York, 1971) p. 7.
17. *Godey's Lady's Book*, January 1878.
18. *Atlantic Monthly*, December 1873.
19. *Godey's Lady's Book*, February 1878.
20. R. W. Emerson, 'The Young American', in *Nature, Addresses and Lectures* (London, 1903) p. 366.
21. Ibid, p. 345.
22. A. de Tocqueville, *Democracy in America*, P. Bradley (ed.), trans H. Reeve, and further corrected by F. Bowen, 2 vols (New York, 1945) vol. 2, p. 214.
23. J. Bryce, *The American Commonwealth*, rev. edn, 2 vols (New York, 1910) vol. 2, p. 795.
24. R. Kipling, *American Notes* (New York, 1891) p. 28.
25. A. de Tocqueville, *Democracy in America*, vol. 2, p. 203.
26. N. Baym, 'Portrayal of Women in American Literature 1790–1870', in M. Springer (ed.) *What Manner of Woman?* (Oxford, 1978) p. 213.
27. E. Earnest, *The American Eve in Fact and Fiction* (Illinois, 1974).
28. R. W. Emerson, 'The Young American', p. 366.
29. A. de Tocqueville, *Democracy in America*, vol. 2, p. 212.
30. J. Bryce, *The American Commonwealth*, vol. 2, p. 807.
31. Ibid, vol. 2, p. 809.
32. H. James, *The American Scene* (New York, 1907) pp. 332–3.
33. D. Boorstin, *The Americans: The National Experience* (New York, 1965) p. 92.
34. A. de Tocqueville, *Democracy in America*, vol. 2, p. 198.
35. Ibid, vol. 2, p. 201.
36. J. Fenimore Cooper, *Notions of the Americans Picked up by a Travelling Bachelor*, 2 vols (New York, 1963) vol. 1, p. 193.
37. B. Welter, *Dimity Convictions*, p. 20.
38. A. de Tocqueville, *Democracy in America*, vol. 2, pp. 198–9.
39. See, for instance, R. W. Emerson, 'Nature', in *Nature, Addresses and Lectures.*
40. See, for instance, R. W. Emerson, 'The Young American', in *Nature, Addresses and Lectures.*
41. P. J. Eakin, *The New England Girl* (Athens, Georgia, 1976) p. 221.
42. M. Fuller, *Woman in the Nineteenth Century*, pp. 62–3.
43. W. D. Howells, *Heroines of Fiction*, 2 vols (London, 1901) vol. 1, p. 12.

44. Ibid, vol. 1, p. 189.
45. J. Goode, 'Woman and the Literary Text', in J. Mitchell and A. Oakley (eds), *The Rights and Wrongs of Women* (Harmondsworth, 1976), p. 218.
46. G. Allen, *The Woman Who Did* (London, 1895) p. 56.
47. Ibid, p. 18.
48. Ibid, p. 241.
49. G. Meredith, *The Egoist*, 3 vols (London, 1879) vol. 1, p. 212.
50. Ibid, vol. 1, p. 112.
51. See J. Goode, 'Woman and the Literary Text', p. 245.
52. C. G. Burke, 'Report from Paris: Women's Writing and the Women's Movement', in *Signs*, vol. 3, no. 4 (1978) p. 853.
53. J. Goode, 'Woman and the Literary Text', p. 247.
54. Ibid, p. 255.
55. See P. Thomson, *The Victorian Heroine: A Changing Ideal, 1837–1873* (London, 1956).
56. P. Rahv, 'Paleface and Redskin', in *Image and Idea*, rev. edn (London, 1957).
57. L. Fiedler, *Love and Death in the American Novel*, 2nd edn (London, 1966).
58. M. Rugoff, *Prudery and Passion: Sexuality in Victorian America* (London, 1972) p. 97.
59. W. Wasserstrom, *The Heiress of all the Ages* (Minneapolis, 1959) p. 24.
60. N. Baym, *Woman's Fiction*.
61. E. Wharton, *The Age of Innocence* (London, 1966), p. 55.
62. W. D. Howells, *The Lady of the Aroostook* (Boston, 1879), pp. 229–30.
63. E. J. Sabiston, 'The Prison of Womanhood', in *Comparative Literature* 25 (1973), p. 338.
64. H. Adams, *Esther* (New York, 1961) p. 231.
65. Ibid, p. 306.
66. P. J. Eakin, *The New England Girl*, p. 134.
67. Ibid, p. 19.

2: 'THE SCARLET LETTER'

1. N. Hawthorne, *The Scarlet Letter* (Boston, 1850), pp. 36–7.
2. Ibid, p. 37.
3. Ibid, p. 93.
4. H. James, *Hawthorne* (London, 1879), p. 112.
5. Hawthorne, *The Scarlet Letter*, p. 95.
6. Ibid, p. 320.
7. Ibid, p. 321.
8. H. James, *Hawthorne*, p. 114.

3: THE EARLY WORK

1. Q. Anderson, *The American Henry James* (London, 1958), p. 9.
2. J. C. Rowe, *Henry Adams and Henry James* (Cornell, 1976), p. 38.
3. For instance, H. James, *The Sacred Fount* (New York, 1901).

4. For instance, H. James, 'The Turn of the Screw'; 'The Jolly Corner'; in *The Complete Tales of Henry James*, L. Edel (ed.), 12 vols (London, 1962–4).

5. For instance, H. James, 'The Beast in the Jungle'; 'The Altar of the Dead'; in *The Complete Tales of Henry James*.

6. H. James, letter to T. Perry, 20 September 1867, in *Henry James's Letters*, L. Edel (ed.), (London, 1974) vol. 1, p. 77.

7. Ibid, p. 77.

8. W. D. Howells, 'Mr James's Daisy Miller', in A. Mordell (ed.), *Discovery of a Genius: William Dean Howells and Henry James* (New York, 1961) p. 181.

9. For instance, the American girls in 'Travelling Companions' (1870); 'Guest's Confession' (1872); and 'The Last of the Valerii' (1874); in *The Complete Tales of Henry James*. Also Gertrude Wentworth in *The Europeans* (London, 1878) and Bessie Alden in 'An International Episode', in *The Complete Tales of Henry James*.

10. For instance, Lizzie Acton in *The Europeans*, or the girls described in 'A Bundle of Letters' (1879) in *The Complete Tales of Henry James*. However, Daisy herself is the best example of the American girl as the innocent, blank surface.

11. See W. Veeder, *The Lessons of the Master* (Chicago, 1975) for an analysis of James's use of contemporary popular fiction.

12. With the amount of material available I have had to be selective, but of the early James not only is *Washington Square* (1881) interesting in this context, but also *Roderick Hudson* (1875). A comparison between Mary Garland, the pale, serious and moral American girl, and Christina Light as the Europeanised version, might prove comparable in some ways to aspects of *Daisy Miller* in that the polarised qualities of the two women are on display for the purpose of their effect on a man, Roderick. Christina tends to burst through the constraints of being a sign for Roderick and to be brought to our attention as herself finding her function limiting. Perhaps this is why she reappears in a later novel, *The Princess Casamassima*.

13. R. W. Butterfield, 'The American', in J. Goode (ed.), *The Air of Reality: New Essays on Henry James* (London, 1972) p. 19.

14. R. Poirier, *The Comic Sense of Henry James* (London, 1960) p. 63.

15. H. James, Preface to *Daisy Miller*, in *The Art of the Novel* (New York, 1962) p. 270.

16. Ibid, p. 270.

17. J. Goode, 'Sue Bridehead and the New Woman', M. Jacobus (ed.) *Women Writing and Writing About Women* (New York, 1979) p. 103.

18. Ibid, p. 101.

19. See R. N. Foley, *Criticism in American Periodicals of the Works of Henry James from 1866 to 1916* (Washington, 1944) and R. Gard (ed.), *Henry James: The Critical Heritage* (London, 1968).

20. P. J. Eakin, *The New England Girl* (Athens, Georgia, 1976) p. 12.

21. C. Wegelin, *The Image of Europe in Henry James* (Dallas, 1958) p. 78.

22. J. Williamson, *Decoding Advertisements* (London, 1978), p. 73.

23. See J. Fryer, 'The American Princess', in *The Faces of Eve: Women in the Nineteenth-century American Novel* (New York, 1976) for a discussion of the development from innocence to self-reliance in the American girl.

24. M. Mackenzie, *Communities of Honor and Love in Henry James* (Cambridge, Mass., 1976) p. 38.

4: 'THE PORTRAIT OF A LADY'

1. A. Kettle, from 'An Introduction to the English Novel', in W. T. Stafford (ed.), *Perspectives on James's 'The Portrait of a Lady'* (London, 1967) p. 105.
2. H. James, Preface to *The Portrait of a Lady*, in *The Art of the Novel* (New York, 1962) p. 51.
3. W. D. Howells, 'Henry James Junior', in R. Gard (ed.), *Henry James: The Critical Heritage* (London, 1968) p. 130.
4. H. A. Huntingdon, Review of *The Portrait of a Lady*, in R. Gard (ed.), *Henry James: The Critical Heritage*, p. 111.
5. Unsigned Review of *The Portrait of a Lady*, in R. Gard (ed.), *Henry James: The Critical Heritage*, pp. 98–100.
6. E. Fawcett, Review of *The Portrait of a Lady*, in R. Gard (ed.), *Henry James: The Critical Heritage*, p. 144.
7. H. E. Scudder, Review of *The Portrait of a Lady*, in R. Gard (ed.), *Henry James: The Critical Heritage*, p. 109.
8. J. Berger, *Ways of Seeing* (Harmondsworth, 1972), p. 46.
9. See E. J. Sabiston, 'The Prison of Womanhood', *Comparative Literature* 25 (1973) pp. 336–51.
10. J. Goode, 'Woman and the Literary Text', in J. Mitchell and A. Oakley (eds.), *The Rights and Wrongs of Women* (Harmondsworth, 1976) p. 230.

5: WOMEN IN THE PUBLIC WORLD: 'THE BOSTONIANS', 'THE PRINCESS CASAMASSIMA' AND 'THE TRAGIC MUSE'

1. See, for instance, L. H. Powers, *Henry James and the Naturalist Movement* (Michigan, 1971).
2. For instance Q. Anderson, *The American Henry James* (London, 1958); T. Tanner, *The Reign of Wonder* (Cambridge, 1965); J. Porte, *The Romance in America* (Middletown, 1969).
3. F. W. Dupee, *Henry James* (London, 1951) p. 149.
4. J. Fetterley, *The Resisting Reader: A Feminist Approach to American Fiction* (Bloomington, 1978), ch. on the Bostonians.
5. C. T. Samuels, *The Ambiguity of Henry James* (Urbana, 1971) p. 103.
6. H. James, *The Notebooks*, F. O. Matthieson and K. P. Murdock (eds) (Oxford, 1961) p. 47.
7. J. Fetterley, *The Resisting Reader*, p. 114.
8. See L. Edel, Introduction to A. James, *The Diary* (New York, 1964), pp. 9–11.
9. D. Howard, '*The Bostonians*', in J. Goode (ed.), *The Air of Reality: New Essays on Henry James* (London, 1972) pp. 71–2.
10. Ibid, p. 79.
11. B. Lee, *The Novels of Henry James* (London, 1978) p. 26.
12. F. W. Dupee, *Henry James*, p. 160.
13. M. Geismar, *Henry James and his Cult* (London, 1964) pp. 71–2.
14. Q. Anderson, *The American Henry James*, pp. 201–2.
15. D. J. Gordon and J. Stokes, 'The reference of *The Tragic Muse*', in J. Goode (ed.) *The Air of Reality*, p. 161.
16. R. Poirier, *The Comic Sense of Henry James* (London, 1960) p. 182.

17. H. James, Preface to *The Tragic Muse*, in *The Art of the Novel* (New York, 1962) p. 89.
18. D. J. Gordon and J. Stokes, '*The Tragic Muse*', in J. Goode (ed.) *The Air of Reality*, p. 158.
19. F. W. Dupee, *Henry James*, pp. 162–3.
20. M. Geismar, *Henry James and his Cult*, p. 104.
21. H. James, Preface to *The Tragic Muse*, p. 91.

6: THE NOVELS OF THE 1890s

1. See W. Isle, *Experiments in Form: Henry James's Novels 1896–1901* (Cambridge, Mass., 1968); L. Edel, *The Life of Henry James* (Harmondsworth, 1977).
2. H. James, *The Notebooks*, F. O. Matthieson and K. P. Murdock (eds) (Oxford, 1961) p. 129.
3. See J. Fryer, 'The Great Mother', in *The Faces of Eve: Women in the Nineteenth-century American Novel* (New York, 1976) for a discussion of older women in James.
4. H. James, Preface to *The Spoils of Poynton*, in *The Art of the Novel* (New York, 1962) p. 129.
5. Ibid, p. 130.
6. Ibid, p. 131.
7. H. James, Preface to *What Maisie Knew*, in *The Art of the Novel*, p. 142.
8. Ibid, p. 149.
9. J. Mitchell, '*What Maisie Knew*: Portrait of the Artist as a Young Girl', in J. Goode (ed.), *The Air of Reality: New Essays on Henry James* (London, 1972) p. 173.
10. See H. James, Preface to *The Awkward Age*, in *The Art of the Novel*, pp. 98–118.
11. S. de Beauvoir, *The Second Sex*, trans. H. M. Parshley (Harmondsworth, 1974) pp. 172–3.
12. Ibid, p. 626.

7: 'THE WINGS OF THE DOVE'

1. N. Hawthorne, *The Scarlet Letter* (Boston, 1850) p. 320.
2. J. Williamson, *Decoding Advertisements* (London, 1978) p. 71.
3. Q. Anderson, *The American Henry James* (London, 1958) p. 236.
4. H. James, Preface to *The Wings of the Dove*, in *The Art of the Novel* (New York, 1962) p. 288.
5. Ibid, p. 294.
6. Ibid, p. 302.
7. J. C. Rowe, *Henry Adams and Henry James* (Cornell, 1976) p. 195.
8. J. Goode, 'The Pervasive Mystery of Style: *The Wings of the Dove*', in J. Goode (ed.), *The Air of Reality: New Essays on Henry James* (London, 1972).
9. R. W. Emerson, essay on 'Wealth' in *The Conduct of Life* and *Society and Solitude* (London, 1896) p. 74.
10. Ibid, p. 82.
11. Ibid, p. 90.

12. Ibid, p. 102.
13. G. Santayana, *The Genteel Tradition* (Cambridge, Mass., 1967) p. 86.
14. H. James, *Hawthorne* (London, 1879) pp. 168–9.
15. N. Hawthorne, *The Marble Faun* (Ohio, 1968) pp. 52–3.
16. H. James, *Hawthorne*, p. 168.
17. N. Hawthorne, *The Marble Faun*, p. 461.
18. H. James, 'Mr Froude's Short Studies', in *Literary Reviews and Essays*, A. Mordell (ed.) (New York, 1957) p. 273.
19. L. Fiedler, *Love and Death in the American Novel*, 2nd edn (London, 1966); M. Geismar, *Henry James and his Cult* (London, 1964); J. A. Ward, *The Imagination of Disaster: Evil in the Fiction of Henry James* (Lincoln, Nebraska, 1961).
20. J. Goode, 'The Pervasive Mystery of Style', in Goode (ed.), *The Air of Reality*, p. 207.
21. Ibid, p. 269.
22. J. C. Rowe, *Henry Adams and Henry James*, p. 171.
23. Ibid, p. 174.

8: 'THE GOLDEN BOWL'

1. C. Lévi-Strauss, *The Elementary Structures of Kinship*, trans. J. Harle Bell, J. R. von Sturmer and R. Needham (London, 1969) p. 54.
2. J. C. Rowe, *Henry Adams and Henry James* (Cornell, 1976) p. 228.
3. N. Lebowitz, *The Imagination of Loving* (Detroit, 1965) p. 130ff.
4. S. B. Purdy, *The Hole in the Fabric: Science, Contemporary Literature and Henry James* (Pittsburgh, 1977) p. 176.
5. For instance, Q. Anderson, *The American Henry James* (London, 1958).
6. Q. Anderson, *The American Henry James*, p. 282.
7. G. Pearson, 'The Novel to End all Novels: *The Golden Bowl*', in J. Goode (ed.), *The Air of Reality: New Essays on Henry James* (London, 1972) p. 315.
8. Ibid, p. 311.
9. Ibid, p. 311.
10. J. C. Rowe, *Henry Adams and Henry James*, p. 222.
11. S. B. Purdy, *The Hole in the Fabric*, p. 176.

Bibliography

HENRY JAMES

Collected Editions

The Novels and Tales of Henry James, 24 vols (New York, 1907–9).
The Complete Tales of Henry James, Edel, L. (ed.), 12 vols (London, 1962–4).

Works Published Separately

The American (London, 1879).
The American Essays, Edel, L. (ed.), (New York, 1956).
The American Scene (New York, 1907).
The Art of the Novel (New York, 1962).
The Bostonians (London, 1886).
The Europeans, 2 vols (London, 1878).
The Future of the Novel, Edel, L. (ed.), (New York, 1956).
Hawthorne (London, 1879).
Henry James's Letters, Edel, L. (ed.), vol. 1 (London, 1974).
The Letters of Henry James, Lubbock, P. (ed.), 2 vols (New York, 1920).
Literary Reviews and Essays, Mordell, A. (ed.), (New York, 1957).
The Notebooks, Matthieson, F. O. and Murdock, K. P. (eds), (Oxford, 1961).
Notes on Novelists (London, 1914).
The Other House (New York, 1896).
The Painter's Eye, Sweeney, J. L. (ed.), (London, 1956).
Roderick Hudson (London, 1875).
The Sacred Fount (New York, 1901).
Selected Literary Criticism, Shapira, M. (ed.), (London, 1963).
Washington Square (New York, 1881).
Watch and Ward (Boston, 1878).

For a complete list of James's work consult:
Edel, L. and Laurence, D. H., *A Bibliography of Henry James* (London, 1961).

OTHER WORKS CITED

Adams, H., *Democracy* and *Esther* (New York, 1961).
———— *The Education of Henry Adams* (New York, 1931).
Allen, G., *The Woman Who Did* (London, 1895).
Anderson, C. R., *Person, Place and Thing in Henry James's Novels* (Durham, North Carolina, 1977).

Anderson, Q., *The American Henry James* (London, 1958).
Appignanesi, L., *Femininity and the Creative Imagination* (London, 1973).
The Atlantic Monthly (1873, 1874 and 1878).
Auerbach, E., *Mimesis*, trans. W. R. Trask (Princeton, 1953).
Banta, M., *Henry James and the Occult* (Bloomington, 1972).
Bantock, G. H., 'Morals and Civilization in Henry James', *Cambridge Journal* 7 (1953) pp. 159–81.
Baym, N., *Woman's Fiction: A Guide to Novels By and About Women in America, 1820–1870* (Ithaca, 1978).
Beauvoir, S. de, *The Second Sex*, trans. H. M. Parshley (Harmondsworth, 1974).
Berger, J., *Ways of Seeing* (Harmondsworth, 1972).
Boorstin, D., *The Americans: The National Experience* (New York, 1965).
Brown, C. B., *Alcuin: A Dialogue* (New York, 1971).
Bryce, J., *The American Commonwealth*, rev. edn, 2 vols (New York, 1910).
Buitenhuis, P., *The Grasping Imagination* (Toronto, 1970).
———— 'From Daisy Miller to Julia Bride: A Whole Passage of Intellectual History', *American Quarterly* 11 (1959) pp. 136–46.
Burke, C. B., 'Report from Paris: Women's Writing and the Women's Movement', *Signs*, vol. 3, no. 4 (1978), pp. 843–56.
Cargill, O., *The Novels of Henry James* (New York, 1961).
Chase, R., *The American Novel and Its Tradition* (London, 1958).
Conrad, S. P., *Perish the Thought: Intellectual Women in Romantic America* (New York, 1976).
Cooper, J. F., *Notions of the Americans Picked up by a Travelling Bachelor*, 2 vols (New York, 1963).
Cornillon, S. P. (ed.), *Images of Women in Fiction* (Bowing Green, Ohio, 1973).
Coward, R. and Ellis, J., *Language and Materialism* (London, 1977).
Cowie, E., 'Woman as Sign' *m/f* 1 (1978) pp. 49–63.
Crews, F. C., *The Tragedy of Manners* (New Haven, Connecticut, 1957).
Delamont, S. and Duffin, L., *The Nineteenth-Century Woman* (New York, 1978).
Douglas, A., *The Feminization of American Culture* (New York, 1977).
Dupee, F. W., *Henry James* (London, 1951).
———— (ed.), *The Question of Henry James* (London, 1947).
Eakin, P. J., *The New England Girl* (Athens, Georgia, 1976).
Earnest, E., *The American Eve in Fact and Fiction* (Illinois, 1974).
Edel, L. (ed.), *Henry James: A Collection of Critical Essays* (Englewood Cliffs, 1963).
———— *The Life of Henry James* (Harmondsworth, 1977).
Eliot, G., *Middlemarch* (Harmondsworth, 1965).
Ellman, M., *Thinking About Women* (London, 1979).
Emerson, R. W., *The Conduct of Life* and *Society and Solitude* (London, 1896).
———— *Nature, Addresses and Lectures* (London, 1903).
Falk, R. P., *The Rise of Realism* (Durham, North Carolina, 1953).
Feidelson, C., *Symbolism and American Literature* (Chicago, 1953).
Ferguson, M. A., *Image of Women in Literature* (Boston, 1973).
Fetterley, J., *The Resisting Reader: A Feminist Approach to American Fiction* (Bloomington, 1978).
Fiedler, L. A., *Love and Death in the American Novel*, 2nd edn (London, 1966).
Foley, R. N., *Criticism in American Periodicals of the Works of Henry James from 1866/1916* (Washington, 1944).

Fowler, R., *Linguistics and the Novel* (London, 1977).
Foucault, M., *The History of Sexuality Volume One: An Introduction*, trans, R. Hurley (New York, 1980).
Fryckstedt, O. W., *In Quest of America* (Cambridge, Mass., 1958).
Fryer, J., *The Faces of Eve: Women in the Nineteenth-century American Novel* (New York, 1976).
Fuller, M., *Woman in the Nineteenth Century* (New York, 1971).
Gard, R., (ed.), *Henry James: The Critical Heritage* (London, 1968).
Geismar, M., *Henry James and his Cult* (London, 1964).
Gissing, G., *The Odd Women* (London, 1968).
Godey's Lady Book (1878).
Goode, J., (ed.), *The Air of Reality: New Essays on Henry James* (London, 1972).
————— 'Woman and the Literary Text', in J. Mitchell and A. Oakley (eds), *The Rights and Wrongs of Women* (Harmondsworth, 1976).
Graham, K., *Henry James: The Drama of Fulfillment* (Oxford, 1975).
Grenander, M. E., 'Henry James's Cappricciosa' *PMLA75* (1960) pp. 309–19.
Gross, T. L., *The Heroic Ideal in American Literature* (New York, 1971).
Gurnick, V. and Moran, B. K., (eds), *Woman in Sexist Society* (New York, 1971).
Hardy, T., *Jude the Obscure* (Harmondsworth, 1980).
Harper's Weekly (1884, 1885 and 1876).
Hawthorne, N., *The Blithedale Romance* (Boston, 1883).
————— *The House of Seven Gables* (Boston, 1883).
————— *The Marble Faun* (Ohio, 1968).
————— *The Scarlet Letter* (Boston, 1850).
Herrick, R., *Together* (Greenwich, Connecticut, 1962).
Holland, L. B., *The Expense of Vision* (Princeton, 1964).
Holmes, O. W., *Elsie Venner* (Boston, 1892).
Howard, D., Lucas, J., Goode, J. (eds), *Tradition and Tolerance in Nineteenth Century Fiction* (London, 1966).
Howells, W. D., *A Chance Acquaintance* (Boston, 1873).
————— *A Foregone Conclusion* (Boston, 1875).
————— *Heroines of Fiction*, 2 vols (London, 1901).
————— *The Lady of the Aroostook* (Boston, 1879).
————— 'The Latest Avatar of American Girlhood', *Literature* 2 (1899) pp. 57–8.
————— *A Modern Instance* (Boston, 1882).
————— *The Undiscovered Country* (Boston, 1880).
————— *W. D. Howells as Critic*, Cady, E. H. (ed.), (London, 1973).
Isle, W., *Experiments in Form: Henry James's Novels 1896–1901* (Cambridge, Mass., 1968).
Jacobus, M. (ed.), *Women Writing and Writing About Women* (New York, 1979).
James, A., *The Diary*, with an introduction by Edel, L. (ed.), (New York, 1964).
James, H. Senior, *Substance and Shadow: or, Morality and Religion in Their Relation to Life* (Boston, 1863).
James, W., *Essays in Radical Empiricism and A Pluralistic Universe*, Perry, R. (ed.) (New York, 1971).
Janeway, E., *Man's World, Woman's Place* (New York, 1971).
Jefferson, D. W., *Henry James* (London, 1960).
Johnson, W. S., *Sex and Marriage in Victorian Poetry* (London, 1975).
Jung, C. (ed.), *Man and His Symbols* (London, 1978).

Kelley, C. P., *The Early Development of Henry James*, rev. edn (Urbana, 1965).

Killham, J., *Tennyson and 'The Princess'* (London, 1958).

Kipling, R., *American Notes* (New York, 1891).

Kraft, J., *The Early Tales of Henry James* (Illinois, 1969).

Krook, D., *The Ordeal of Consciousness in Henry James* (Cambridge, 1962).

Lawrence, D. H., *Studies in Classic American Literature* (London, 1937).

Lebowitz, N., *The Imagination of Loving* (Detroit, 1965).

Lee, B., *The Novels of Henry James* (London, 1978).

Lévi-Strauss, C., *The Elementary Structures of Kinship*, trans. J. Harle Bell, J. R. von Sturmer and R. Needham (London, 1969).

———— 'Introduction à l'oeuvre de Marcel Mauss', in Mauss, M., *Sociologie et Anthropologie* (Paris, 1950).

———— 'The Structural Study of Myth', in Sebeok, T. A. (ed.), *Myth: A Symposium* (Bloomington, 1955).

Lewis, R. W. B., *The American Adam* (Chicago, 1955).

Lubbock, P., *The Craft of Fiction* (London, 1921).

Mackenzie, M., *Communities of Honor and Love in Henry James* (Cambridge, Mass., 1976).

Marks, E., 'Women and Literature in France', *Signs* 4 (1978), pp. 832–42.

Martineau, H., *Society in America*, 3 vols (London, 1837).

Marx, L., *The Machine in the Garden* (New York, 1964).

McCarthy, H. T., *The Expatriate Perspective* (Rutherford, 1974).

Meredith, G., *Diana of the Crossways* (London, 1894).

———— *The Egoist*, 3 vols (London, 1879).

Mill, J. S., *The Subjection of Women* (London, 1869).

Miller, C. and Swift K., *Words and Women* (Harmondsworth, 1979).

Millett, K., *Sexual Politics* (New York, 1971).

Miner, E. R., 'Henry James's Metaphysical Romances', *Nineteenth Century Fiction* 9 (1954) pp. 1–21.

Mitchell, J., *Psychoanalysis and Feminism* (Harmondsworth, 1975).

Mordell, A. (ed.), *Discovery of a Genius: William Dean Howells and Henry James* (New York, 1961).

Mull, D. M., *Henry James's Sublime Economy* (Connecticut, 1973).

Patmore, C., *The Angel in the House* (London, 1866).

Peirce, C. S., 'Speculative Grammar', in *Collected Papers of Charles Sanders Peirce*, Hartshorne, C. and Weiss, P. (eds), 6 vols (Cambridge, Mass., 1960).

Piaget, J., *The Origin of Intelligence in the Child*, trans. M. Cook (London, 1953).

———— *Structuralism*, trans. C. Maschler (London, 1971).

Poirier, R., *The Comic Sense of Henry James* (London, 1960).

Porte, J., *The Romance in America* (Middletown, 1969).

Powers, L. H., *Henry James and the Naturalist Movement* (Michigan, 1971).

———— (ed.), *Henry James's Major Novels* (Michigan, 1973).

Praz, M., *The Hero in Eclipse in Victorian Fiction*, trans. A. Davidson (London, 1956).

Propp, V., *Morphology of the Folktale*, trans. L. Scott (Texas, 1968).

Purdy, S. B., *The Hole in the Fabric: Science, Contemporary Literature and Henry James* (Pittsburgh, 1977).

Rahv, P., *Image and Idea*, rev. edn (London, 1957).

Robinson, L., *Sex, Class and Culture* (Bloomington, 1978).

Rowe, J. C., *Henry Adams and Henry James* (Cornell, 1976).

Rugoff, M., *Prudery and Passion: Sexuality in Victorian America* (London, 1972).

Sabiston, E. J., 'The Prison of Womanhood', *Comparative Literature* 25 (1973) pp. 336–51.

Samuels, C. T., *The Ambiguity of Henry James* (Urbana, 1971).

Santayana, G., *The Genteel Tradition* (Cambridge, Mass., 1967).

Saussure, F., *Course in General Linguistics*, Bally, C. and Sechehays, A. (eds), trans. W. Baskin (London, 1960).

Sears, S., *The Negative Imagination* (Cornell, 1968).

Sheppard, E. A., *Henry James and 'The Turn of the Screw'* (Auckland, 1974).

Smith, H. N., *Democracy and the Novel* (New York, 1978).

Spender, D., *Man Made Language* (London, 1980).

Springer, M. (ed.), *What Manner of Woman?* (Oxford, 1978).

Stafford, W. T. (ed.), *Perspectives on James's 'The Portrait of a Lady'* (London, 1967).

Stevenson, E., *The Crooked Corridor: A Study of Henry James* (New York, 1949).

Tanner, T. (ed.), *Henry James* (London, 1968).

———— *The Reign of Wonder* (Cambridge, 1965).

Thomson, P., *The Victorian Heroine: A Changing Ideal, 1837–1873* (London, 1956).

Tocqueville, A. de, *Democracy in America*, Bradley, P. (ed.), trans. Reeve, H., and further corrected by Bowen, F., 2 vols (New York, 1945).

Veeder, W., *The Lessons of the Master* (Chicago, 1975).

Wagenknecht, E., *Eve and Henry James* (Norman, 1978).

Walcutt, C. C., *Man's Changing Mask* (Minneapolis, 1966).

Wallace, R., *Henry James and the Comic Form* (Michigan, 1975).

Ward, J. A., *The Search for Form* (North Carolina, 1967).

———— *The Imagination of Disaster: Evil in the Fiction of Henry James* (Lincoln, Nebraska, 1961).

Wasserstrom, W., *The Heiress of all the Ages* (Minneapolis, 1959).

Wegelin, C., *The Image of Europe in Henry James* (Dallas, 1958).

Weinstein, P., *Henry James and the Requirements of the Imagination* (Cambridge, Mass., 1971).

Welter, B., *Dimity Convictions* (Athens, Ohio, 1976).

Wharton, E., *The Age of Innocence* (London, 1966).

Williamson, J., *Decoding Advertisements* (London, 1978).

Willen, G. (ed.), *A Casebook on Henry James's 'The Turn of the Screw'* (New York, 1959).

Wollen, P., *Signs and Meaning in the Cinema*, 3rd edn (London, 1972).

Yeazell, R. B., *Language and Knowledge in the Late Novels of Henry James* (Chicago, 1976).

Index

Literary criticism has often identified the extent to which women exist as symbols, or "signs", pointing to a range of meanings and values: woman as the dove, madonna, temptress or earth mother, sexual or spiritual, fickle or faithful, womanly, feminine, inspirational or deceiving. But for whom do these ideals, meanings and inspiration exist? And what effect does this process have on the woman herself – whether within the confines of the novel or in a wider cultural sense? In this book these questions are explored through some of the major works of Henry James.

This is the first full-length study of the ways in which James uses heroines – as distinct from central male characters – and the starting point is the use he made of the "American girl", a figure (or an idea) caught in her most popular form in James's *Daisy Miller*. In a long line of heroines from Daisy Miller through Isabel Archer to Milly Theale and Maggie Verver (and encompassing the "English girls" like Maisie, and Nanda of *The Awkward Age*) James explores the conflict between woman's function as sign and representer of meaning for her society – her obligation to be visible, to be feminine, to be judged – and her own struggle into "consciousness", that major Jamesian concern. James himself wrote, in the preface to *The Portrait of a Lady*, that what was different about his treatment of Isabel Archer was that her story mattered first and foremost to *her* and not simply in its meaning or value to those around her.

The struggle to develop a female consciousness, the threats implicit in sexuality, in marriage, in poverty and dependence, the individualistic counterbalances attempted through wealth, intelligence and wit – the presence of these tensions in James's novels raises a series of questions which are intrinsic to much of the feminist theory being debated today.